A HISTORIOGRAPHY OF THE MODERN SOCIAL SCIENCES

A Historiography of the Modern Social Sciences includes essays on the ways in which the histories of history, anthropology, sociology, psychology, economics, and political science have been written since the Second World War. In drawing together chapters written by leading historians of each discipline, the book reveals significant parallels and contrasts that serve as a basis for a comparative interdisciplinary historiography, in which not only forces specific to individual disciplines but also social, political, and intellectual developments outside are seen to shape the various social science disciplines. The book invites historians, including historians of the different social sciences, who often see them in fragments, to look beyond disciplinary boundaries and to contemplate the possibility of a historiography of the social sciences as a whole.

Roger E. Backhouse is Professor of the History and Philosophy of Economics at the University of Birmingham, where he has taught since 1980. He currently holds a Leverhulme Trust Major Research Fellowship to write an intellectual biography of Paul Samuelson. He is the coeditor of *The History of the Social Sciences since 1945* (Cambridge University Press, 2010); *The Unsocial Social Science? Economics and Neighboring Disciplines since 1945* (2010); and *The Cambridge Companion to Keynes* (Cambridge University Press, 2006). He is author of *The Ordinary Business of Life* and *The Penguin History of Economics*. He has written for a number of journals, including *Economica*, the *Journal of Economic Perspectives*, *History of Political Economy*, the *Journal of the History of Economic Thought*, and the *Journal of Economic Methodology*.

Philippe Fontaine is Professor of Economics in the department of economics at the École normale supérieure de Cachan and an Honorary Fellow of the Institut universitaire de France. In 2003–2004, he was Ludwig Lachmann Research Fellow in the department of philosophy at the London School of Economics and Political Science. He is the coeditor of *The History of the Social Sciences since 1945* (Cambridge University Press, 2010); *The Unsocial Social Science? Economics and Neighboring Disciplines since 1945* (2010); and *The Experiment in the History of Economics* (2005). He has written for a number of journals, including the *British Journal of Sociology*, *Economics and Philosophy*, *History of Political Economy*, *Isis*, the *Journal of the History of Economic Thought*, and *Science in Context*. He has been the associate editor of *Revue de philosophie économique*. In 2005, he received the Best Article Award from the Forum for History of Human Science. In 2008, he was the recipient of the *prix d'excellence en sciences sociales* from the Foundation Mattei Dogan/CNRS.

A Historiography of the Modern Social Sciences

Edited by

ROGER E. BACKHOUSE

University of Birmingham, United Kingdom

PHILIPPE FONTAINE

École normale supérieure de Cachan, France

CAMBRIDGE
UNIVERSITY PRESS

CAMBRIDGE
UNIVERSITY PRESS

32 Avenue of the Americas, New York NY 10013-2473, USA

Cambridge University Press is part of the University of Cambridge.

It furthers the University's mission by disseminating knowledge in the pursuit of education, learning and research at the highest international levels of excellence.

www.cambridge.org
Information on this title: www.cambridge.org/9781107037724

First published 2014

A catalogue record for this publication is available from the British Library

Library of Congress Cataloguing in Publication data
A historiography of the modern social sciences / edited by Roger E. Backhouse, Philippe Fontaine.
pages cm
Includes bibliographical references and index.
ISBN 978-1-107-03772-4 (hardback)
1. Social sciences – History. 2. Economics – History. 3. Historiography. I. Backhouse, Roger, 1951– editor of compilation. II. Fontaine, Philippe, 1960– editor of compilation.
H51.H5754 2014
300.72–dc23 2014015325

ISBN 978-1-107-03772-4 Hardback

Contents

Notes on Contributors

Robert Adcock is Assistant Professor of Political Science at George Washington University. His research focuses on nineteenth- and twentieth-century Anglo-American political and social thought, especially the history and methods of the modern social sciences, and the politics of knowledge. He has most recently published *Liberalism and the Emergence of American Political Science: A Transatlantic Tale* (Oxford University Press, 2014) and previously coedited *Modern Political Science: Anglo-American Exchanges since 1880* (Princeton University Press, 2007).

Roger E. Backhouse is Professor of the History and Philosophy of Economics at the University of Birmingham. He currently holds a Leverhulme Trust Major Research Fellowship to write an intellectual biography of the economist Paul A. Samuelson. He is author of *The Ordinary Business of Life* (Princeton University Press, 2002), *The Penguin History of Economics* (Penguin, 2002), and *Capitalist Revolutionary: John Maynard Keynes* (Harvard University Press, 2011, with Bradley W. Bateman) and with Philippe Fontaine has edited two books on the history of postwar social science.

Charles Camic is John Evans Professor of Sociology at Northwestern University. He was previously Martindale-Bascom Professor of Sociology at the University of Wisconsin-Madison. From 1999 to 2004, he served (along with Franklin Wilson) as editor of the *American Sociological Review*. Recent publications include *Social Knowledge in the Making* (University of Chicago Press, 2011), edited with Neil Gross and Michèle Lamont, and *Essential Writings of Thorstein Veblen* (Routledge, 2011), edited with Geoffrey Hodgson. He is completing a book on the development of Thorstein Veblen's economic ideas.

James H. Capshew serves on the faculty of Indiana University, in the Department of History and Philosophy of Science and Medicine, where he teaches courses on the scientific dimensions of society, the history and culture of the modern university, and the environmental humanities, among other topics. Author of *Psychologists on the March: Science, Practice, and Professional Identity in America, 1929–1969* (Cambridge University Press, 1999), he was editor of *History of Psychology* (2006–2009) and subject editor for psychology of the *New Dictionary of Scientific Biography* (Scribner, 2008). Much of his work in the history of psychology investigates the tension between disciplinary agendas and institutional constraints and opportunities in the scientific community, particularly in the post–World War II period. He has long-standing interests in biography, historiography, and the social organization of scholarship.

Philippe Fontaine is Professor of Economics at the École normale supérieure de Cachan and an Honorary Fellow of the Institut universitaire de France. His research focuses on cross-disciplinary research ventures in postwar American social science, especially the relationships between economics and other social sciences. His recent publications include *The History of the Social Sciences since 1945* (Cambridge University Press, 2010) and *The Unsocial Social Science? Economics and Neighboring Disciplines since 1945* (Duke University Press, 2010), both edited with Roger E. Backhouse.

Henrika Kuklick was a Professor Emerita in the Department of History and Sociology of Science at the University of Pennsylvania, where she had taught since 1975. Her research interests included the development of the human science disciplines in the American university, and what role science played in justifying colonial settlement in North America, southern Africa, and the Middle East; and she taught courses in the history of the human sciences, the history of the field sciences, and the sociology of knowledge. Her books include *The Imperial Bureaucrat: Colonial Administrative Service in the Gold Coast, 1920–39* (Hoover Colonial Series, 1979); *The Savage Within: The Social History of British Anthropology, 1885–1945* (Cambridge University Press, 1991); and the edited collection *A New History of Anthropology* (Blackwell, 2008). She received her B.A. from Brandeis University, her M.A. from the University of London, and her doctorate from Yale University. Dr. Kuklick passed away in 2013.

Kevin Passmore is Professor of History at Cardiff University. In the field of historiography, he has edited with Stefan Berger and Heiko Feldner, *Writing*

History: Theory and Practice (Bloomsbury, 2010). On the history of modern France, he has published *The Right in France from the Third Republic to Vichy* (Oxford University Press, 2013). He also writes on fascism and has just published a revised edition of his *Fascism: A Very Short Introduction* (Oxford University Press, 2014). He currently holds a Leverhulme Trust Major Research Fellowship to write *France 1940: The Maginot Line in History, Society, and Culture.*

1

Introduction

Roger E. Backhouse and Philippe Fontaine

The literature on historiography is large and diverse. From characterizing the main stages in historical research to picking out "great men," from identifying leading schools and main ideas to clarifying the differences between professional and lay historians, from describing what historians write about to explaining their methods, from noting the significance of history for the social sciences to pointing out the usefulness of the social sciences to historians, from writing about what historians actually do to deliberating about what they should do, historiographers carry out an impressive range of activities.

Within a field spanning several millennia and covering numerous geographical areas, it is not unusual to distinguish various forms of historiography according to "temporal and spatial characteristics" (Lorenz 2011, p. 14). As it concerns Western societies since the Second World War, this book remains within that tradition. It offers an illustration of what historians regard as more "particular and concrete" forms of historiography. At the same time, it flirts with more "general and abstract" forms of historiography (Lorenz 1999) in arguing that, because of the commonality of problems facing social scientists after the Second World War, it makes sense to go beyond disciplinary boundaries to contemplate a history of the social sciences as a whole. It also argues that something can be learned about the way the history of history is written from considering the historiographies of the different social sciences within a comparative interdisciplinary framework. The chapters that follow represent the first steps in that direction.

The essential starting point is the rise of the social sciences since the Second World War, covered in the next section, for it provides the background to their increased consideration in the historical literature in the past twenty-five years. In particular, an important part of this history is that the social sciences achieved their more significant place in economic, political, social, and cultural life, in large part, through cross-disciplinary engagements guided by a common problem-oriented approach. We then turn to the existing historiography, arguing that recent work has laid the foundations for moving from largely disciplinary histories – of psychology, sociology, anthropology, economics, and political science – to a history of the social sciences as a whole. This is followed by the central section, in which we argue for a comparative interdisciplinary historiography of the social sciences. In the final section, we explain how the chapters that follow take us toward that goal.

The Rise of the Social Sciences after 1945

It is well known that the natural sciences played an enormous role in the Second World War and that their prestige was greatly enhanced, both in government and in society at large. The atomic bomb and radar were just the most visible results of a research effort that was recognized by those in the military and in government to have been crucial to winning the war (on British developments, see Edgerton 2011), but social scientists were also heavily involved in the war effort (Backhouse and Fontaine 2010a, pp. 186–9). Psychologists played an important role in screening military personnel, dealing with psychological casualties and appraising the enemy (Herman 1995; Capshew 1999). Anthropologists were needed because of their knowledge of many of the societies and cultures in which fighting was taking place, especially in the Pacific (Price 2008). Economists were likewise involved in economic planning, in intelligence, and in a number of activities soon to be identified under the umbrella "operations research" (Mirowski 2002; Guglielmo 2008). The bombing of Pearl Harbor introduced new geographical "realities" that existing maps could hardly render (Schulten 2001) so that American cartography entered a new era, as illustrated by the role of geographers in the Office of Strategic Services (Barnes 2006), which also employed historians. In much of this work, social scientists were working in multidisciplinary teams, alongside natural scientists and engineers.[1]

After the Second World War, though some businessmen and politicians objected to peacetime government involvement in science, the natural scientists were able to capitalize on their wartime achievements, especially

[1] Talcott Parsons offered a valuable presentation of the war record of social scientific research in a draft – "Social Science: A Basic National Resource" – submitted to the Social Science Research Council in 1948 and subsequently published with an instructive introduction by Klausner and Lidz (1986, pp. 79–101).

as the Cold War developed. Instrumental to this process was the report *Science: The Endless Frontier* (1945), produced by a committee headed by Vannevar Bush, head of the wartime Office of Scientific Research and Development (for an official history of OSRD, see Baxter 1968 [1946]). This report supported the case for government sponsorship of science by arguing for the importance of new knowledge obtained through basic research as a prerequisite to social progress. It was concerned primarily with the natural sciences, reflecting the lesser authority of the social sciences in the eyes of policy makers at the time. Indeed, while the war had profound effects on the social science disciplines, their practitioners failed to capitalize on their wartime activities in the way that natural scientists were able to do. Strong reservations as to their scientific legitimacy and social usefulness persisted in political and business circles: For some, the phrase "social science" was sufficient to suggest social policy or, even worse, socialism. Thus when the National Science Foundation (NSF) was established, assuring long-term federal support for scientific research, the social sciences were not formally excluded, but they were lumped with "other sciences" so that it was hard for them to get support (Larsen 1992, p. 39). Yet, with problems of human welfare being made increasingly central to the social science enterprise and its gradual endorsement of the "scientific study of man" – an approach that favored the quantitative dimension of social phenomena – by the mid-1950s the social sciences had regained most of their wartime confidence, as illustrated by increased recognition within NSF.[2]

Increasingly recognized as an important source of new knowledge (notably by private foundations and think tanks), the social sciences played a growing role in shaping the perception of policy makers of society and its problems. As much as they inspired a view of society according to which intervention was not only possible but also desirable, they offered tools that allowed for better-informed decisions and subtler understanding of current societal transformations. The techniques of social science spread through every area of American life. As Dorothy Ross (2003, p. 229) has argued, "The liberal Enlightenment vision of a progressive modern society guided

[2] On the centrality of human welfare to the social science enterprise, see the *Report of the Study for the Ford Foundation on Policy and Program* – the so-called Gaither Report of 1949. Geiger (1993, p. 104) notes that "American social science was far more vigorous by 1956, and much less in need of reformation, than had been the case at the end of the 1940s." As noted by Larsen (1992, p. 39), "social scientists were found to be needed at NSF before their programs were judged to be worthy of support." The role of the sociologist Harry Alpert was central to the recognition of the social sciences at NSF (see Solovey and Pooley 2011).

by science gained energy and urgency from the defeat of fascism, the disintegration of colonial empires, and the threat of communism." Meeting this challenge required not only the systematic design of policies to transform society – avoiding those that had created economic and social chaos, encouraged the rise of fascism, and strengthened communism in the interwar period – but also the construction of a scientific approach to human behavior. This need for social science was met by the expansion of higher education and growing support from national governments and foundations, notably Rockefeller and Ford. Countries outside the Soviet sphere imported American models for the organization of science, supported by the United Nations Educational, Scientific and Cultural Organization (UNESCO).[3]

It was not just the academic and policy-making elites who ultimately appropriated the results of social scientific research. Though they may not have thought of what they were encountering in this way, members of the public were also exposed to techniques and ideas that originated in the social sciences. To take but a few examples, social surveys, polling, and election studies – developed by sociologists, psychologists, and political scientists – became a part of everyday life (Igo 2007) as much as maps entered the national culture with the help of geographers' recreation of the world (Schulten 2001). Similarly, it is hard to imagine popular discussions of economic policy without ideas such as "Keynesianism" and "monetarism," let alone without concepts such as "national income" or "money supply" (Parsons 1990).

If the increasing importance of the social sciences is well known, both to historians and to social scientists themselves, their extensive connections deserve better appreciation. As was mentioned earlier, one aspect of wartime activities was the organization of research into multidisciplinary teams, which continued long after the war's end. An early example was the Russian Institute, established at Columbia in 1946, but many research institutes and centers were subsequently created to undertake research on the Soviet Union. The creation of cross-disciplinary teams did not stop with area studies – the cross-disciplinary enterprise par excellence. At Harvard, the Russian Research Center coexisted with the Laboratory (and Department) of Social Relations, established in 1946; at Chicago the committee structure encouraged exchanges among social scientists and even between social

3 This draws on Ross (2003, pp. 229–34), which contains extensive references to document these claims. On the attempt by social scientists associated with UNESCO to institutionalize American disciplines on an international scale, see Selcer (2009).

and natural scientists, occasioning various projects such as that of creating an Institute devoted to the mental sciences under the psychologist James G. Miller; at Michigan, Donald Marquis and Rensis Likert helped form or attract to the university a number of cross-disciplinary teams such as the Survey Research Center, the Research Center for Group Dynamics, or the Mental Health Research Institute. This was a time when cross-disciplinary relationships flourished in the social sciences, reflecting a problem-oriented approach in which disciplinary boundaries were unhesitatingly minimized.[4]

However, by the 1970s cross-disciplinary research ventures had largely declined, provoking fears of excessive specialization. Crowther-Heyck (2006) has analyzed this phenomenon through the lens of patronage systems, pointing out that the rise of the system organized around the NSF and the National Institutes of Health, different from the preceding system, played a significant role in the perception of social scientific fragmentation. Another way of looking at the problem is to recall that cross-disciplinary research ventures did not imply the same degree of participation from different social scientists. For instance, when joining multidisciplinary teams, geographers may have been less confident of their added value than were sociologists.[5] Social scientists did not play the same role either. For example, there were differences between the attitudes of psychologists and economists in that psychology's protean identity allowed for greater flexibility and readier accommodation of other disciplines' demands than did economists'

4 Crowther-Heyck (2006, p. 421) notes that there were "nearly 250 new interdisciplinary social science research institutes created in the first twenty years after the war." Abbott (2001, chap. 5) recalls usefully that cross-disciplinary research ventures presuppose disciplines.

5 Barnes (2006, pp. 158–9) recalls the difficulties of geographers after the reorganization of the Research and Analysis Branch of the Office of Strategic Services (OSS). While this reorganization, with its new regional geographical focus, should have benefited geographers, it actually penalized them. By compelling geographers to interact with other social scientists and adopt a problem-oriented approach, this reorganization brought out various deficiencies in their training and more generally their inability to translate their skills into the larger cross-disciplinary framework imposed by military intelligence. In his description of geography's wartime service, Stone (1979) emphasizes the need for geographers to cross disciplinary boundaries and to confer with specialists in other disciplines, but minimized geographers' deficiencies in that respect. On the side of sociology, cross-disciplinary contacts strengthened during the war, "continuing a process of interdisciplinarity that had its roots in the movement for the SSRC in the 1920s" (Abbott and Sparrow, p. 294). More importantly, after the postwar campaign for scientific legitimacy (Haney 2008, chap. 2), Parsons was able to place sociology at the center of a cross-disciplinary enterprise, involving both anthropology and psychology, which other sociologists participating in multidisciplinary teams could use as an inspiration.

widespread endorsement of the utility maximization framework. This suggests that despite strong cross-disciplinary interactions within the social sciences during the war and in the two decades following it, disciplinary claims to expertise over various social problems did not disappear though they may have been less perceptible when the cross-disciplinary mood dominated.

When the emphasis shifted away from interdisciplinarity toward specialization, there was some incentive for social scientists to reaffirm their own discipline's expertise in addressing a variety of society's issues. It then became apparent that the authority accorded different forms of disciplinary knowledge varied enormously. That was a side effect of what can be described as an increased segmentation in the analysis of society following the decline of the Parsonian paradigm.[6] Gradually abandoning the view of society as a functional whole, with its various segments playing an instrumental role, in favor of a conception of society in which they are considered in isolation from each other, social scientists could entertain the belief that the logic of society could be reduced to the working of one of these segments only. Subsequently, it became possible for some social scientists to claim expertise over human behavior in a variety of situations, economic, political, and social, and accordingly to appear as competent analysts of society as a whole. Of course, some social sciences were more successful at this than were others, as illustrated by the psychologization of American society in the 1960s and the increasing dominance of an individualistic economic discourse in Western societies from the 1970s.

Before the Second World War, psychology enjoyed some recognition inside and outside the university, but its growth was circumscribed. After the war, it outgrew the bounds of professionalization and came to pervade most spheres of life (see Herman 1995, chap. 1): it became "a veritable worldview" promising "to satisfy the hunger for values and the desire for affirmation" at a time when traditional beliefs were becoming harder to hold (p. 5). There was an enormous rise in the number of clinical psychologists, therapy achieving a centrality to American life unknown before the war when it had been the preserve of the insane, the affluent,

[6] Brian Barry (1970 [1978], p. vi) has described part of this development in the context of writing about politics. He notes: "What does seem defunct … is the notion, introduced by Durkheim and elaborated by Parsons, that the way to explain some feature of a society is to show how it relates to other aspects of the society to form part of a functional whole." This fits well into the story told by Rodgers (2011), though he does not mention Parsons.

and the avant-garde. The popularity of works such as David Riesman's *The Lonely Crowd* (1950), centered on the study of the American character, and C. Wright Mills's *White Collar* (1951), with its emphasis of a form of social alienation, illustrates the way psychology permeated thinking about the structure of society. Mills went so far as to claim, "We need to characterize American society of the mid-twentieth century in more psychological terms, for now the problems that concern us most border on the psychiatric" (p. xx; quoted in Herman 1995, p. 7).

The increasing dominance of an economic discourse endorsing an individualistic perspective from the mid-1970s culminated with the political revitalization of market liberalism (Kelley 1997; see also Cockett 1995 and Mirowski and Plehwe 2009). It was closely allied to the weakening of a view of society in which individuals were shaped by their place in society, which influenced their life chances, social norms, and even their personalities.[7] Gradually, individuals were increasingly seen as isolated agents making rational choices. Notions of society fractured, undermining the intellectual basis on which many postwar social institutions rested (Rodgers 2011). The fracturing of the idea of the social was associated with an increasing focus on economics – the social science that was viewed as having developed the tools for analyzing market interactions between isolated individuals – at the expense of sociology and, to a certain extent, psychology.[8] Economists, more and more, defined their discipline as analyzing rational choice, a definition that minimized the importance of the social. The understanding that there were realms of life that could not be reduced to money and that should be kept outside the sphere of the market gradually broke down (see Offer 2006).[9] At the policy level, that conception translated itself into the belief that problems of society could be solved by acting on one of its segments, as when neoliberals argued that, being the best coordinating device,

[7] The argument in this paragraph is taken from Rodgers (2011), drawing in particular on the prologue.

[8] A paradoxical illustration of the growing significance of the individualistic perspective in economics can be observed in Harvey Leibenstein's (1979) argument that a branch of economics was missing: micro-micro theory. Taking the example of economics in the 1930s, a time when the movement of the discipline was in the macro direction, Leibenstein argued that, unlike other sciences, economics had not necessarily moved toward the study of smaller and smaller entities, as illustrated by the fact that, when they spoke about decision units such as firms or households, economists had in mind collections of individuals not individuals. Leibenstein mostly hoped to draw attention to a number of problems associated with the role of individuals in multiperson decision units. His was clearly an individualistic perspective and one that gained prominence in the years that followed.

[9] The provision and distribution of blood provide a telling illustration of the commodification of society from the 1970s (see Fontaine 2002).

the market mechanism should be gradually substituted for other forms of social coordination.[10]

The increased importance of the social sciences in society since the Second World War has coincided with their gradual estrangement from the past but has resulted in an increased willingness on the part of social scientists who write the histories of their disciplines to cover recent developments. At the same time, it has encouraged historians of science, intellectual historians, and even sociologists to pay more attention to the emergence of a distinctive academic culture in the social sciences, recognition of which was delayed by the customary partition of the intellectual life of Western societies into the natural sciences and humanities.[11]

From Disciplinary Histories to the History of the Social Sciences

The history of the social sciences after the Second World War is primarily written by social scientists, many of them interested in legitimizing current theoretical orientations or resuscitating older ones. Some social scientists may show greater historical sensibility (Geary 2008), but as a rule "discipline history," as Collini (1988) called it, focuses on one particular discipline and tends to ignore its relationships with others, with sociologists writing about the history of sociology, psychologists writing about the history of psychology, economists writing about the history of economics, and so on.

In recent years, however, there have been attempts to take a more general perspective. As historians of science, intellectual historians, and even sociologists have turned increasingly to the study of the postwar era, greater attention has been paid to the social sciences as a whole (e.g., Ross 1991; Wagner, Wittrock, and Whitley 1991; Smith 1997; Wagner 2001; Porter and Ross 2003; Chapoulie 2005; Isaac 2007, 2009; Heilbron, Guilhot, and Jeanpierre 2008; Backhouse and Fontaine 2010a). Though they often had to rely on historical work by practicing social scientists whose orientations were clearly in the disciplinary mold, these researchers endorsed approaches that were not necessarily motivated by the current concerns of practitioners of the social science disciplines. Instead, they combined disciplinary

[10] This perspective was vigorously promoted by free-market think tanks and other organizations and taken up enthusiastically by politicians, mostly on the Right. However, as Rodgers (2011) makes clear, it went much deeper than this.

[11] Kagan (2009, p. vii) motivated the writing of *The Three Cultures* by the observation that "the changes in the sciences and research universities over the past half-century had rendered Snow's analysis a bit archaic."

histories within narratives that put more store on the relations between social scientific work and the transformations of Western societies.[12]

The work by Dorothy Ross (1991) and Peter Wagner, Björn Wittrock, and Richard Whitley (1991) marked a first step in the attempt to consider the social sciences as a whole.[13] Ross's *The Origins of American Social Science* (1991) related the rise of American social science to broader intellectual and cultural developments in American society. Initially an import from Europe, where modern understandings of history had been developed in the eighteenth century, the social sciences were seen as having emerged in response to what she called "the crisis of American exceptionalism" in the period after the Civil War. The Progressive era formed the common background to the emergence of the distinct disciplines of economics, sociology, and political science. The section titled "Progressive Social Science, 1896–1914" was the only part of the book, albeit a significant one, in which these social sciences were assigned separate chapters, for when Ross returned to the challenges to liberal exceptionalism and the rise of scientism, discussions of these three social sciences were again integrated. Unfortunately, the

12 Not so long ago, it was not unusual to see the history of the social sciences as a whole relegated to a secondary role in history of science journals. For example, when Hamilton Cravens (1985) wrote on the history of the social sciences in a special issue of *Osiris* devoted to "historical writing of American science," the emphasis in the volume was clearly on the natural sciences. Yet, history of science journals are now increasingly hospitable to articles and even symposia dealing with the social sciences (Kaiser and Heyck 2010; Isaac 2011; Fontaine 2015).

13 An argument against placing the shift from disciplinary history to the history of the social sciences as a whole in the early 1990s is that the "social history of the social sciences" had emerged at least a decade earlier under the influence of the sociologist Pierre Bourdieu, informing a detailed analysis of the growth of the social sciences in France between 1945 and the late 1960s (for instance, see Drouard 1982). Centred on a sociology of knowledge in which disciplines are the crucial level of analysis, this literature considers ideas through the social conditions of their production and circulation, and views history as the mere instrument of a reflexive science. It can be seen as offering disciplinary-centred insights into the past of a variety of social science disciplines, though its accounts remained geared toward defending the progress of scientific reason (Bourdieu 1995). A recent illustration of the genre is to be found in Heilbron, Lenoir and Sapiro's *Pour une historie des sciences sociales* (2004), a collection of essays that does not primarily concern the postwar era and hardly covers the whole social sciences. Renewed interest in the history of the social sciences can also be found in the activities of the *Société française pour l'histoire des sciences de l'homme*, created in the mid-1980s, which demonstrated a great variety of approaches and eventually prompted the reconsideration of disciplinary history even though the discussions preceding the formation of the *Société* were conducted within a framework that stresses the discipline as the relevant level of historical analysis (see Blanckaert 1993). Interestingly, the two foreigners present at the founding colloquium of the *Société*, Collini (1988, p. 399) and Charles C. Gillispie (1988, p. 380), expressed uneasiness at such a frame of analysis.

book stopped in the late 1920s, leaving open the question of the relationships between interwar and postwar developments.

Though contributions in Wagner, Wittrock, and Whitley (1991) offered valuable historical insights and considered parallels and contrasts among the social science disciplines, most chapters were not centered on the postwar era. Moreover, even though the book covered a wide range of broad historical issues, including international variations in the structures of intellectual fields, the special place of political science among social sciences, the possibility of a science of society, the institutionalization of economics, and a comparative perspective on the structuration of the social sciences, its editors meant it as a contribution to the sociology of the social sciences more than their history. Accordingly, they endorsed "structuration theory" à la Giddens and "theory of practice" à la Bourdieu so as to propose a view of the transformations of social scientific knowledge that strove to combine social forces and human agency.[14]

Later in the decade there appeared an impressive book, Roger Smith's *The Fontana History of the Human Sciences* (1997). Smith's aim is a history of scientific attempts to understand humankind, which, though it overlaps considerably, is not the same as a history of the social sciences. However, it is fair to comment that it offers a picture of the social sciences that is, to say the least, unusual. His inclusion of seventeenth and eighteenth century political economy and his consideration of a substantial discussion of academic sociology in the nineteenth century suggest that he sees these disciplines as an integral part of the human sciences. However, when it comes to the twentieth century they are completely absent, for his final section – comprising roughly a third of the book – is headed "Psychologies in the 20th Century." Once disciplines are consolidated (economics in the eighteenth century, sociology in the nineteenth, and presumably psychology

[14] Though the influence of Bourdieu on the writing of the history of the social sciences by sociologists has been especially significant from the 1980s, mention should be made of Raymond Boudon's "Comment écrire l'histoire des sciences sociales?" (1992), an article closing a special issue of *Communications* devoted to the beginnings of the human sciences. There, against the background of a critique of Wolf Lepenies' approach to the history of sociology in *Die drei Kulturen*, which had been recently translated into French, Boudon offered a number of general considerations on the writing of the history of the social sciences. In particular, he deplored the decreasing attention to sociology's production of scientific knowledge among its historians. Notwithstanding a quick reference to anthropology whose boundaries with sociology have often been permeable, Boudon equated the history of the social sciences with the history of sociology and cannot therefore be associated with the effort to consider the history of the social sciences as a whole. His article reflected nonetheless a widespread belief among sociologists that their discipline was the core discipline in the study of society.

in the twentieth) they drop from his view. In a sense, therefore, it is not a history of the social sciences so much as a history of their emergence. Political science and anthropology are conspicuous by their absence. This can be rationalized by arguing that Smith's concern is with scientific attempts to understand human nature, rather than attempts to understand human interactions. When economics and sociology had established the conceptions of human nature on which their analyses of human interactions were to be based (academic political science being concerned solely with interactions from the start, and hence absent), they cease to be part of Smith's history.

At the turn of the century, Wagner (2001) proposed to reconsider the history of the social sciences with a view to changing the common perception that the twentieth century was the time of their emergence and consolidation. In place of this perception, Wagner offered a conception of the history of the social sciences in which they refer to a number of *problématiques* associated with the onset of political modernity. His notion of the history (and sociology) of the social sciences is intimately connected with a project of enriching conceptual debates in current social theory.

Wagner contributed two essays to *The Modern Social Sciences* (2003), edited by Theodore Porter and Ross as volume VII of *The Cambridge History of Science*. Starting with the Enlightenment, this landmark collection of essays covers a slightly smaller time span than Smith's book but its range is much broader. Conventional disciplinary boundaries are absent from the chapters on the period running from the eighteenth century to the 1880s, again with the exception of economics, covered in chapters on "continental political economy" and "British economic theory," and a chapter on "history and historicism." Themes include naturalism, socialism, scientific ethnography, the psyche, and Marxism. In part II, the coverage turns to the histories of social science disciplines, with an essay by Ross on the "changing contours of the social science disciplines," preceding essays on statistics, psychology, economics, political science, sociology, anthropology, geography, along with one on history and the social sciences.

Though this offered the most comprehensive history of the social sciences then available, for the period after the current disciplinary structure of the social sciences emerged, the book's coverage was limited. There is the essay with which Ross introduced part II, which does include two short sections spanning the years 1945–2000. There is also part III, which contains instructive essays on the social sciences in Africa, Latin America, and major Asian countries and does consider postwar developments. There are finally fourteen chapters on the social sciences and public life offering valuable discussions of topics from managing the economy and business, to social welfare, education, the child, psychiatry, and cultural relativism. There is much material here that covers more than one social science but with the exception of Wagner's essay "The Uses of the Social Sciences," these are isolated topics, with the result that there is no systematic coverage of the development of the social sciences as a whole, or of the interactions among them. Covering more than a century, and moreover a century during which the social sciences had expanded enormously, the disciplinary chapters in the Porter and Ross volume could not attempt anything like a full coverage of the second half of the twentieth century, this being met by chapters on six social science disciplines.

In the wake of Porter and Ross's *The Modern Social Sciences*, Chapoulie (2005) proposed to go beyond the disciplinary mold associated with "conventional history" to emphasize extra-disciplinary factors. His insistence on the social sciences as going concerns encouraged an historical approach in which disciplines were not reified even if their influence on the production and dissemination of social scientific work was acknowledged. Chapoulie's framework complicated disciplinary histories of the social sciences by suggesting the significance of extra-disciplinary factors and by implying that a comparative perspective may be of some use when considering the transformations of the social sciences disciplines.

By the late 2000s, the literature attained critical mass and efforts to derive lessons from existing historiography began to flourish. In a survey article, Joel Isaac (2007) strove to define the main characteristics of the historiography of the social sciences in postwar America by placing them within the broader perspective of the boom of Cold War studies. Combining three strands of literature – "the history of science, the cultural turn in Cold War studies, and the history of the birth of the human science professions in the United States" – he showed that though the Cold War stood as one important context for considering the evolution of the social sciences in the postwar era, interwar and turn-of-the-century developments deserved serious attention as well. In addition, Isaac noted that much work remained to be done to write the history of the social science disciplines and that consideration should be given to developments in neighboring fields, suggesting that not only intra- but also extradisciplinary factors mattered.

While Isaac's account focused on Cold War America, Heilbron, Guilhot, and Jeanpierre (2008) opted for an approach in which the customary distinctions among the local, the national, and the international were deemphasized in favor of transnational factors. By suggesting that the developments in the social sciences since 1945 should be studied in the light of various transnational relations, as supported by international scholarly institutions, the transnational mobility of scholars, and the politics of transnational exchange of nonacademic institutions, the authors opened the way toward a more nuanced understanding of the relation between the American disciplinary structure and those of other countries. Whereas much of the literature on the modern social sciences has made a serious effort to cross disciplinary boundaries, Heilbron, Guilhot, and Jeanpierre draw attention to connections across national boundaries. To the extent that national traditions are often associated with different disciplinary structures, it should be clear that a transnational perspective cannot but emphasize extradisciplinary factors when considering the history of individual social science disciplines.

While the field was still expanding, Isaac (2009) was in a position to look for parallels and contrasts among various efforts undertaken by intellectual historians, sociologists, historians of science, and practicing social scientists to analyze the Cold War reformation of the social sciences. Isaac's historiographical effort concentrated on the theory-practice dyad, offering a new perspective in which theory was defined as a practical activity. On this view, social-scientific theories are not seen as mere instruments of policy making; they are practical before all, standing as forms of subculture. Isaac's historical approach not only goes beyond the preoccupations of practitioners of a particular discipline, but also considers the nature of human-scientific theorizing in a way that emphasizes the role of extradisciplinary factors.

Roger Backhouse and Philippe Fontaine's *The History of the Social Sciences since 1945* (2010a) juxtaposed disciplinary histories with a view to shedding light on parallels and contrasts among the histories of psychology, economics, political science, sociology, social anthropology, and geography. The closing chapter drew on these disciplinary histories to sketch an account of the history of the social sciences as a whole, paying particular attention to the extensive cross-disciplinary engagements that took place in the period after 1945. This involved challenging the notion, central to the self-identity of some disciplines, that after 1945, the social sciences had developed in isolation from each other. In another volume, *The Unsocial Social Science?* (2010b), Backhouse and Fontaine (2010b) explored interactions between economics (probably the most isolationist of the social sciences) and other social sciences. Case studies of such interactions were the prelude to arguing that disciplinary identities were formed, at least in part, as a result of interactions among the social sciences.

During the 2010s important work (Fleck 2011; Isaac 2012; Solovey and Cravens 2012; Solovey 2013; Cohen-Cole 2013) has been published that tackles the relationship between developments in social scientific work and transformations of Western societies from a variety of angles. These works show that the history of the social sciences since 1945 can hardly be limited to the work of practicing social scientists and that departures from discipline history are now so significant that it becomes difficult to produce histories of social science that do not take extradisciplinary factors into account.

To a lesser extent, a broader perspective on the history of the social sciences since 1945 can also be found in various subfields of history in which there has been a gradual realization of the significance of social scientific ideas. Take political and diplomatic history. In the late 2000s, David Engerman (2007, pp. 600–1) could still write, "Diplomatic historians should now take the next steps: to analyze ideas as seriously as we analyze interests, to take monographs as seriously as memos, and to rank the work of professors on par with that of policymakers and film producers." By that time, international history, if not diplomatic history, had already registered that research on the history of international relations could not but benefit from considering the role of social scientists in building postwar ideologies, most notably modernization (Latham 2000; Gilman 2003). With his study of America's Soviet experts, Engerman (2009) himself offered a convincing demonstration of the synergies to be expected from a combination of diplomatic and intellectual history.[15]

The same can be said of economic history. The influence of Keynes and the Keynesian revolution, a phrase that (rightly or wrongly) linked the emergence of new economic and social policies with developments in economics (see Backhouse and Bateman 2011), made it more difficult for economic historians – especially as some of them were trained as economists – to ignore the role of Keynesian ideas in Western societies.[16] The institutionalization of the relationships between the production of economic knowledge

15 The phrase "Cold War social science," which, as noted by David Engerman (2010), is often used to point out the influence of national security concerns over the production and diffusion of social scientific knowledge, evidences as much the impact of the social sciences on political life and can even be interpreted as a sign of lesser latitude for political historians to produce narratives of political events in which the role of the social sciences would be ignored. As early as the mid-1980s, Conrad Russel (1985, p. 12), professor of British history, wrote, "no political historian should be ignorant of what is going on in other sorts of historical research" and mentioned the history of ideas among the latter.

16 Following suit, Peter Clarke (1985, 18), who was then working on the thinking of Keynes, remarked, "It seems, at first sight, an odd project for a political historian with no qualifications in economic theory behind him." Interestingly Clark reminded his readers of Keynes's apophthegm: "Practical men, who believe themselves to be quite exempt from any intellectual influences, are usually the slaves of some defunct economist."

and policy making represented in the United States by the establishment of the Council of Economic Advisers and in many countries by the increased recruitment of economists to government service gave economic theories a prominence that they had not had before the war (Bernstein 2001) and that was largely confirmed by the rediscovery of the market in the past twenty-five years.[17]

The same is also true of social and cultural history. Although cultural history grew at the expense of social history from the 1970s before it eventually got its "revenge" in the 1990s (Burke 2008 [2004]), there is a sense in which both subfields may be said to have pursued imperialistic ambitions and influenced the writing of history in general. Yet, of the two, cultural history seems to have paid more attention to the power of ideas, and in recent years the connections between cultural and intellectual history have come under greater scrutiny, as illustrated by the cultural turn in Cold War studies (Isaac 2007, pp. 731–3).[18]

In the preceding literatures, the focus of which is not the histories of particular social science disciplines but the broader political, economic, social, and cultural context in which they operate, it is not unusual for scholars to emphasize the significance of what Isaac (2012, p. 60) has termed the "interstitial academic spaces," in which a variety of cross-disciplinary research ventures developed with some success.[19] In view of that development, it seems especially opportune to consider more closely the possible benefits of a comparative interdisciplinary historiography. This book makes an attempt in that direction by juxtaposing the various historiographies of the social sciences – taken as historiographical case studies – in order to establish that the parallels and differences between them are of interest (see also Isaac 2007, 2009).

17 Fourcade (2009) offers a detailed account of the relationships between economists and society in the United Kingdom, the United States, and France in the twentieth century. It should be noted that in the preceding paragraphs we are not so much concerned with the conviction that gradually emerged after the Second World War that understanding historical events should be strongly informed by knowledge produced in the social sciences and that history could make use of techniques taken from the social sciences, as with the role of social scientific ideas in society and its transformations. Revel (2003, pp. 403–4) usefully distinguishes between two types of confrontation and collaboration between history and the social sciences in the twentieth century.

18 Ron Robin's (2001) *The Making of the Cold War Enemy* illustrates the benefits attached to combining cultural and intellectual history.

19 At Harvard the "interstitial academy" corresponded to a "collection of clubs, discussion groups, societies, pedagogical programs, seminars, and marginal departments and schools" (Isaac 2012, p. 60).

Toward a Comparative Interdisciplinary Historiography

Given our interest in comparative interdisciplinary historiography, it might seem counterproductive to structure the book the way we have done, with separate chapters on individual social sciences. However, at the moment, this is probably the only sensible way to approach the problem because it reflects the way the bulk of the literature has evolved. Separate literatures have developed – on the individual social sciences and on historical problems that relate to the social sciences more generally – with the result that many of those who write on the history of the social sciences are well informed about their niche but show little awareness of historiographical developments within contexts other than their own. There has been limited interaction among social scientists writing about the way the history of their own disciplines has been written. As a result it is necessary to turn to specialists in the different social sciences to survey the historiography of their own field, for they can take to the table significant literatures with which the small number of historians working on the social sciences as a whole are not familiar. There has also been limited interaction between such social scientists and those writing on historiography more generally. Having developed historiographies of their own, the former tend to neglect general historiography as a context or inspiration for their own work.[20] There is thus a shortage of cross-disciplinary comparisons of historiographical traditions in the different social sciences that echoes disciplinary historians' neglect of cross-disciplinary engagements. In order to achieve such a comparative interdisciplinary historiography, one needs first to form a clear idea about the existing disciplinary historiographies so as to be able to account for historiographical developments within disciplines on the basis of either disciplinary or extradisciplinary factors.

Both historians tout court and social scientists writing the histories of their own disciplines need to be convinced to take the historiography of the social sciences as a whole more seriously. Historians interested in general

[20] Historians have a much longer tradition of reflection on the practice of writing history from which historians of the social sciences can learn. In particular, they have addressed the critical question of the relationships between history and the social sciences (Iggers 2005 [1997], part two; Burke 2005 [1993], chap. 1) and that of the use of their methods in history writing. Intellectual historians have further grappled with specific problems confronted by historians of the social sciences, such as interpreting texts written in times very different from our own (Collini 1985) and investigating the relationships of ideas to action (Mattson 2002).

historiography have traditionally had little to say about the history of the social sciences as a whole though increased interest in the period since 1945 has prompted greater attention to the social sciences (e.g., Bentley 1997 and Iggers 2005). Historians sometimes exhibit a form of indifference toward the history of ideas, which resembles that demonstrated by current practitioners of social science. Though the past is undeniably the province of historians, past ideas often seem to fall within other, less accessible, provinces. Because it involves a relation with texts, which does not necessarily occur in other types of history (Collini 1985, p. 46), intellectual history raises issues that may seem foreign to political, economic, and social historians. Yet, its reinvention in recent decades, with increased attention paid to the interactions between texts and contexts and the rapprochement with cultural history, though it does not challenge the distinctiveness of the field, has certainly increased its appeal to historians. A number of works (Geary 2008, 2013; Specter 2009; Isaac 2009; Behrent 2009; Sackley 2012) published in the new journal *Modern Intellectual History*, for instance, have demonstrated the relevance of histories of the social science for issues of broader historical interest.

Similarly, historians of the various social sciences need to be convinced to consider the historiography of their own disciplines in the context of the historiography of other social sciences. Contrary to what is often assumed, interdisciplinary relationships and the stability of departmental structure in post–Second World War social sciences need to be considered together, not to be opposed. As intellectual historians concerned with previous centuries have long recognized, today's disciplinary boundaries previously did not exist, and letting them frame past writing, as when Adam Smith is viewed as contributing to the modern discipline of economics, is misleading. Even in the decades after the Second World War, a period in which it is widely assumed that disciplinary identities were fixed, cross-disciplinary engagements were sufficiently widespread to justify taking them into consideration in writing the history of individual social sciences.[21]

For instance, it would seem unreasonable for historians of British anthropology to ignore the history of sociology or for historians of U.S. anthropology to neglect the history of psychology. Likewise, with some leading political scientists actively participating in cross-disciplinary research

[21] Cross-disciplinary research took on several forms, from juxtaposing various disciplinary viewpoints on a variety of society's problems (labor-management relations, crime, social maladjustment, etc.), to more ambitious attempts to combine various social science methods (culture and personality) or to use natural science methods in the study of social phenomena (the behavioral sciences movement).

ventures in the postwar era, there is good reason for historians of political science to be attentive to the history of other social sciences such as sociology, psychology, or economics, with which political science interacts within the field of policy sciences. The same applies to economics, which offers interesting examples of engagements with other social sciences, even though it is generally considered the most isolationist of the social sciences, in the sense that most of its practitioners claim that interactions with the other social sciences have been insignificant, stressing instead its connections with mathematics and the natural sciences (see Backhouse and Fontaine 2010b).

Clearly, the question of the significance of the historiography of the social sciences as a whole for both historians at large and historians of individual social sciences cannot be separated from the discussion of the nature of historical research. General histories that subordinate human agency to social structures or are based on narrow conceptions of human agency may leave little room for the ideas that motivate action – confining them to the superstructural level – and even less for social scientific ideas. In contrast, when the realm of ideas is taken as one human activity among others, historians have every reason to concern themselves with the history of the social sciences if only to get a better grasp of the relations between scientific and lay knowledge.

Last but not least, one important reason for comparing the historiography of the various social sciences after the Second World War is that, as the following essays show, all of them have become, in varying degrees, estranged from their past. This shift has precipitated the emergence of a new category of social scientists whose interest in the past has distinguished themselves from their peers. Social scientists have written about the past of their disciplines ever since disciplinary boundaries began to be defined, but till recently this was in a context where historical approaches were firmly embedded in the social sciences themselves. When the social sciences became less historical, those concerned with the historiography of the social sciences were placed in an awkward position, unlike historians of history, who could still write on historiography without taking off their disciplinary caps. For social scientists in general, the weakening of the link with history meant less familiarity with the various attempts "to understand past human experience" (Collini 1985, p. 46), which in turn explains in part why the historiography of the social sciences and the history of history have moved away from each other in the postwar era. There are variations from one social discipline to another, but there is no question that the general trend toward the dismissal of the past in social science makes a difference in the way the history of the social sciences has been written.

The Chapters That Follow

The growing importance of the social sciences in society motivates this volume, aimed at both persuading historians at large that the historiographies of the social sciences may be relevant to the writing of history of history and introducing historians of individual social sciences to the ways the history of social sciences other than their own is written.

"History and Historiography since 1945," by Kevin Passmore, is placed first because it provides a useful vantage point from which to look at the historiography of other social sciences, as considered in the other chapters. It offers a helpful characterization of postwar history organized around four periods. Relative decline of political history in the decade and a half after 1945 was followed in the 1960s by an affirmation of social history, with its marked eclecticism. Then, one witnesses the emergence of the "cultural turn" in the 1990s and a shift of emphasis from social to cultural history. Finally, a "transnational turn" occurred, whereby he describes the emergence of a series of works emphasizing "the mutual construction of cultures and the instability of their meanings." Needless to say, Passmore does not wish to suggest that this periodization implies that different types of history can be confined to historical periods. Political history, social history, and cultural history, as well as economic history, have coexisted right through the period. His point is that the importance attached to these different types of history and their prominence in both universities and society at large have changed. Passmore's periodization is helpful because, throughout the period, these developments have been accompanied by growing recognition by historians of the accomplishments of social sciences, to the point where it has not been unusual for historians to turn to social scientists for inspiration.

To some extent, these four historical moments can be read in terms of the changing relationships between history and social sciences. The period of dominance of political history predated the expansion of the social sciences after the Second World War so that the reason why that subfield is sometimes seen as having been unscientific may simply be that perceptions of what constitutes science were different before and after the war. Another factor, probably more significant, is that political history came to be seen as having placed too much importance on the intentions lying behind the actions of important people: Those who sought to construct a more scientific history after the war preferred to find explanations in economic and social factors rather than subjective elements.[22]

As is well known, the rise of social history, at least in its *Annales* version, was accompanied by a repositioning of history at the centre of the social sciences with a view to making it displace sociology as the main federating discipline (Revel 1979). This is not to say that Annalistes underestimated other social sciences. They saw them as an integral part of their vision of history, which explains in turn why social scientists such as sociologists, geographers, and anthropologists were interested in the *Annales* approach (see Burke 1990, p. 101–5).[23]

The "cultural turn" can be characterized by increased attention to meaning. As a result, it went with a turn to philosophy and literary criticism, as suggested by Passmore. However, that is not the whole story. While some social scientists considered the meaning ascribed by agents to the world to be irrelevant to the construction of knowledge, others did not. In that sense, the "cultural turn" of the 1990s also revealed a turn to social sciences. As early as in the 1960s and up to the 1990s, cultural historians turned to anthropology for inspiration, with Clifford Geertz standing as the most prominent figure with his "interpretative theory of culture" (Burke 2008 [2004], p. 37). More generally, the idea that social scientists cannot do without representations that the individuals being studied form about social phenomena, though not dominant in postwar social science in general, was far from negligible in those social sciences in which the method of participant observation was central, anthropology being the main example. Historians have gradually become more sensitive to this idea and in the process accepted the need to allow for a variety of viewpoints on reality, its construction and meaning.

Finally, it is unclear whether transnational history, which Passmore associates with the "transnational turn," corresponds to a new form of

[22] At the same time, it should be noted that from the 1950s social historians explored more seriously the possibilities of utilizing insights from psychology and psychiatry in history writing but that development often concerned irrational motivation (Brand 1970, pp. 70–5).

[23] Lepetit (1996, p. 34–5) recalls that the dominant role of *Annalistes* within the Sixth Section can also be explained by the lack of serious institutional competitors in the wake of the Second World War. Likewise, he notes connections with the project of unification of the social sciences as called for by Durkheimian sociology though he insists that *Annalistes* did not recognize themselves in its imperialistic ambitions and relegating of other social sciences to secondary roles (pp. 35, 38). On the influence of other social sciences on the development of the *Annales* project, see Coutau-Bégarie (1989, esp. pp. 82–108).

relationship between history and social science. As we have seen, this new orientation has affected the history of the social sciences (Heilbron et al. 2008; Selcer 2009). It appears that the questions that historians working in transnational history consider most important are often regarded as central in the subfield of international relations, suggesting that historians and political scientists may have something to learn from each other.

Passmore's periodization illustrates that in thinking of the history of history it makes sense to pay some attention to the historiographies of the social sciences because some of them have played an important role in historical research. We have already pointed to the role of anthropology in postwar historical writing especially in cultural history. A better understanding of the historiography of anthropology may prove helpful therefore to illuminate the acclimatization of anthropological concepts, methods, and theories in history. In her essay in this volume, Henrika Kuklick draws an interesting, if debatable, conclusion to the effect that as "a discipline, anthropology is more complex than any of the other social sciences" (Chapter 3, pp. 89–91). Anthropologists, who have made a profession of comparative studies of human societies, finding many significant differences among them, have good reason to think of social scientists' common presuppositions about humankind as unduly simplistic. The complexity alluded to by Kuklick is therefore part of the self-image anthropologists have constructed for their discipline, but it is also the result of anthropologists' belief that other social scientists have experienced difficulty in their attempts to incorporate meaning in their theoretical constructs. After all, Kuklick's remark about the complexity of (sociocultural) anthropology can be read as an indication of its moving away from the social sciences toward the humanities and accounts for its influence in history with its dual footing in the social sciences and humanities.

Though sociology has often been associated with anthropology for its use of the method of participant observation, its role within the social sciences has been even more significant especially because of is integrative ambitions after the Second World War. As "students of society," sociologists have frequently felt it more difficult to resist imperialistic ambitions and accordingly assigned other social sciences an ancillary role. As is well known, economics experienced similar temptations from the 1960s, but economists did not share in the objective of a general theory of social systems that characterized the Parsonian enterprise from the 1950s and dominated American sociology into the 1960s.

Charles Camic provides an instructive account of the historiography of sociology between 1945 and 2012. His essay documents sociologists' ambivalence toward the history of their discipline, which expresses itself in the changing nature of scholarship on the history of sociology, but may also reveal the changing role of history in sociology itself. Camic distinguishes three periods: 1945 to 1969, 1970 to 1999, and 2000 to 2012. Though it is not his intention to suggest that these three periods should be taken rigidly, he nonetheless acknowledges that they facilitate the description of the movement of the history of sociology from the periphery to the center of the discipline and back to its periphery. The ideas of philosophers such as Foucault and Kuhn were taken up both by historians of sociology and by mainstream sociologists, causing history of sociology to move to the center of the discipline. Similarly, the production of encyclopaedic surveys that linked historical traditions in sociological research positioned the history of sociology at the center of mainstream debates. This was in marked contrast to economics, where the ideas of Foucault and Kuhn never penetrated the mainstream. This contrast reflected sociology's lack of a central unifying theoretical structure such as that found in economics. Yet, in other ways, there were parallels with the history of economics: For example, there was a turn toward archival research and a move from the study of ideas to investigating what Camic calls the material aspects of the history of sociology. Finally, the presence of the history of sociology at the heart of the discipline may have helped the establishment of the specialized *Journal of the History of Sociology*, but it did not prevent its disappearance.

In his essay on the historiography of psychology, James H. Capshew also resorts to a tripartite periodization – 1945 to the late 1960s, the late 1960s to the early 1990s, and the past twenty-odd years – which culminates with the preservation of the history of psychology as part of the psychology discipline and its affirmation within the history of science field. Capshew argues that psychology's scientific legitimacy and academic status in the immediate postwar era made concerns over its history secondary to preoccupations about its theoretical advancements. Conditions changed gradually when some began to think of the history of psychology as a neglected area in the late 1950s and early 1960 and tried hard to convince others of the same opinion that something needed to be done about this, resulting in the launching of the *Journal of the History of the Behavioral Sciences* in 1965, followed, some thirty years later, by *History of Psychology*, a journal specifically devoted to psychology's past. Ever since, the field has prospered, giving increased attention to postwar developments.

In economics, too, the establishment of specialized journals played an important role. After the Second World War, economics became a more mathematical, technical discipline and economists were increasingly unwilling to see its history as meriting a place in the curriculum or in general in economics journals. As a result, journals such as *History of Political Economy*, established in 1969, became important in providing places where such work could be published. With a few notable exceptions, its main practitioners, though they might be trained as economists and work in economics departments, were scholars whose reputation rested on their historical research, unlike in the previous generation, where the most eminent historians of economics were drawn from the ranks of leading economic theorists.

As their field changed from being an activity that was widely, though not universally, considered part of economics to a specialized field whose relationship to its parent discipline was increasingly contested, questions were naturally raised about where historians of economics belonged and how they should be conceiving their subject. Economists, to an extent not found in any other social science, evolved a narrow mainstream based on a relatively small set of techniques – to use language favored by many other social scientists, the victory of "positivism" was complete – creating an identity problem for those economists who continued to engage in historical scholarship. Historians of economics had to face the question of whether they remained practitioners of their discipline to a degree historians of other social sciences did not. One of the complications not found in other social sciences is that the group of scholars contending that history of economic thought should be seen as part of economics included many who wished to challenge, if not reject outright, its prevailing "mainstream." Marxists, post-Keynesian, Austrians, and other "heterodox" economists whose work was largely ignored by most economists as leading nowhere found history of ideas a useful niche from which to defend their approach to economics. Such arguments not only reinforced the divide between this group of historians and those wanting to move closer to intellectual history or history of science, but also provided mainstream economists with further reasons to reject historical work.

Robert Adcock, discussing the historiography of political science, exemplifies a completely different orientation in which disciplinary histories are seen as being written by political scientists for other political scientists. Thus although Adcock's chapter covers engagements with intellectual history, represented, for example, by Quentin Skinner, and though there were repeated calls within the field to be "historical," he does not see this as having fed an identity crisis comparable with that found in the history of economics; perhaps this is linked to the existence of disaggregated scholarly identities in the field and of a subfield – political theory – that has long cultivated a rich relationship with the history of political thought. As with sociology and psychology but unlike with economics, it was never possible to hold the view that political science might be a unified field centered on a specific technical apparatus. As with sociology, the historiography of political science was tied up with the disputes over the way the highly fragmented discipline of political science should be approached.

As indicated at the outset of this Introduction, as long as the history of the social sciences was tied to the needs of the subject disciplines, there was arguably little scope for a comparative interdisciplinary historiography. As a history of the social sciences as a whole has gradually taken shape, however, it becomes possible for social scientists and historians as well to have a broader view of the main developments of the social sciences since 1945 and therefore to form a better idea of their parallels and contrasts. In so doing, it may be hoped that our historical knowledge of the social sciences – which has so far been so influenced by the division of labor between historians of different disciplines – be supplemented with a better appreciation of interdisciplinary considerations.

References

Abbott, Andrew. 2001. *Chaos of Disciplines.* Chicago and London: University of Chicago Press.

Abbott, Andrew, and James T. Sparrow. 2007. "Hot War, Cold War: The Structures of Sociological Action, 1940–1955." In *Sociology in America: A History*, ed. Craig Calhoun. Chicago and London: The University of Chicago Press.

Abella, Alex. 2007. *Soldiers of Reason: The RAND Corporation and the Rise of the American Empire.* Boston: Houghton Mifflin.

Amadae, Sonja M. 2003. *Rationalizing Capitalist Democracy: The Cold War Origins of Rational Choice Liberalism.* Chicago and London: The University of Chicago Press.

Backhouse, Roger E., and Bateman, Bradley W. 2011. *Capitalist Revolutionary: John Maynard Keynes.* Cambridge, MA: Harvard University Press.

Backhouse, Roger E., and Fontaine, Philippe, eds. 2010a. *The History of the Social Sciences since 1945.* Cambridge: Cambridge University Press.

2010b. *The Unsocial Social Science? Economics and Neighboring Disciplines since 1945.* Annual supplement to Volume 42 of History of Political Economy. Durham, NC: Duke University Press.

Barnes, Trevor J. 2006. "Geographical Intelligence: American Geographers and Research and Analysis in the Office of Strategic Services, 1941–1945," *Journal of Historical Geography* 32.1:149–68.

Barry, Brian. 1970. *Sociologists, Economists and Democracy.* Chicago and London: The University of Chicago Press, 1978.

Baxter, James Phinney. 1968. *Scientists against Time*, 3rd ed. Boston: Little, Brown. Reprinted Cambridge, MA: MIT Press. First published in 1946.

Behrent, Michael C. 2009. "Liberalism without Humanism: Michel Foucault and the Free-Market Creed, 1976–1979," *Modern Intellectual History* 6.3:539–68.

Bentley, Michael, ed. 1997. *Companion to Historiography.* London: Routledge.

Bernstein, Michael A., 2001. *A Perilous Progress: Economists and Public Purpose in Twentieth-Century America.* Princeton, NJ, and Oxford: Princeton University Press.

Blanckaert, Claude. 1993. "La Société française pour l'histoire des sciences de l'homme. Bilan, enjeux et 'questions vives,'" *Genèses* 10:124–35.

Boudon, Raymond, "Comment écrire l'histoire des sciences sociales?" *Communications* 54:299–317.

Bourdieu, Pierre. "La Cause de la science: Comment l'histoire des sciences sociales peut servir le progrès de ces sciences," *Actes de la recherche en sciences sociales* 106–107:3–10.

Brand, Jeanne L. 1970. "The Social Historian and the History of Psychiatry." In *Psychiatry and Its History: Methodological Problems in Research*, ed. George Mora and Jeanne L. Brand. Springfield, IL: Charles C. Thomas.

Burgin, Angus. 2012. *The Great Persuasion: Reinventing Free Markets since the Depression.* Oxford: Oxford University Press.

Burke, Peter. 1990. *The French Historical Revolution: The* Annales *School, 1929–1989.* Oxford: Polity Press.

2005. *History and Social Theory*, 2nd ed. Ithaca, NY: Cornell University Press. First published in 1993.

2008. *What Is Cultural History?* 2nd ed. Cambridge: Polity. First published in 2004.

Burrow, John. 1966. *Evolution and Society: A Study in Victorian Social Theory.* Cambridge: Cambridge University Press.

2009. *A History of Histories.* London: Penguin.

Bush, Vannevar. 1945. *Science – the Endless Frontier: A Report to the President on a Program for Postwar Scientific Research.* Washington, DC: National Science Foundation, reprinted in 1960.

Capshew, James H. 1999. *Psychologists on the March: Science, Practice, and Professional Identity in America, 1929–1969.* Cambridge: Cambridge University Press.

Chapoulie, Jean-Michel. 2005. "Un cadre d'analyse pour l'histoire des sciences sociales," *Revue d'histoire des sciences humaines* 13:99–126.

Clark, Peter. 1985. "What Is Political History?" *History Today* 35.1:17–18.

Cockett, Richard. 1995. *Thinking the Unthinkable: Thinks-Tanks and the Economic Counter-Revolution, 1931–1983.* London: Fontana Press.

Cohen-Cole, Jamie. 2013. *The Open Mind: Cold War Politics and the Sciences of Human Nature.* Chicago: University of Chicago Press.

Collini, Stefan. 1985. "What Is Intellectual History?" *History Today* 35.10:46–8.

1988. "'Discipline History' and 'Intellectual History': Reflections on the Historiography of the Social Sciences in Britain and France," *Revue de synthèse* 3–4:387–99.

Coutau-Bégarie, Hervé. 1989. *Le Phénomène Nouvelle Histoire: Grandeur et décadence de l'école des* Annales, 2nd ed. Paris: Economica.

Crowther-Heyck, Hunter. 2006. "Patrons of the Revolution: Ideals and Institutions in the Postwar Behavioral Science," *Isis* 97.3:420–46.

De Pillis, Mario S. 1967. "Trends in American Social History and the Possibilities of Behavioral Approaches," *Journal of Social History* 1.1:37–60.

Drouard, Alain. 1982. "Réflexions sur une chronologie: Le développement des sciences sociales en France de 1945 à la fin des annèes soixante," *Revue française de sociologie* 23.1:55–85.

Edgerton, David. 2011. *Britain's War Machine: Weapons, Resources and Experts in the Second World War.* New York: Oxford University Press.

Elton, G. R. 1985. "What Is Political History?" *History Today* 35.1:11–12.

Engerman, David C. 2007. "Bernath Lecture: American Knowledge and Global Power," *Diplomatic History* 31.4:599–622.

2009. *Know Your Enemy: The Rise and Decline of America's Soviet Experts.* Oxford: Oxford University Press.

2010. "Social Science in the Cold War," *Isis* 101.2:393–400

Fleck, Christian. 2011. *A Transatlantic History of the Social Sciences: Robber Barons, the Third Reich ad the Invention of Empirical Social Research.* London: Bloomsbury Academic.

Fontaine, Philippe. 2002. "Blood, Politics, and Social Science: Richard Titmuss and the Institute of Economic Affairs, 1957–1973," *Isis* 93.3:401–34.

2015. "Introduction: The Social Sciences in a Cross-disciplinary Age," *Journal of the History of the Behavioral Sciences*, special issue.

Foster, Roy. 1985. "What Is Political History?" *History Today* 35.1:14–15.

Fourcade, Marion. 2009. *Economists and Societies: Discipline and Profession in the United States, Britain, and France, 1890s to 1990s.* Princeton, NJ, and Oxford: Princeton University Press.

Geary, Daniel. 2008. "Every Social Scientist Her Own Historian," *Modern Intellectual History* 5.2:399–410.

2013. "Children of *The Lonely Crowd*: David Riesman, the Young Radicals, and the Splitting of Liberalism in the 1960s," *Modern Intellectual History* 10.3:603–33.

Geiger, Roger L. 1993. *Research and Relevant Knowledge: American Research Universities since World War II.* New York and Oxford: Oxford University Press.

Gillispie, Charles C. 1988. "History of the Social Sciences," *Revue de synthèse* 3–4:379–85.

Gilman, Nils. 2003. *Mandarins of the Future: Modernization Theory in Cold War America.* Baltimore and London: John Hopkins University Press.

Guglielmo, Mark. 2008. "The Contribution of Economists to Military Intelligence during World War II," *Journal of Economic History* 68.1:109–50.

Haney, David P. 2008. *The Americanization of Social Science: Intellectuals and Public Responsibility in the Postwar United States.* Philadelphia: Temple University Press.

Heilbron, Johan, Nicolas Guilhot, and Laurent Jeanpierre. 2008. "Toward a Transnational History of the Social Sciences," *Journal of the History of the Behavioral Sciences* 44.2:146–60.

Heilbron, Johan, Remi Lenoir, and Gisèle Sapiro (with the collaboration of Pascale Pargamin). 2004. *Pour une histoire des sciences sociales: Hommage à Pierre Bourdieu.* Paris: Fayard.

Herman, Ellen. 1995. *The Romance of American Psychology: Political Culture in the Age of Experts.* Berkeley, Los Angeles, and London: University of California Press.

Iggers, Georg G. 2005. *Historiography in the Twentieth Century: From Scientific Objectivity to Postmodern Challenge.* Middletown, CT: Wesleyan University. First published in 1997.

Igo, Sarah E. 2007. *The Averaged American: Surveys, Citizens, and the Making of a Mass Public*. Cambridge, MA: Harvard University Press.

Isaac, Joel. 2007. "The Human Sciences in Cold War America," *Historical Journal* 50.3:725–46.

2009. "Tangled Loops: Theory, History, and the Human Sciences in Modern America," *Modern Intellectual History* 6.2:397–424.

2011. "Introduction: The Human Sciences and Cold War America," *Journal of the History of the Behavioral Sciences* 47.3 (special issue on The Human Sciences and Cold War America):225–31.

2012. *Working Knowledge: Making the Human Sciences from Parsons To Kuhn*. Cambridge, MA, and London: Harvard University Press.

Kagan, Jerome. 2009. *The Three Cultures: Natural Sciences, Social Sciences, and the Humanities in the 21st Century*. Cambridge: Cambridge University Press.

Kaiser, David, and Heyck. 2010. "Introduction," *Isis* 101.2 (New Perspectives on Science and the Cold War):362–6.

Kelley, John L. 1997. *Bringing the Market Back In: The Political Revitalization of Market Liberalism*. New York: New York University Press.

Klausner, Samuel Z. and Victor M. Lidz, eds. 1986. *The Nationalization of the Social Sciences*. Philadelphia: University of Pennsylvania Press.

Larsen, Otto N. 1992. *Milestones and Millstones: Social Science at the National Science Foundation, 1945–1991*. New Brunswick, NJ, and London: Transaction.

Latham, Michael E. 2000. *Modernization as Ideology: American Social Science and "Nation Building" in the Kennedy Era*. Chapel Hill and London: University of North Carolina Press.

Leibenstein, Harvey. 1979. "A Branch of Economics Is Missing: Micro-Micro Theory," *Journal of Economic Literature* 17.2:477–502.

Lepetit, Bernard. 1996. "Les *Annales*: Portrait de groupe avec revue." In *Une école pour les sciences sociales: De la VIe section à l'École des hautes études en sciences sociales*, ed. J. Revel and N. Wachtel. Paris: Les Éditions du Cerf & EHESS.

Lorenz, Chris. 1999. "Comparative Historiographies: Problems and Perspectives," *History and Theory* 38.1:25–39.

2011. "History and Theory." In A. Schneider and D. Woolf, eds. *The Oxford History of Historical Writing*, Vol. 5: *Historical Writing Since 1945*. Oxford: Oxford University Press.

Mills, C. Wright. 1951. *White Collar: The American Middle Classes*. New York: Oxford University Press.

Mirowski, Philip. 2002. *Machine Dreams: Economics Becomes a Cyborg Science*. Cambridge: Cambridge University Press.

Mirowski, Philip, and Dieter Plehwe, eds. 2009. *The Road from Mont Pelerin: The Making of the Neoliberal Thought Collective*. Cambridge, MA: Harvard University Press.

Offer, Avner. 2006. *The Challenge of Affluence: Self-Control and Well Being in the United States and Britain since 1950*. Oxford: Oxford University Press.

Parsons, Wayne. 1990. *The Power of the Financial Press: Journalism and Economic Opinion in Britain and America*. New Brunswick, NJ: Rutgers University Press.

Porter, Theodore M., and Dorothy Ross, eds. 2003. *The Cambridge History of Science*, Vol. 7: *The Modern Social Sciences*. Cambridge: Cambridge University Press.

Price, David H. 2008. *Anthropological Intelligence: The Deployment and Neglect of American Anthropology in the Second World War.* Durham, NC, and London: Duke University Press.

Revel, Jacques. 1979. "Histoire et sciences sociales: Les paradigmes des *Annales*," *Annales. Économies, Sociétés, Civilisations* 34.6:1360–76.

2003. "History and the Social Sciences." In *The Cambridge History of Science*, Vol. 7: *The Modern Social Sciences*, ed. T. M. Porter and D. Ross. Cambridge: Cambridge University Press.

Riesman, David. 1950. *The Lonely Crowd: A Study of the Changing American Character.* New Haven, CT: Yale University Press.

Robin, Ron. 2001. *The Making of the Cold War Enemy: Culture and Politics in the Military-Intellectual Complex.* Princeton, NJ, and Oxford: Princeton University Press.

Rodgers, Daniel. 2011. *Age of Fracture.* Princeton, NJ: Princeton University Press.

Ross, Dorothy. 1991. *The Origins of American Social Science.* Cambridge: Cambridge University Press.

2003. "Changing Contours of the Social Science Disciplines." In *The Cambridge History of Science*, vol. 7: *The Modern Social Sciences*, ed. T. M. Porter and D. Ross. Cambridge: Cambridge University Press.

Russel, Conrad. 1985. "What Is Political History?" *History Today* 35.1:12–13.

Sackley, Nicole. 2012. "Cosmopolitanism and the Uses of Tradition: Robert Redfield and Alternative Visions of Modernization during the Cold War," *Modern Intellectual History* 9.3:565–95.

Schulten, Susan. 2001. *The Geographical Imagination in America, 1880–1950.* Chicago and London: The University of Chicago Press.

Selcer, Perrin. 2009. "The View from Everywhere: Disciplining Diversity in Post-World War II International Social Science," *Journal of the History of the Behavioral Sciences* 45.4:309–29.

Smith, Roger. 1997. *The Fontana History of the Human Sciences.* London: Fontana.

Specter, Matthew. 2009. "Habermas's Political Thought, 1984–1996: A Historical Interpretation," *Modern Intellectual History* 6.1:91–119.

Solovey, Mark. 2013. *Shaky Foundations: The Politics-Patronage-Social Science Nexus in Cod War America.* New Brunswick, NJ, and London: Rutgers University Press.

Solovey, Mark, and Hamilton Cravens, eds. 2012. *Cold War Social Science: Knowledge Production, Liberal Democracy, and Human Nature.* New York: Palgrave Macmillan.

Solovey, Mark, and Jefferson D. Pooley. 2011. "The Price of Success: Sociologist Harry Alpert, the NSF's First Social Science Policy Architect," *Annals of Science* 68.2:229–60.

Stone, Kirk H. 1979. "Geography's Wartime Service," *Annals of the Association of American Geographers* 69.1:89–96.

Wagner, Peter. 2001. *A History and Theory of the Social Sciences.* London: Sage.

Wagner, Peter, Björn Wittrock, and Richard Whitley, eds. 1991. *Discourses on Society: The Shaping of the Social Science Disciplines.* Dordrecht, Boston and London: Kluwer.

2

History and Historiography since 1945

Kevin Passmore

Historians are as inclined as ever to divide the past into great ages: traditional, premodern, modern, postmodern, colonial, postcolonial, global, feudal, capitalist, et cetera. Historiographers have been particularly attracted to these watersheds. They may claim that inexorable external forces, such as modernization or globalization, break down old certainties and necessitate a new way of writing history appropriate to new times. The shift from social to political history after 1945 and then the cultural turn of the 1990s were both presented in that way. Historiographers may also evoke heroic precursors, great historians, and theoreticians, men and women who possessed privileged insight not only into historical method, but into the very movement of history. The work of these canonical scholars possesses quasi-biblical status, and it must be elucidated and commented upon. Historians sometimes forget to historicize when their own discipline is at stake. A major contention of this essay is that while periodization is unavoidable, one must not reify periods or mistake chronological categorization for explanation.

It would be unfair to charge historians with ignorance of the problems of these ways of writing history. In 1947, Sir Maurice Powicke wittily dismissed teleologies thus:

> To track down every nerve in the body politic and locate each impulse, as though they carried some secret message, is as futile as to read the rivulets that compose the upmost reaches of the Thames as a foresight of the wharves and shipping in the spacious estuary. (Powicke 1947, p. 340, cited in Bentley 2005, p. 113)

An admirer of R. G. Collingwood, Powicke urged historians to examine intellectual contexts and human action. Yet he did not consistently heed his own advice, not least because he believed that intellectual history was a window into the development of the national character. A few years later,

E. P. Thompson advocated beginning with the collective action of ordinary people rather than with abstractions, but he too failed in practice to break with grand narratives, for he often depicted capitalism as a catastrophe of external origin visited on hitherto harmonious working-class life. More recently, some historians have used Michel Foucault's concept of governmentality to critique the idea of progress through neoliberal marketization only to substitute for it a pessimistic grand narrative of their own. Finer reading of historical writing than I can undertake in this essay reveals that certain tensions – methodological holists against methodological individualists, constructivists against realists, materialists against idealists, for example – have been more or less continually present, including within individual works. At the same time, the actual disposition of competing positions in terms of access to institutional power has varied greatly. I shall focus on the broader question of why grand narratives and turns have persisted in spite of awareness of their problematic nature.

The sociology of knowledge tradition provides some help with this paradox. Academic advancement, publication opportunities, and respect within the discipline require historians to demonstrate the "wider implications" of their work. Connecting it with familiar generalizations about the course of history is a good way to do so, given that these notions are so well rooted in politics, journalism, and elsewhere. Indeed, we may turn to the Cambridge school of intellectual history for additional help with our problem, for Stefan Collini has argued that preoccupation with genius and the historiographical canon has obscured the broad intellectual context of historical writing (Collini 1988). We shall see that both historiography and historical writing have been situated within a belief in grand narratives, reified periodization, national stereotypes, resurgences from the collective past, and ideas about elites and masses. These ideas could be traced back to nineteenth-century crowd psychology, as modified by certain strands of positivist social science. Only from the 1960s have historians challenged systematically these approaches, without ever eliminating their legacy.

Another reason for exaggeration of the explanatory power of turning points is that historians have used them as weapons in both specific historical controversies and disputes about the shape of the discipline, thus universalizing particular vantage points (Noiriel 1996, p. 327). More specifically, methodological innovators have been tempted to lump together previous work as positivist or empirical, only to find themselves denounced similarly by advocates of newer paradigms. As Gérard Noiriel puts it, positivism is a "custard pie … thrown in the most contradictory of causes" (Noiriel 1996, pp. 111–16). Those on the receiving end of such accusations may respond with an alternative cyclical periodization, involving the decline of historical method. In fact, historical methods have always been more diverse than many historiographies would suggest – even more so if we take geography into account and if we remember the methodological eclecticism of the work of individual historians.

Rather than categorizing historical work in terms of periods, it is more revealing to examine practical use of methods for particular purposes from particular perspectives. However, we cannot ignore historical turns. Whatever we might think, many historians have believed them to be important, and have positioned their work in relation to them. Of course, there was little certainty concerning what these turns entailed, and so theoretical reference points do not correlate neatly with historical practice. And in the cut and thrust of debate, historians often take positions different from those with which they begin. Privileging the practical use of methods allows us to overcome fruitless debates about the relative importance of continuity and change in historical writing and whether or not there was a cultural turn, for instance, for the answer depends on one's perspective and definition of a turn.[1] Another advantage of beginning with perspectives is that it reveals that allegedly different positions can be more compatible than protagonists in historiographical disputes have realized – as Steve Rigby showed for the Brenner debate concerning the origins of agrarian capitalism, which once so exercised medieval historians (Rigby 1995). With these considerations in mind, I shall explore and problematize some of the conventional turns in historical writing – social and cultural and transnational.

Before I do so, two points require elucidation. First, my arguments apply to historiography defined broadly: to histories of the whole discipline, to history in particular countries, periods, or fields. Historiography may involve critique of concepts, the chronology of interpretative fashions, or social or cultural histories of academic life. Insofar as most historians position themselves in relation to previous work in their field, they are all historiographers. The term "historiography" may include abstract philosophies of history and methodological discussions of issues such as objectivity, explanation, structure and agency, causation, and the status of history

[1] Arguably, the dispute in the recent *American Historical Review* forum between Judith Surkis and Julia Adeney Thomas concerning the reality or otherwise of the cultural turn revolves around an irresolvable dispute about definition of a turn. Both implicitly assume that they can measure the past of the discipline against what a turn really is, and then universalize what can actually only be a perspective. In fact, from different perspectives one may see either diversity or unity. My preference is to examine the multiple meanings and uses in practice of "turns" (Surkis 2012; Thomas 2012).

as a science. I have included them only where they have a direct bearing on practical historical writing.

Second, my essay is itself a perspective. It reflects my knowledge as a French specialist in a Welsh university. Typically, my department is divided between a minority of monolingual historians of England and a bi- or multilingual majority of historians of Wales, Europe, and Asia. I know the francophone historiography of France at first hand, but that of other countries only through the vast anglophone scholarship on them (Evans 2009). No historian possesses a global perspective, but historians' views are not reducible to national labels either. History has always been transnational, dialogic and multivocal, and inseparable from global economic and cultural power relationships. However, as Robert Adcock reminds us in this volume, neither the inevitability of construction, selection, and perspective nor the prevalence of professional rivalries absolves us from examining the relative coherence and plausibility of historical interpretations – including interpretations of the history of history.

The Swan Song of Political History: 1945–60

In *What Is History?* (1962), a text still regularly prescribed as undergraduate reading in British universities, E. H. Carr caricatured previous historical writing as preoccupied with high politics, empirical, and hypocritically objectivist, and advised historians to learn from social science. His answer to the question of what made one historian more objective than another was to ask which of them better understood the direction of history – as, one presumes, Carr believed himself to do. His targets were the British followers of the founder of modern historiography, Leopold von Ranke. Yet Rankeans were not simply inductivists. Ranke had denied that the sources simply spoke for themselves; documents reflected a "spirit," expressed in nations and states, that must be grasped through intuition. This combination of inspiration and science, Rankeans believed, rendered German methods superior to dry French positivism (Iggers 1984, pp. 17–23). In fact, political historians across the West all used concepts familiar to crowd psychologists – elite, mass, national psychology, and progress. Establishment historians may have focused largely on politics, but they were implicitly or explicitly theoretical and did not neglect society, even if their politics differed from Carr's.

Political history was strongest in West Germany, where scholars had to define themselves against East German Marxism. West German historians were well placed to resist novelty because the grip of the professoriate on new appointments was so firm. Yet German history was not entirely divorced from the social science of the day. Gerhard Ritter claimed in 1946 that the purpose of the historian was to uncover racial peculiarities within peoples (Berger 1997, pp. 25–6). Teleologies and crowd psychology handily disposed of Nazism: Even the anti-Nazi Golo Mann argued that Hitler's ability to hypnotize the mass had diverted Germany from its true path, while Friedrich Meinecke and others revealed that path to be the Atlantic Alliance and Europe of nation-states. Totalitarianism theory, integral to Western non-Marxist social science, reinforced this interpretation. For instance, Hans Rothfels held that the roots of Nazism were not to be found specifically in Germany, but in the vulnerability of European mass society to totalitarianism. He assumed the strain-anomie-breakdown-reintegration model inherited from crowd psychology (Mann 1974; Berger 1997, pp. 40–8). German historians demanded high standards of scholarship, but used their monopoly on "historical science" to prevent revision of nationalist history. Interestingly, German pioneers of social history, such as Werner Conze and Theodor Schieder, had begun their careers in the National Socialist *Volksgeschichte* (people's history) movements of the 1930s. They transformed this racist history into a social history fit for the supposed realities of the new "technical-industrial era" (Welskopp 2010).

Meanwhile, British political historians semiunwittingly reworked social science concepts. The preeminent historians – Herbert Butterfield, Geoffrey Elton, and Lewis Namier – were primarily historians of politics, and Elton was especially hostile to social scientists, whom he charged with constructing abstractions that "always failed the test of facts." In *The Practice of History* (1967) he counterpoised his Rankeanism to Carr's *What Is History?*; in his revealingly entitled *Return to Essentials* (1991) he related modern historiography as decline in the face of threats from Marxists, Whigs, and deconstructionists.

Yet Elton's practical work implicitly combined social scientific categories with national stereotypes. He held that the English possessed an ability to reconcile order with liberty that he contrasted to the ethos of the German regime from which he had fled, and he saw English history as the working out of those characteristics (W. Palmer 2001, pp. 8–9). His histories of the "Tudor revolution in government" narrated England's development from the traditional monarchy of Henry VII to modern nation-statehood under Henry VIII, impelled by Thomas Cromwell's reforms (Elton 1953; Slavin 1990). Elsewhere, Elton quoted Max Weber, and saw specialization, secularization, and the nation-state as the key to the historical process (Elton 1963, pp. 274–97). To borrow Trotsky's representation of Lenin, Cromwell was the "midwife of history," leading his country to self-realization. Elton presents Cromwell as the epitome of English virtues; he always "proceeds with circumspection, while making plain the direction in which his intentions lay" (Elton 1973, p. 33). Mutatis mutandis, Elton saw professionalism and distrust of preconceived blueprints as essential to objectivity in historical writing – Elton casts himself in the historiographical role of Cromwell (Elton 1967).

Social science is rarely explicit in Elton's work. In the case of Namier it is obvious. Namier's histories of eighteenth-century English politics were neither narrowly political nor stories of great men pursuing high-minded goals in the manner of Cromwell. Namier attacked the Whig story of progress. He pioneered the method of "collective biography" or "prosopography"; he constructed detailed life stories of members of parliament, their property holdings, commercial ties, patronage networks, and club membership, and argued that personal advancement mattered more than the struggle between Whig and Tory (Namier 1929; Namier 1930).

While Namier was Rankean in his rejection of generalization, he nevertheless felt that Sigmund Freud had unlocked the link between politicians' private and public lives. He denied that men acted in response to reason: "What matters most is the underlying emotions, the music, compared to which ideas are a mere libretto, often of very inferior quality" (Namier 1955, p. 4). Namier approved Marx's view that politics were based on interests, but he was very right-wing – E. P. Thompson called him an "inverted Marxist" (Thompson 1965, p. 23). Namier borrowed a cynical view of the masses (the "ham") from Vilfredo Pareto, thus blending politics with crowd psychology and elitism.

Butterfield's *Whig Interpretation of History* (1931) was a major reference point for British historians, even if its strictures against teleology were mostly honored in the breach. The paradox applied to Butterfield himself. On the one hand, he criticized the Protestant and parliamentary Whigs for triumphalism and dividing the world into friends and enemies of progress. On the other hand, he felt that historians could judge from a plane higher than the Whigs' Protestantism or Lord Acton's Catholicism. Butterfield also criticized Namier for neglecting the positive role of the masses (Bentley 2005, pp. 154–8).

Butterfield's anti-Whig manifesto is important too because it essentialized the history of the discipline. Michael Bentley points out that Butterfield classed as Whigs certain historians who in their time stood on opposite sides of the political divide. In effect, Butterfield invented the category "Whig," thus "othering" the disciplinary past (Bentley 2005, pp. 92–3).

Notwithstanding, Butterfield correctly highlighted the presence of teleologies in British historical writing. A glance at British social history in this period confirms the point.

Contrary to subsequent accounts, British social history, including radical social history, began long before the 1960s. Interestingly, it was methodologically related to the fear (or idealization) of the masses and progress narratives that we saw in political history. A major debate concerned the consequences of (historically inevitable) industrialization. John Clapham saw it as progressive while R. H. Tawney saw it as a human catastrophe, at least until Christian-socialist ethics moralized it. George Kitson Clark, in *The Making of Victorian England* (1962), wrote in terms that the crowd psychologist Gustave Le Bon would have recognized: England was in a state of transition from the old to the new order, and so "promiscuity, animalism, brutality and grossness" prevailed. Demagogic Chartists and Gladstonian liberals exploited this potential for evil, but the manufacturing common sense protected the mass from totalitarianism (Taylor 1997, pp. 160–1).

Harold Perkin was more to the left, but shared similar concepts. Perkin was influenced by Max Weber, and like the German sociologist, Perkin was indebted to crowd psychology (Baehr 1990). Perkin conceived the crowd as an organism that possessed a mind with drives. In *The Structured Crowd*, he called for historians to write "the natural history of the body politic, exposing and explaining its ecology, anatomy, physiology, pathology and, since the body politic may be assumed to exist on more than the physical plane, its psychology too" (Perkin 1981, pp. 9, 16). As a left-winger, Perkin looked to a managerial elite rather than manufacturers; he embraced trade unionism and felt that the working class could generate an elite of its own, able to structure the mass.

In France, the *Annales* was then acquiring international fame. Ernest Labrousse, who succeeded Marc Bloch at the Sorbonne, was a Marxist who emphasized the relationship between economic crises, grasped through analysis of price series, and the revolutions of 1789 and 1848. Yet the influence of Marxism on the *Annales* was limited. Even Labrousse's own disciples rejected his economic determinist Marxism. More important was Durkheim's holist social science, with its functionalism, traditional-modern evolution, and assumption of unitary social entities held together by a "collective conscience." Also influential was the positivism of the Durkheimian economist François Simiand, who derived laws of development from the comparison of a series of cases. Annalistes advocated scientific social history, which they saw as superior to unscientific political history. They shared more with American modernization theorists than with Marxism and were especially interested in the work of W. W. Rostow, for whom British industrialization depended as much on Protestantism and nationalism as on economics (Burguière 2006, pp. 142–5, 163; Rostow 1949).

Fernand Braudel (who had invited Rostow to contribute to the *Annales*) was more representative of the *Annales* than Labrousse (Burguière 2006, pp. 169–70). Braudel advocated "total history," which meant both interdisciplinarity and division of society into three levels with corresponding temporalities. Historians, he argued, must focus not on politics or economic conjunctures, the first and second levels, respectively, but on the interaction of deep geographical, meteorological, economic, agricultural, demographic structures that changed almost imperceptibly over the "longue durée." Braudel's *Annales* also broke with national-political history in that they focused on regions (albeit mainly of France) and transnational units such as his own Mediterranean world. Whereas Labrousse concentrated largely on France, the *Annales* under Braudel's influence extended its reach globally, covering topics from colonial Peru to beasts of burden in ancient North Africa. Historians of Wales were among those who were attracted to the *Annales* rejection of national frameworks (Williams 1980).

Emmanuel Le Roy Ladurie's *Les Paysans de Languedoc* (1966) is a classic total history of a medieval region, drawing together geography, demography, psychology, economy, and society, and it compares Languedoc with Catalonia. It is also compatible with the functionalisms, interactions, temporal lags, and diverse paths to modernity of the more nuanced versions of modernization theory, as found in Norbert Elias's civilizing process and in Rostow. In this vein, Le Roy Ladurie evoked the dysfunctional contradiction between Languedoc's backward demographic and economic conditions and the advanced development of the state and culture, and added that the exile of their elites provoked outbursts of hysteria in the persecuted Protestant peasant mass (Burguière 2006, pp. 174, 177, 183).

Following in the tradition of Marc Bloch, the *Annales* presented their social history as more appropriate to the requirements of modern society. They cast their rivals of Sciences Po (the popular name for the Institut d'études politiques, a higher education and research institution specializing in the social sciences) as advocates of an outdated political history. In fact, the two sides shared methodological assumptions, not least because inductivist political history had never been as influential in France as the *Annales* narrative would have it (Sirinelli 1992, pp. xviii–xxii; Noiriel 1988, pp. 60–1). Both the Annalistes and their rivals rooted individual behavior in reified geographical "mentalities" or "temperaments," with their crowd psychology baggage – the difference was that the *Annales* focused on regional and transnational rather than political-national mentalities. Analogous concepts had been imported into both through the geography of Vidal de la Blache, the electoral geography of André Siegfried, and the ethnology of Lucien Lévy-Bruhl, all of which owed much to crowd psychology (Le Goff 1974). In 1946, the Sciences Po historian François Goguel reaffirmed the importance of deep mental structures in politics, through his examination of the parties of "order" and "movement" (Goguel 1946; Sirinelli 1992).

In America politics remained the primary focus of historical writing, but the notion that politics should be studied using social scientific methods was equally strong. The influential Charles Beard had argued in the 1930s that although social science could not be as exact as natural science, it could nevertheless establish laws based on observed repetitions of conduct (Beard 1934). In the 1950s, Beard's economic determinist understanding of the American Revolution, dating back to 1913, remained important. Beard saw the revolution as a conflict between, on the one hand, debtors, small farmers, and wealthy landowners, and, on the other, rich capitalists. The latter used the new federal Constitution to curb the democratic tendencies of the small farmers, but in 1800 planters and small farmers worked together to establish Jeffersonian democracy. Beard's emphasis on class conflict possessed affinities with Marxism. Yet Beard was at least as much a left liberal and a precursor of modernization theorists. Like Perkin, Beard was convinced that the twentieth century would generate the triumph of the rationalizing industrial corporation in a planned economy, and that the most important question was whether the agent of planning would be Marxian socialism, industrial feudalism, or his own preference, social democracy. Otherwise put, industrial concentration was an external force, to which classes and societies adapted in different ways, as must historical writing. Beard's arguments anticipated the many later twentieth-century works that compared pathways to modernization (Beard 1913; Beard 1915; Noble 1985, pp. 26–8; Barrow 2000).

After 1945, several American historians dropped Beard's emphasis on conflict for a more conservative consensus vision. In 1965, John Higham published his Whiggish history of the profession, in which he celebrated the triumph of objectivism over the "ideological" history of the 1930s (Higham 1965). Some historians opposed a moralistic view of the past to Beard's economic determinism, while others developed a version of modernization theory that showed the United States as both unique and a model for the world. For modernization theorists, conflict did not produce progress, but caused status anxiety (or anomie) – a concept with roots in crowd psychology (Tyrrell 2011).

The "Social Turn"

The preceding narrative problematizes the view that social history was invented in the 1960s (Taylor 1997). It was already a leading force in France, and elsewhere particular kinds of social science informed political histories. There is more truth in the contention that the 1960s brought about a new historical method that extended the range of sources and developed new ways of reading them. Rather than focus on reified social groups and structures, British Marxists such as Edward Thompson emphasized the self-creation of social groups in conditions of unequal conflict and power – they wrote "history from below." American Marxists also went in search of the agency of the working class, but more modestly saw themselves as heralds of a "new" social history. These historiographical developments were far from original in themselves. Thompson cited the eighteenth-century thinker Giambattista Vico, as a precedent for Marx's contention that men [*sic*] make history but not in circumstances of their own choosing (Thompson 1965, p. 353). But they did bring about a partial reconfiguration of history in the academy. Moreover, new social histories emerged just as figures at the junction of history and sociology, notably Charles Tilly, critiqued the functionalist concepts on which earlier generations of historians had drawn. Also important was the import of social and political conflicts into the universities thanks to relative democratization of access. Some social historians endeavored to expand the practice of academic history beyond university departments.

From the perspective of protagonists, conflicts among political historians, Marxists, and non- or anti-Marxist social historians were acrimonious. Controversy covered issues such as the primacy of domestic or foreign policy in German history, the role of coercion and consent in maintaining social hierarchy in Anglo-Britain, the extent to which American slaves possessed an independent culture, and the validity of the Marxist view of class as opposed to the Weberian multidimensional approach.

From a *post hoc* perspective, it is evident that there was also some agreement. Progress narratives and crowd psychology were too subtly entrenched in Western historiography to disappear overnight. Critics accused Thompson of merely celebrating agency rather than historicizing it (Giddens 1987). We shall see that Thompson reverted to functionalism when his understanding of agency broke down. The persistence of older forms of social science was particularly evident in the way that social historians wrote the history of the profession. Broad-brush intellectual teleologies, national stereotypes, and external social forces continued to dominate. Alternative methods emerged gradually, and never won out completely.

The *Annales* still focused more on social structure than on agency. Use of computers enabled extension of Labrousse's economic history, especially of early-modern France. Genuinely scientific history seemed possible, as quantification revealed patterns that were invisible to people in the past (Burguière 2006, p. 132). Interest in quantification was not confined to the *Annales*. In Britain, it was more indebted to classical economics than in France, but shared the same tendency to see Western developments as paradigmatic. Faith in the scientific status of economic history was strongest in the United States, where R. W. Fogel projected trends backward to suggest that the role of railways in U.S. industrialization had been exaggerated (Hudson 2010).

In 1979, Jacques Le Goff's collection *La nouvelle histoire* reaffirmed the preeminence of the *Annales* in French social history (to the point of triumphalism, some said) and did not depart radically from Braudel's methods. A decade on, in a new preface, Le Goff struggled to convince readers that the *Annales* was still historiographically progressive. To ward off challenges, he resorted to the classic tactic of depicting challengers as resurgences from the past. He urged his colleagues to guard against "the revenge of traditional or neo-traditional historians who resemble the post-revolutionary émigrés who returned having 'learned nothing and forgotten nothing.'" He warned against "young or old historians who are simply reactionary" (Le Goff 1988, p. 15; Middell 2010, p. 119).

This recourse to teleology was part of a struggle to define and capture the *Annales* movement. Le Goff's target was the emergence of national and political history within the *Annales*. Pierre Nora's massive *Lieux de mémoire* collection (1984–6) focused on *national* memory, which assumed implicitly that the nation was like a person, with a psychology and a memory. François Furet, meanwhile, critiqued the Marxist view of the French Revolution using classic progress narratives, and argued that if France was to become genuinely modern, it must break with the Jacobin legacy (communism). The *Annales* turned to the great subjects of French political history, just as Sciences Po historians began to emphasize common ground with the *Annales* (Furet 1985; Furet 1995; Nora 1987; Sirinelli 1992, pp. vii–x).

Annales histories shared functionalism with "American" modernization theory, then entering its heyday. Modernization theory's core concepts were the shift from tradition to modernity, comparison of national cases, functionalism, internalization, and use of models to measure and classify objectively discrete social phenomena. For modernization theorists, stability was the natural state of society; conflict derived from backward-looking resistance to modernization. Along with the *Annales*, modernization theorists widened the subject matter of history to include topics such as emotions and childhood. Examples include Pieter Spierenberg's account of the modernization of manners and private life and Edward Shorter's history of the modern family (Spierenburg 1991; Shorter 1977).

In Germany, too, social history advanced without breaking entirely with the past. From one angle, Fritz Fischer's *Germany's War Aims in the First World War* (1961) represented a radical departure from established history. He used quasi-Marxist concepts to argue that in 1914 Germany had risked world war to secure economic hegemony over Eastern Europe. Otherwise, Fischer's reliance on diplomatic documents was familiar, and his claim that Germany was entirely responsible for the war was a mirror image of the conservative view that it was the victim of the other powers. Subsequently, historians such as Hans-Ulrich Wehler developed a sophisticated version of modernization theory in which anachronistic aristocratic counterelites indoctrinated the masses through education and conscription, resisted democracy, and drove Germany down a "special path" (*Sonderweg*) toward Nazism. Only the latter's catastrophic defeat permitted Germany to modernize (Iggers 1984, pp. 83–180).

Georg Iggers, the leading Western expert on European historiography, applied the *Sonderweg* narrative in a way that paralleled Le Goff's defense of the *Annales*. For Iggers, the German historical establishment represented an academic equivalent of the aristocracy, attached to the preindustrial past and resistant to modern British, French, and American methods. German historians' fetishization of the state ensured that civil society was poorly developed, and so historians refused to expand their interest into economic and social issues (Iggers 1997, pp. 41, 66; Berger 1997, pp. 21–48). In effect, the absence of a bourgeois revolution ensured that German historiography failed to modernize.

The major theoretical innovations of the period originated with those who focused not on social and mental structures, but on the rationality of ordinary people, their acquisition of self-knowledge through pursuit of collective interests, and their influence upon the course of history. The new trend included the British Marxists, German champions of *Alltagsgeschichte* (the history of everyday life), the microhistory of the Italian Carlo Ginzburg, and the American Herbert Gutman's reinterpretation of slave culture (Gutman 1976). Theoretically, these historians simultaneously rejected "bourgeois" social science and Stalinist Marxism.

On the margins of history and sociology, Marxism and modernization theory, Charles Tilly argued that social movements did not act blindly, but used "repertoires of collective action" (Tilly 1964). Thompson's *Making of the English Working Class* (1963) showed that workers did not mindlessly respond to the evolution of the mode of production, but experienced the industrial revolution as an assault on their rights as "free-born Englishmen". George Rudé exploded Le Bon's view that the crowd was motivated by elemental passions; he researched its social composition, its members' ideas and objectives, and the changing nature of protest in history. Participants in the crowd were not inordinately affected by anomie, but were respected members of the community (Rudé 1964). Ginzburg showed that the early modern peasantry possessed a culture of its own, not dependent on that of the elites (Ginzburg 1981).

"Historians of the people" attempted to expand historical writing socially. In France, Marxist history had since the 1930s possessed a limited presence in the universities, particularly in the field of the French Revolution, and was closely linked to the Communist Party. In 1960, the party founded the interdisciplinary Institut Maurice Thorez, linking activists to university historians. Marxist history in France declined with the Communist Party, and history from below in the British sense hardly developed there. At Ruskin College Oxford, Raphael Samuel linked academic and amateur historians with activists through the History Workshop movement. In West Germany, too, History Workshops sprouted; they were linked to the *Alltagsgeschichte* movement and played an important part in reworking the Nazi past.

Ultimately, these initiatives were absorbed into the academic mainstream, not least because there was a contradiction at their heart. Peoples' historians wanted the people to speak for themselves, but expected professional historians to train them to do so. Even Thompson could not quite escape the communist vanguardism of his past, while Samuel claimed that without Marxist stiffening, people's history would degenerate into nostalgia (Samuel 1981). Glen Jordan, in an account of the development of a people's history movement in Cardiff Docklands, denounces the elitism of "Rankean" history, but is coy about his own role as a professional academic in the movement.

However innovative they were, people's historians struggled to free themselves from older assumptions about reified social structure, partly because it was present in an influential reading of Antonio Gramsci, in which reified classes' struggles against each other for ideological hegemony. Ginzburg, for instance, used Gramsci to criticize Bloch's privileging of the homogeneous psychology of a given period over class conflict, but saw classes as things; he combined Gramsci with a determinist reading of the linguistic theory of M. M. Bakhtin to buttress the notion of an absolutely autonomous peasant culture (Ginzburg 1972; Zambelli 1985, pp. 985–6). The American historian Eugene Genovese used the concept of hegemony to emphasize social control. He may have subtitled his book "The World the Slaves Made," but he stressed slaves' internalization of slave owner values rather than agency.

Meanwhile historians of Italy drew upon Gramsci's view of the Risorgimento as a failed "bourgeois" revolution that had not produced a genuinely modern national society (Davis 1979). That too opened Marxists to "bourgeois" views of history. Gramsci urged the working-class movement to assume the historically necessary task of completing the national-bourgeois revolution and to that end advocated popular front alliances of socialist and democratic forces. Thompson advanced similar arguments about England, where, he argued, the working class had (or should have) assumed the progressive cause that the bourgeoisie had "betrayed" out of fear of Jacobinism (Thompson 1963, pp. 466–77).

Following this logic, Thompson advocated a sort of historiographical popular frontism, with nationalist connotations: Marxist historians would take the historiographical leadership from bourgeois functionalists while adopting the best of the English radical tradition – they would translate foreign traditions into "an English tongue" (Thompson 1979a, p. 37; B. D. Palmer 1994, pp. 11–15). His "Time, Work-Discipline and Industrial Capitalism" illustrates his consequent methodological eclecticism. He cites the *Annales* as a precedent for his analysis and recounts an epochal shift from a naturally and religiously regulated world to one rationalized by time, a process that begins with the elites and is initially resisted in popular culture, but is eventually "internalized" thanks to the intensity with which injunctions against time wasting were repeated by employers, clergy, and schoolteachers. Working-class agency, he implies, is confined to the transition to capitalism (Thompson 1967). His arguments share much with the modernization theory and functionalism that he criticized elsewhere.

The essay also confirms Samuel's regretful suggestion that left-wing people's history shared much with right-wing critiques of mass society derived from Durkheim and Le Bon (Samuel 1981, p. xii). Indeed, Thompson was not above feminizing and racializing the crowd, and he ascribed to the English working class a blend of English method and Irish excitability. He evokes the recalcitrance of Irish and colonial workers to time discipline and suggests that mothers of young children have "an imperfect sense of time" (Thompson 1963, pp. 469–85; 1967, pp. 79, 91–3; J. W. Scott 1988). Methodological eclecticism is evident in each strand of history from below.

Women's history owed as much to liberal modernization theory as to Marxism (not to speak of radical feminism). In the modernizing camp, Patricia Branca argued that in nineteenth-century France, middle-class women led the way in emancipation. They did not abandon the family, but became freer within it. They achieved more loving relationships within nuclear families, abandoning the less affective relationships of traditional society. The family was a stepping-stone toward female emancipation in a modern society (Branca 1978). Other historians of women assumed the primacy of class over gender. Elizabeth Roberts controversially argued that because women controlled the family purse strings, they were not really oppressed by working-class men; only bourgeois men possessed power over women (Roberts 1985). Still others used the concept of patriarchy to show the undifferentiated oppression of women throughout history, but their advocacy of women's separatism also left room for women's agency (Bennett 1996).

Some historians of women emphasized agency in the Thompsonian vein. Claudia Koonz argued that the (functionalist) totalitarianism model of Nazism reduced women to passive objects of Nazi ideology; she countered that millions of bourgeois women joined Nazi organizations in the belief that they were furthering women's cause (Koonz 1988). Others rejected the optimistic modernization narrative in favor of the argument that capitalism and rationalization had destroyed a golden age of relative sexual complementarity. Bonnie Smith argued that in the mid-nineteenth century, men and women had worked side by side in the businesses of northern France, but that capitalist concentration separated the male and female spheres and confined women to the family. Nevertheless, Smith uses psychoanalytic methods to argue that through charitable work women attempted to moralize the male world of politics (Smith 1981).

In India, the subaltern studies movement issued from disillusion with successor regimes in formerly colonial states. It took issue with a historiography that had hitherto been written from the perspective of two elite groups: the colonial British and Indian nationalists. The former held that the British had taught liberty and parliamentary government to Indians – in other words they modernized the country. The latter saw the independence movement as united behind the bourgeois leadership of Gandhi's Congress, which awoke the mass of Indians to political life; enlightenment, once again, spread downward (Guha 1982). Subaltern historians recast nationalism as popular, just as Thompson had reworked the English national tradition with the working class at its heart. Subaltern studies spawned a vast historiography of the Indian peasantry, showing its active contribution to nationalism, and its reappropriation of Western ideas in native idiom. For instance, Shahid Amin argued that Gandhi's message of national unity was invoked by the people against their landlords, whom they criticized for unpatriotic alliance with the British (Amin 1984). Like labor and women's historians, Indian historians often posited a golden age, in which peasants of different religions lived harmoniously before capitalism and colonialism produced disharmony.

To explore resistance to capitalism, patriarchy, and colonialism, labor, women's, and subaltern historians developed new ways of reading sources. Thompson had struggled with the problem of understanding subjects who had left no traces in the archives. He sometimes argued that it was sufficient to "listen" to the sources to hear the importance of class (Thompson 1979b, pp. 18–19), but got into a terrible tangle when considering eighteenth-century societies in which the word "class" was not explicit in the sources (Thompson 1978). He and others turned to anthropology, which taught that historians did not have to read sources simply for the conscious intentions of their authors. They used reading against the grain, thick description, and visual sources.

The turn to anthropology confirmed the eclecticism of social history. Anthropology could be integrated into historiography partly because some versions were rooted in a Durkheimian method to which historians were accustomed. Sir Keith Thomas's seminal work on magic is a case in point, in that it reads meaning from modernization. Thomas accepted Bronisław Małinowski's view that magic met people's alleged innate need for explanation of phenomena that they could neither understand nor control, and he attributed magic's decline not to the emergence of new technology, as Małinowski did, but to the rise of scientific rationalism (Thomas 1971, pp. 767–800). Marxists sometimes used Durkheimian anthropology in similar ways, as Thompson did in his aforementioned essay on capitalist time.

Historians also used the symbolic anthropology of Claude Lévi-Strauss and Clifford Geertz, for it seemed to provide a means to show how workers, women, and peasants viewed the world. Symbolic anthropology was central to Le Roy Ladurie's immensely successful *Montaillou* (1975) and to *Alltagsgeschichte*, while the ever-eclectic Thompson used it in his account of the moral economy of the poor (Thompson 1971; Burguière 2006, pp. 177–9). Ginzburg's *Ecstasies: Deciphering the Witches' Sabbath* (1991) bears the imprint of Lévi-Strauss's anthropology, in that a microhistory provides the links to all human stories. Some critics felt that symbolic anthropology could lead to a new idealism, a charge also leveled at the cultural turn of the 1990s.

The "Cultural Turn"

The expression "linguistic turn" was first used at an intellectual history conference at Cornell in 1980, in which Dominick LaCapra and Hayden White were prominent. Their desire to treat intellectual works as texts and to liberate their discipline from subservience to social context subsequently became an attack on social history generally and on historians' naïve reliance on facts (LaCapra and Kaplan 1982). By the early 1990s, historians across the discipline were evoking a "cultural turn." Some of its advocates share with earlier innovators the conviction that they are the avant garde of a new epoch characterized by imperatives that render older approaches irrelevant. Thus, Julia Adeney Thomas argues that the linguistic turn could not be submitted to prior meanings but could only be understood in the light of future possibilities; she cites Nietzsche to the effect that the greatest thoughts are understood most slowly (Thomas 2012).[2] Yet we saw in the previous section that social historians had not neglected culture. In different ways, British Marxists, Gramscians, and *Annales* historians had made it central to their work, for instance, through engagement with cultural anthropology. Their methods and concerns would not be entirely abandoned after the "turn," sometimes in opposition to new methods, sometimes in harmony. While controversy mostly concerned poststructuralism, other methods of reading texts, such as those of Mikhail Bakhtin and the Cambridge school, were also important (Surkis 2012). That is not to say that the linguistic/cultural turns are irrelevant, for the historiographical landscape has changed, if not necessarily in ways that advocates of various kinds of cultural history wanted it to change. As attention shifts to meaning, previously central topics such as the causes of the French and Russian Revolutions now attract little notice.

The French philosopher-historian Michel Foucault was an obligatory reference point for poststructuralists. Inevitably historians' reception of his work was selective, and it could support multiple readings anyway. On the one hand, Foucault rejected academic history for legitimizing the disciplinary society rather than challenging it. Political historians might have been one target of Foucault's denial that the choices of rational, autonomous individuals provided the motor and meaning of historical action. Foucault's critique of progress narratives could also be read as an attack on modernization

2 Her essay illustrates the problems of reification of periodization. She argues that climate change is such a threat that it renders all previous historical work irrelevant. One may agree that it raises new questions about the past, but it can hardly explain everything that is happening in the present, let alone the past.

theory. While the latter stressed evolutionary change, Foucault described sharp breaks in overarching systems of meaning (*epistemes*), an idea that alienated some Annalistes, but might have been more attractive to Marxists, had Foucault not dismissed socialism as another instance of the disciplinary Enlightenment project.

Foucault considered himself to be an archaeologist and genealogist of knowledge rather than a historian. Nevertheless, his work appealed to some historians. Marxists recognized in his *L'Ordre du discours* a version of their own theory of ideology, in which institutions constrain through prohibition, rejection, and division. Institutions "give a person a place, honour, and disarm him/her" (Foucault 1971, p. 9). Advocates of non-Marxist social science could accept his contention that rationalization meant extension of control because it conceded that there was indeed a universal process in history – had not Weber seen modernity as an iron cage? Neither were Foucault's *epistemes* incompatible with those versions of modernization theory that saw traditional and modern as dichotomies (McNay 1994, pp. 93–4; Berkhofer 1995, p. 224).

Ironically, those scholars who are most critical of "modernist history" are most prone to resort unwittingly to progress narratives and determinism and to essentialize historical practice. From the late 1980s, cultural critics and historians such as Robert Berkhofer, Keith Jenkins, and Alun Munslow began to popularize the ideas of Foucault and the literary critic Hayden White. From the latter, postmodernists learned that history was a narrative in which emplotment was more important than any relationship with facts. If history was still to be written, it must imitate postmodern art and draw attention to itself as a constructed artifact, notably through mixing of genres (Jenkins 1991; Munslow 1997; Munslow and Rosenstone 2004; Berkhofer 1995).

In practice, this radical skepticism coexisted with explicit reification of periods and implicit functionalist social science. Interestingly, Munslow had begun his career with a statistical-sociological analysis of racial assimilation in Boston (Munslow 1986); Robert Berkhofer's jargon-laden first book used behaviorism and functionalism to understand social processes (Berkhofer 1969). Jenkins came to postmodernism via a doctoral dissertation on the philosophy of Nietzsche, yet he too mirrors progress narratives in his account of the history of methods. He argues that we are living through an epochal shift from the modern to the postmodern, and he uses something like Weberian ideal types to characterize each period. Not only does Jenkins distinguish traditional and modern epochs in casually conventional terms, but he uses similar logic to oppose modern and postmodern *epistemes.* The cause of the shift is equally familiar: external "secularising, democratising, computerising and consumerising pressures." Now, Jenkins argues, modernist certainties have collapsed along with the idea that there is a single truth, so we have no choice but to embrace the multiple possibilities of postmodern times (Jenkins 1991, pp. 59–70). In practice, reception of postmodernism has been uneven. Some have resisted stubbornly; others more or less consciously combine postmodern methods with older ones, producing something new in the process.

Historians in Foucault's native country were generally resistant to linguistic theory, but briefly there was a vogue for it and historians could not avoid dialogue with Foucauldian historians in the longer term. Indeed, the *Annales*'s emphasis on deep structures over agency had influenced Foucault, and in 1974, the Annaliste historian of antiquity Paul Veyne described Foucault as the "complete historian" (Noiriel 1996, pp. 104–5, 111; Jones and Porter 1994, pp. 7–9). Yet the relative homogeneity and entrenched power of the École des hautes études en sciences sociales (EHESS) and Sciences Po restricted innovation, and both institutions had already developed their own versions of cultural history. The Sciences Po historian Serge Berstein defended the Durkheimian concept of political culture from multiple criticisms. He described a political culture as an ethos, internalized by all members of a national community, which neutralized nondominant ideas (Berstein 1992). More convincingly, Pierre Bourdieu and others developed an alternative constructivism, linking the formation of categories in academic and social discourse to social action. In Germany, too, poststructuralism had relatively little impact, for historians associated Foucault with their least favorite philosopher, Nietzsche, whom they saw as a critic of the Enlightenment. In Germany, modernization theory resisted criticism better than elsewhere, perhaps because of the influence of Jürgen Habermas, who conceded that modernization had its dark side (Dinges 1994).

Meanwhile, Britain and the United States experienced theory wars. In 1980s Britain, in a context of defeat and defensiveness for the labor movement, some Marxists began to rethink their methods. Particularly controversial was Gareth Stedman Jones's application of linguistic theory to the history of Chartism. Stedman Jones denied that the point of departure must be "some conception of class or occupational consciousness." Language was not directly referential and so historians must attend to its "linguistic form" and "start from what Chartists actually said or wrote." He claimed that class was "a discursive rather than an ontological reality, the central effect being to explain languages of class from the nature of politics rather than the character of politics from the nature of class" (Stedman Jones

1982; Stedman Jones 1983, pp. 6–8). Stedman Jones accepted that British Marxists' emphasis on the relative autonomy of cultures had paved the way for linguistic analysis, but went further, arguing that political ideas actually shaped people's understanding of class. He was nevertheless prepared to examine social context and did not engage deeply with linguistic theory (Lawrence and Taylor 1993).

The same cannot be said of the major protagonist in the next wave of controversy: Patrick Joyce. Whereas Stedman Jones revised Marxist understandings of culture, Joyce's background was in non-Marxist social science. His earlier work had represented a classic application of pre–linguistic turn social science: "Deference" and "internalization" were the key terms in work that harks back to Kitson Clark's previously cited *The Making of Victorian England* (Taylor, 1997, p. 165; Joyce 1980, pp. xxi, 222–5). Joyce's *Visions of the People* (1991) did not take poststructuralist theory much beyond the notion that nineteenth-century workers thought in terms of "the people" rather than class. He later acknowledged that *Visions* did not break with social determinism, for it had assumed that popular identity derived from an existential experience of poverty. Joyce developed further the implications of poststructuralist linguistic theory in *Democratic Subjects* (1994), in which he explored the construction of the middle-class reform movement from a combination of religious, literary, and dramatic tropes.

In America, gender theory was instrumental in spreading the linguistic turn to historical practice. Joan Wallach Scott systematized ideas about gender that had been floating around for some time (J. W. Scott 1986). She criticized women's history for assuming that femininity was unproblematically the product of biology and instead argued for the linguistic construction of gender in a context of unequal power. Following Foucault, she argued that gender inequalities were intrinsic to the binary operation of power and used Derrida's deconstruction technique to reveal the protean character of historical gender identities. She added that gendered ideas could signify the whole system of power in society. Jeanne Boydston identifies the kinship of Scott's concept of gender to social-science models – it is a thing with intrinsic properties rather than a genuinely historical category. For Boydston, distinctions between male and female may have been nearly universal in history, but their relationship to the distribution of power has varied (Boydston 2008).

Scott's work paralleled Edward Said's *Orientalism* (1978). Said's demonstration that depiction of the East as irrational, passive, volatile, and mysterious had been used to legitimate imperialism was compatible with older histories of empire. His originality lay in using poststructuralist theory to show that the entire tradition of Western rationality and progress was dependent on the "other" of the irrational East, and so imperialism could not therefore be dismissed as a blip in an otherwise progressive Western tradition, separate from liberal domestic cultures. Many historians have extended this insight. For instance, Todd Shepard argues that Algerian independence undermined the French assimilationist model, according to which education would eventually raise indigenous peoples to the level of the French. Consequently, a new emphasis on the whiteness of the French race accompanied decolonization, and Algerian immigrants to France were excluded from rights that they had previously possessed (Shepard 2006).

Subaltern historians also engaged with poststructuralism. Dipesh Chakrabarty proposed to "provincialise Europe." Like Said, he argued that Europeans assumed the universality of categories of progress and freedom that in reality derived from particular circumstances. European scholars wrongly supposed that non-Europeans possessed no meaningful ways of understanding the world, and that whatever ideas colonized peoples did possess would eventually be superseded by Western ones. But Chakrabarty did not discount Western thought entirely. Like subaltern historians, he examined the ways in which it was redefined in the colonial context. For instance, Marxist categories could be reworked through confrontation with race to allow for difference; capitalism never completely subsumed social life, but existed in tension with solidarities that were not essential to the reproduction of capital. In his historical work on Bengal, Chakrabarty argued that the Western concepts of civil society were both essential and inadequate to understanding social life (Chakrabarty 2000; Majumdar 2010, pp. 44–62).

Chakrabarty's work is postcolonial in that it breaks the binary opposition between colonized and colonizer that had (allegedly) structured the historiography of anticolonial struggle. Postcolonialists stress connections and conflicts; Western ideas structure formerly colonized societies, and vice versa. Chakrabarty's work is also methodologically eclectic, for he explores the role of capitalism in history without recourse to essentialism, and without neglecting the ideas and languages that people used to make sense of the world. Chakrabarty also rejects implicitly top-down readings of Foucault, evident in Said's assumption that colonial peoples were silenced as the negative term of a binary opposition (Chaudhuri 2004; Downs 2010, pp. 92–101). Chakrabarty is representative of historians who combine cultural and social history, especially the latter's emphasis on the rationality-in-a-context of historical actors.

This same quest led other scholars to engage with alternative linguistic theories and sociologies, arguably better able to historicize and transcend structure and agency than the social history of the 1960s and 1970s had been. Some turned to Mikhail Bakhtin (1895–1975), for whom a text is not a self-referential system of disembodied signs; rather it is "multivocal," containing the voices of the author, his/her sources, and the anticipated responses of the audience (Bakhtin 1981; Arnold 1998). Like Bakhtin, the already cited Cambridge school read classic texts in the context of the conventions of rhetoric, as well as dialogue with other authors in the intellectual and social contexts of their production. They emphasize the possibility for reinterpretation and misunderstanding of ideas as they are appropriated in unexpected contexts and combined with others (Skinner 2002; Lawrence 2010, pp. 212–13). The Cambridge school places more emphasis than Bakhtin had upon speech as a social act. In that respect, its methods converge with those of historians who used the concepts of Bourdieu, for whom languages were interventions in struggles for power and resources. In the field of anthropology, James C. Scott argued that the subaltern did not uncritically absorb the dominant ideology. S/he might have to collude outwardly with their powerful ideas, but the "hidden transcript" shows that the subaltern questions, adapts, or rejects it out of the hearing of the ruler (J. C. Scott 1991).

In practical historical work, Evelyn Brookes Higginbotham used Bakhtinian methods to show that discourses of race in the American South simultaneously dehumanized black people, justified exploitation, and served as a focus for black nationalism (Higginbotham 1993). William Gould combined Bakhtin with Skinner to examine not discourse, but the repertoire of languages used by Indian nationalists. He argues that the apparently inclusive secular languages of Congress nationalists actually contained a version of Hinduism that in practice excluded Muslims (Gould 2004). In the field of early modern English history, Andy Wood combined Thompsonian concerns with James C. Scott's ideas to understand popular politics. He argued that when defeated rebels humiliated themselves before their masters they were asserting the conditions of their allegiance (Wood 2001). Without necessarily referring to specific theories, historians of women have produced an enormous body of work in this vein, in fields from the history of unmarried mothers to the involvement of women in fascist movements.

Linguistic theory, poststructuralist or not, has been used relatively infrequently in general histories of historical writing. Explicitly poststructuralist historiography still largely consists of abstract discussion of objectivity, causes, and agency, combined with periodized accounts of disciplinary history. Alun Munslow's *History of History* (2012), despite its title and the author's desire to distance himself from the caricature of postmodernism, largely essentializes historical writing prior to the "cultural turn." Ironically, a reviewer uses the contention that the postmodern phase of historical theory is drawing to a close to discredit Munslow's book as outdated (Timmins 2012). More usefully, some historiographers have used poststructuralism to examine the oeuvre of particular historians. Indeed, in this essay I have profited from Arthur Slavin's deconstruction of Geoffrey Elton's work (Slavin 1990).

As for opponents of the cultural turn, they are torn between defending history as a practice or craft and venturing onto the terrain of theory. In the best known response to postmodernism, Richard Evans begins with a chapter on the "history of history," designed to show that historians have never been as certain of their objectivity as postmodern critics believe they are. He adds that postmodernism is just one more external attempt to apply abstract concepts to historiography (Evans 1996). Subsequent chapters revisit epistemological and ontological terrain familiar to readers of *What Is History?* One reviewer commented that Evans reproduced the error of postmodernists, who reduced historiography to the study of a few canonical texts. Both sides, the reviewer continued, should have used the methods of Pocock and Skinner (Ghosh 1998).

To my knowledge, no historiographer has written a general history of historical writing in that way. However, two books show the multiple interpretive possibilities that arise from engaging with postmodernism while remaining within the discipline and accepting that historians are implicated in the social distribution of power.

We saw that Bonnie Smith had used feminist psychoanalytic and social methods to understand the history of bourgeois women in nineteenth-century France. In *The Gender of History* (1998) she combined psychoanalysis with gender theory to show that the conceptualization of rational historical inquiry as male effectively excluded women from the profession. Women represented the irrational other, prone to nervousness and volatility; like "primitive races," women were likely to fetishize documents rather than understand them. Men discounted amateur women's contributions as repetitive and sensual rather than rational. For Smith, out of the trauma of repression, these women produced biographies of prominent women, in which the bodily and sensual countered the abstract universalism of male history.

Second, Peter Novick combines Durkheim, Lévi-Strauss, and Skinner in his account of American historiography. From Durkheim he takes the idea that objectivity was a functional myth holding the American historical profession together. However, this myth allowed for contest and contradiction, as it was used and misused in strategies of professionalization. In the late nineteenth century, Americans misinterpreted Rankeanism as rigid science and used it to exclude amateurs from the profession. The Great War exposed the national and class biases of these allegedly objective historians. That was the context in which Charles Beard promoted his quasi-Marxist view of history as necessarily ideological. The Cold War generated a new faith in objectivity, defined against distortions of history in the Soviet bloc. But in the 1970s polarization between Left and Right reemerged; historiography began to fragment, just as postmodernism undermined faith in objectivity. Novick was pessimistic about the prospects of sound historical knowledge, and oddly given the methods he uses, he does not see a pragmatic middle way between hyperobjectivism and hyperrelativism (Novick 1988).

The "Transnational Turn"

At the time of writing, transnationalism is the touchstone of "interesting work." And since espousal of new methods remains as essential as it ever was to getting a job or to winning a research award, historians of all methodological backgrounds invoke the term. Once again, historians may be guilty of universalizing their particular perspectives through teleological argument: Akira Iriye (2004, pp. 211–12) illustrates the point when he argues that "transnational forces ... have contributed to the growth of transnational consciousness" and that the global age entails a "revolution" in historical method, which he presents in Hegelian terms as a "new synthesis." And like earlier advocates of new methods, transnationalists accuse predecessors of using positivist methods, and more specifically of taking the nation for granted.

Comparative history was indeed positivist insofar as it treated nations as containers for economic and cultural processes, as so many cases that could be compared to produce general laws – a method that provoked recourse to national stereotypes to explain differences. Michel Espagne contended that while nations defined themselves in opposition to other nations, national identities actually rested on ideas that were appropriated and adapted from elsewhere (Espagne 1994). In the ensuing debates, some accused Espagne himself of naturalizing the nation-state, because he envisaged the incorporation of foreign elements within it (Trebitsch 1998). Others sought to reconcile the two sides (Berger 2010). Michael Werner and Bénédicte Zimmermann argue that both comparison and transfer are intrinsic to social relations and to the study of history, and that historians' positioning, questioning, and expertise determine which they privilege (Werner and Zimmermann 2004).

The methods used in transnational history are more eclectic than the idea of a historiographical revolution would suggest. The first scholarly use of the term, in the field of international relations in the 1970s, involved the question of whether supranational organizations are actors in the same way as states allegedly are. From the late 1980s, historians began to expose their profession's role in the construction of the nation-state along with the nation-state's part in the construction of the profession (Berger et al. 1999). Transnationalism encouraged the *Annales* school to rediscover Bloch's ambition to decenter the nation-state, and indeed to publish (ironically with the support of the Institut français, the cultural agent of the French state) an online compendium of articles demonstrating its contribution to global history.[3] Recent transnational histories do not usually focus on the deep structures that had once been the *Annales*'s concern, but in principle they assume that economies transcend the nation-state, and indeed some economic historians have long questioned the national framework.

Transnationalists' emphasis on the mutual construction of cultures and the instability of their meanings also reveals a debt to poststructuralism and its related concepts, especially postcolonialism (Bayly et al. 2006, pp. 1448–52). Just as often, transnational history begins with people and their rational-within-a-context activities (Clavin 2005, p. 422). In studies of international organizations, historians have discarded model building for showing how such bodies work on a personal level (Iriye 2004a). Espagne advocated tracing the movement of ideas across borders, through travelers, commercial exchanges, the translation of books, and newspaper reporting on foreign countries (Espagne 1994; Werner and Zimmermann 2006). Doing transnational history in this way contradicts the notion that historical processes may be explained by "factors" or "influences" external to one's object of research; research focuses precisely on these external objects (Saunier 2004 at 117).

As such, transnational approaches contest modernization narratives. For instance, Sanjay Subrahmanyam draws on postcolonial theory to explore little-known circuits of exchange in the early modern Portuguese empire, Indian Ocean, and Eurasia, from the east Mediterranean to the Moghul controlled Ganges (Subrahmanyam 1997). He problematizes the notion of separate Indian and European civilizations and questions the narrative of Western expansion, modernization, and domination. In a different vein,

[3] See http://annales.ehess.fr/index.php?247; accessed 15 June 2014.

Thomas Bender breaks the link between national histories and modernization. He argues that U.S. history should be denationalized, for the assumption of national unity masks differences within the nation. He calls for history on a variety of scales and asks questions such as, did American missionaries in China identify themselves as Americans or as Protestants? (Bender 2006)

While Subrahmanyam and Bender critique the concept of globalization as an external constraint to which societies must adapt, other advocates of transnationalism might be accused of celebrating (or wishing for) a universal process of homogenization, a world in which everything is connected and in which cooperation matters more than conflict. Akira Iriye speaks precisely of a "global consciousness" – inadvertently presenting a world much as modernization theorists claimed it would be (Iriye 2004b, p. 218; Bayly et al. 2006, pp. 1455–60). Just as historians helped to establish the nation-state they might become protagonists of globalization, or of Americanization universalized as globalization (Saunier 2004, p. 125). In fact, the mere crossing of borders does not necessarily dissolve them, for those who did so, from translators to smugglers and currency speculators, have an interest in maintaining them. Transnational actors, individual or collective, might work against globalization (Clavin 2005, p. 431).

If globalization, like modernization, is not an external force, then historiographers cannot see transnational history as simply the consequence of cheap air travel, the Internet, and economic liberalization. Rather, just as ordinary people have long been both protagonists in and victims of transnational circuits (from sailors who carried plague rats on their ships to international diplomats), so have historians. What have changed are rather the contours, values, and geographical centers of these exchanges. The centers of exchange in the field of historiography have passed from Germany to France and Britain, then to the United States and India. In Europe, transnational approaches are especially relevant because the academic field is structured by the availability of European funding for collaborative projects and the large audience for publication in English.

Conclusion

My narrative provides ample support for the view of Philippe Fontaine and Roger Backhouse that the histories of the social sciences and history have been more entangled than some practitioners claim. Even those who rejected any use of theory wrote practical histories using narratives that were familiar to social science, and indeed they conceptualized the history of their discipline and its place in society using those same theories. Just as social scientists wrote histories of their disciplines without being trained in history, so historians used social science without having been trained in it. That doubtless led to many misunderstandings, but there has also been much common ground between the disciplines and indeed parallel disputes within disciplines. There is no doubt either that historians have used social science selectively as part of struggles for position within their field.

In this chapter I have borrowed from the sociology of knowledge to suggest that historians have used paradigm shifts to categorize historical work and assign value to it. At each point, previous work has been dismissed as tedious amassing of facts or as socially and politically irrelevant. Across the years, the logics have been remarkably similar: Such and such a phenomenon is the foundation of society and so it must be the primary focus of historiography. Elton claimed that since politics ensured that society was a properly structured organism (note the crowd psychology), it must be the core of historiography (Elton 1968, p. 25). Social historians from Marxists to Annalistes held that since reality was social, then history must be social history. Poststructuralists argued that because reality could be known only through language, then historians could only study discourses. In each case, external forces, from civilization to globalization, ensure the primacy of politics, society, or language, and give birth to new epochs that determine the nature of historiography. Following this logic, some historians are supposedly disoriented by the loss of old certainties, but canonical figures understand the movement of history before anyone else does, and (with luck) historians in general ultimately become "conscious" of, say, the inevitability of postmodern or transnational history, just as workers had once became conscious of the inevitability of class struggle. Ultimately, this foundationalist logic depends on arbitrary universalization of a viewpoint, and so it is not surprising that some of those who advocate foundationalism justify it through recourse to (unfalsifiable) intuition (Hobsbawm 1972; Ginzburg 1980, pp. 28–9).

It is a banality to say that historians are necessarily positioned by their inherited knowledge and ways of seeing and by their relationship to the profession, to the state, and to the public demand for knowledge of history. Too often that acknowledgment is an excuse for foundationalism and/or radical relativism. In fact, so long as questions are potentially falsifiable, any perspective potentially has some value; it will explain some things but not others, and one researcher's view may complement rather than contradict another's, so long as it is coherent and compatible with evidence.[4] Any

[4] For a similar analysis see Fulbrook (2002).

coherent interpretation can tell us something, so long as its advantages and disadvantages are clear – historians too rarely mention the latter. At a time when governments expect universities and colleagues to see each other as rivals, it is worth remembering that history is a collaborative effort, even in its reliance on mutual criticism.

References

Amin, S. 1984. "Gandhi as Mahatma: Gorakhpur District, Eastern UP, 1921–2," *Subaltern Studies* 3:1–61.

Arnold, J. H. 1998. "The Historian as Inquisitor: The Ethics of Interrogating Subaltern Voices," *Rethinking History* 2.3:379–86.

Baehr, P. 1990. "The 'Masses' in Weber's Political Sociology," *Economy and Society* 19.2:242–65.

Bakhtin, M. M. 1981. *The Dialogic Imagination: Four Essays*, Austin: University of Texas Press.

Barrow, C. W. 2000. *More Than a Historian: The Political and Economic Thought of Charles A. Beard*, New York: Transaction.

Bayly, C. A. et al. 2006. "AHR Conversation: On Transnational History," *The American Historical Review* 111.5:1441–64.

Beard, C. A. 1913. *An Economic Interpretation of the Constitution of the United States.* New York: Macmillan.

1915. *Economic Origins of Jeffersonian Democracy.* New York: Macmillan.

1934. *The Nature of the Social Sciences.* New York: Charles Scribner.

Bender, T. 2006. *A Nation among Nations: America's Place in World History.* New York: Hill & Wang.

Bennett, J. M. 1996. *Ale, Beer and Brewsters in England: Women's Work in a Changing World, 1300–1600.* Oxford: Oxford University Press.

Bentley, M. 2005. *Modernizing England's Past: English Historiography in the Age of Modernism, 1870–1970.* Cambridge: Cambridge University Press.

Berger, S. 1997. *The Search for Normality: National Identity and Historical Consciousness in Germany Since 1800.* Leamington Spa: Berg.

2010. "Comparative History." In *Writing History: Theory and Practice*, ed. S. Berger, H. Feldner, and K. Passmore. London: Bloomsbury, 161–79.

Berger, S., Donovan, M., and K. Passmore, eds. 1999. *Europe since 1800: Writing National Histories.* London: Routledge.

Berkhofer, R. F. 1969. *A Behavioral Approach to Historical Analysis.* New York and London: Collier Macmillan.

1995. *Beyond the Great Story: History as Text and Discourse*, Cambridge, MA: Belknap.

Berstein, S. 1992. "L'historien et la culture politique," *Vingtième Siècle* 35.1:67–77.

Boydston, J. 2008. "Gender as Question of Historical Analysis," *Gender and History* 20.3:558–83.

Branca, P. 1978. *Women in Europe since 1750*, London: Croom Helm.

Burguière, A. 2006. *L' école des Annales: une histoire intellectuelle.* Paris: Odile Jacob.

Chakrabarty, D. 2000. *Provincializing Europe: Postcolonial Thought and Historical Difference.* Princeton, NJ: Princeton University Press.

Chaudhuri, A. 2004. "In the Waiting-Room of History," *London Review of Books*, 3–8.
Clark, G. Kitson. 1962. *The Making of Victorian England*. London: Methuen.
Clavin, P. 2005. "Defining Transnationalism," *Contemporary European History* 14.4:421–39.
Collini, S. 1988. "'Discipline History' and 'Intellectual History': Reflections on the Historiography of the Social Sciences in Britain and France," *Revue de synthèse* 109.3–4:387–99.
Davis, J. A. 1979. *Gramsci and Italy's Passive Revolution*. London: Croon Helm.
Dinges, M. 1994. "The Reception of Michel Foucault's Ideas on Social Discipline, Mental Asylums, Hospitals and the Medical Profession in German Historiography." In *Reassessing Foucault: Power, Medicine and the Body*, ed. C. Jones and R. Porter. London: Routledge, 181–212.
Downs, L. L. 2010. *Writing Gender History*, 2nd ed. London: Hodder Arnold, 1994.
Elton, G. R. 1953. *The Tudor Revolution in Government: Administrative Changes in the Reign of Henry VIII*. Cambridge: Cambridge University Press.
1963. *Reformation Europe 1517–1559*. London: Fontana.
1967. *The Practice of History*. London: Methuen.
1968. *The Future of the Past*. Cambridge: Cambridge University Press.
1973. *Reform and Renewal*. Cambridge: Cambridge University Press.
1991. *Return to Essentials: Some Reflections on the Present State of Historical Study*. Cambridge: Cambridge University Press.
Espagne, M. 1994. "Sur les limites du comparatisme en histoire culturelle," *Genèses. Sciences sociales et histoire* 17.17:112–21.
Evans, R. J. 1996. *In Defence of History*. London: Granta.
2009. *Cosmopolitan Islanders: British Historians and the European Continent*. Cambridge: Cambridge University Press.
Foucault, M. 1971. *L' Ordre du discours*. Paris: Gallimard.
Fulbrook, M. 2002. *Historical theory*. London: Routledge.
Furet, F. 1985. *Penser la Révolution française*. Paris: Gallimard.
1995. *Le passé d'une illusion: essai sur l'idée communiste au XXe siècle*. Paris: Robert Laffont/Calman-Lévy.
Ghosh, P. 1998. "Laid Down by Ranke," *London Review of Books*, 18–19.
Giddens, A. 1987. "Out of the Orrery: E. P. Thompson on consciousness and history." In *Central Problems in Social Theory: Action, Structure and Contradiction in Social Analysis*. London: Macmillan, 203–43.
Ginzburg, C. 1972. *I benandanti. Stregoneria e culti agrari tra Cinquecento e Seicento*, Torino: Einaudi.
1980. "Morelli, Freud and Sherlock Holmes: Clues and Scientific Method," *History Workshop Journal* 9:5–36.
1981. *The Cheese and the Worms: The Cosmos of a Sixteenth-Century Miller/Carlo Ginzburg*, trans. John Tedeschi and Anne Tedeschi. London: Routledge & Kegan Paul.
Goguel, F. 1946. *La politique des partis sous la IIIe République*. Paris: Seuil.
Goubert, P. 1969. *L' Ancien Régime*. Paris: Armand Colin.
Gould, W. 2004. *Hindu Nationalism and the Language of Politics in Late Colonial India*. Cambridge: Cambridge University Press.

Guha, R. 1982. "On Some Aspects of the Historiography of Colonial India," *Subaltern Studies* 1:37–44.

Gutman, H. G. 1976. *The Black Family in Slavery and Freedom 1750–1925*. Oxford: Blackwell.

Higginbotham, E. B. 1993. *Righteous Discontent: The Women's Movement in the Black Baptist Church, 1880–1920*. Cambridge, MA: Harvard University Press.

Higham, J. 1965. *History: Professional Scholarship in America*. Baltimore: Johns Hopkins University Press.

Hobsbawm, E. 1972. "Karl Marx's contribution to historiography." In *Ideology in Social Science: Readings in Critical Social Theory*, ed. Robin Blackburn. London: Fontana, 265–83.

Hudson, P. 2010. "Economic History." In *Writing History: Theory and Practice*, ed. S. Berger, H. Feldner, and K. Passmore. London: Bloomsbury, 248–66.

Iggers, G. G. 1984. *New Directions in European Historiography*. Middletown, CT: Wesleyan University Press.

1997. *Historiography in the Twentieth Century*. Hanover and London: Weslyan University Press.

Iriye, A. 2004a. *Global Community: The Role of International Organizations in the Making of the Contemporary World*. Berkeley: University of California Press.

2004b. "Transnational History," *Contemporary European History* 13.2:211–22.

Jenkins, K. 1991. *Re-Thinking History*. London: Routledge.

Jones, C., and R. Porter, eds. 1994. "Introduction." In *Reassessing Foucault: Power, Medicine and the Body*. Studies in the social history of medicine. London: Routledge, 1–16.

Jordan, G. 2010. "'Voices from Below': Doing People's History in Cardiff Docklands." In *Writing History: Theory and Practice*, ed. S. Berger, H. Feldner, and K. Passmore. London: Bloomsbury, 330–52.

Joyce, P. 1980. *Work, Society and Politics: The Culture of the Factory in Later Victorian England*. Brighton: Harvester Press.

1991. *Visions of the People*. Cambridge: Cambridge University Press.

1994. *Democratic Subjects: the Self and the Social in Nineteenth-century England*. Cambridge: Cambridge University Press.

Koonz, C. 1988. *Mothers in the Fatherland: Women, the Family and Nazi Politics*. New York: St. Martin's Press.

LaCapra, D., and S. L. Kaplan. 1982. *Modern European Intellectual History: Reappraisals and New Perspectives*. Ithaca, NY: Cornell University Press.

Lawrence, J. 2010. "Political History." In *Writing History: Theory and Practice*, ed. S. Berger, H. Feldner, and K. Passmore. London: Bloomsbury, 209–27.

Lawrence, J., and M. Taylor. 1993. "The Poverty of Protest: Gareth Stedman Jones and the Politics of Language: A Reply," *Social History* 18.1:1–15.

Le Goff, J. 1974. "Les mentalités: Une histoire ambiguë." In *Faire de l'histoire*, ed. P. Nora. Paris: Gallimard, 76–94.

1988. *La Nouvelle histoire*, 2nd ed. Paris: Complexe, 1978.

Majumdar, R. 2010. *Writing Postcolonial History*. London: Bloomsbury.

Mann, G. 1974. *The History of Germany since 1789*. London: Penguin.

McNay, L. 1994. *Foucault: A Critical Introduction*. Cambridge: Polity Press.

Middell, M. 2010. "The Annales." In *Writing History: Theory and Practice*, ed. S. Berger, H. Feldner, and K. Passmore. London: Bloomsbury, 108–22.

Munslow, A. 1986. "The Decline of Ethnic Politics in Boston, 1882–1921." *Proceedings of the Massachusetts Historical Society* 98:116–34.

1997. *Deconstructing History*. London: Routledge.

Munslow, A., and R. A. Rosenstone, eds. 2004. *Experiments in Rethinking History*, London: Routledge.

Namier, L. 1929. *The Structure of Politics at the Accession of George III*. London: Macmillan.

1930. *England in the Age of the American Revolution*. London: Macmillan.

1955. *Personalities and Powers*. London: Hamish Hamilton.

Noble, D. W. 1985. *End of American History: Democracy, Capitalism, and the Metaphor of Two Worlds in Anglo-American Historical Writing, 1880–1980*. Minneapolis: University of Minnesota Press.

Noiriel, G. 1988. *Le Creuset français: histoire de l'immigration, XIXe-XXe siècles*. Paris: Seuil.

1996. *Sur la "crise" de l'histoire*, 2nd ed. Paris: Gallimard, 1996.

2006. *Introduction à la socio-histoire*. Bagneux: Numilog.

Nora, P. ed. 1987. *Essais d'ego-histoire*. Paris: Gallimard.

Novick, P. 1988. *That Noble Dream: The "objectivity Question" and the American Historical Profession*, Cambridge: Cambridge University Press.

Palmer, B. D. 1994. *E. P. Thompson: Objections and Oppositions*. London: Verso.

Palmer, W. 2001. *Engagement with the Past: The Lives and Works of the World War II Generation of Historians*. Lexington: University Press of Kentucky.

Passmore, K. 2008. "The gendered genealogy of political religions theory," *Gender & History* 20.3:644–68.

Paul, H. 2011. "Introduction: Fathers of history," *Storia della Storiografia*, 59–60:224–30.

Perkin, H. 1981. "What Is Social History?" In *The Structured Crowd*, ed. H. Perkin. Sussex: Harvester, 1–27.

Popper, K. 1961. *The Poverty of Historicism*. London: Routledge and Kegan Paul. First published in 1957.

Powicke, Maurice. 1947 *King Henry the Third and Lord Edward*, Vol. I. Oxford: Clarendon.

Rigby, S. H. 1995. "Historical Causation: Is One Thing More Important than Another?" *History* 80.259:227–42.

Roberts, E. 1985. *A Woman's Place: An Oral History of Working-Class Women 1890–1940*. Oxford: Blackwell.

Rostow, W. W. 1949. *British Economy of the Nineteenth Century*. Oxford: Clarendon.

Rudé, G. 1964. *The Crowd in History: A Study of Popular Disturbances in France and England, 1730–1848*. London: Wiley.

Samuel, R. 1981. *People's History and Socialist Theory*. London: Taylor & Francis.

Saunier, P.-Y. 2004. "Circulations, connexions et espaces transnationaux," *Genèses* 57.4:110–26.

Scott, J. C. 1991. *Domination and the Arts of Resistance: Hidden Transcripts*, New Haven, CT: Yale University Press.

Scott, J. W. 1986. "Gender: A Useful Category of Historical Analysis," *The American Historical Review* 91.5:1053–75.

1988. "Women in The Making of the English Working Class." In *Gender and the Politics of History*. New York: Columbia University Press, 68–90.

Shepard, T. 2006. *The Invention of Decolonization: The Algerian War and the Remaking of France*. Ithaca, NY: Cornell University Press.
Shorter, E. 1977. *The Making of the Modern Family*. London: Fontana.
Sirinelli, J.-F. 1992. "Des droites et du politique." In *Histoire des droites en France*, ed. J.-F. Sirinelli. Paris: Gallimard, iii–xlv.
Skinner, Q. 2002. *Visions of Politics*. Cambridge: Cambridge University Press.
Slavin, A. 1990. "Telling the story: GR Elton and the Tudor Age," *Sixteenth Century Journal* 21.2:151–69.
Smith, B. 1981. *Ladies of the Leisure Class: The Bourgeoisie of Northern France in the Nineteenth Century*, Princeton NJ: Princeton University Press.
1998. *The Gender of History: Men, Women, and Historical Practice*, Cambridge, MA: Harvard University Press.
Soboul, A. 1968. "Survivances 'féodales' dans la société rurale du XIXe siècle." *Annales. Économies, Sociétés, Civilisations* 23.5:965–86.
Spierenburg, P. 1991. *The Broken Spell: A Cultural and Anthropological History of Preindustrial Europe*. New Brunswick, NJ: Rutgers University Press.
Stedman Jones, G. 1982. "The Language of Chartism." In *The Chartist Experience: Studies in Working-Class Radicalism and Culture, 1830–60*, ed. James Epstein and Dorothy Thompson. London: Macmillan, 3–57.
1983. "Rethinking Chartism." In *Languages of Class: Studies in English Working-Class History 1932–1982*. Cambridge: Cambridge University Press.
Subrahmanyam, S. 1997. *The Career and Legend of Vasco da Gama*. Cambridge: Cambridge University Press.
Surkis, J. 2012. "When Was the Linguistic Turn? A Genealogy," *American Historical Review* 117.3:700–22.
Taylor, M. 1997. "The Beginnings of Modern British Social History," *History Workshop Journal* 43:155–76.
Thomas, J. A. 2012. "Comment: Not Yet Far Enough," *American Historical Review* 117.3:794–803.
Thomas, K. 1971. *Religion and the Decline of Magic*. London: Peregrine.
Thompson, E. P. 1963. *The Making of the English Working Class*. London: Penguin.
1965. "The Peculiarities of the English," *Socialist Register* 2:311–62.
1967. "Time, Work-Discipline, and Industrial Capitalism," *Past & Present* 38.1:56 –97.
1971. "The Moral Economy of the English Crowd in the Eighteenth Century," *Past and Present* 50:76–136.
1978. "Eighteenth-century English society: class struggle without class?" *Social History* 3.2:133–65.
1979a. "The Peculiarities of the English." In *The Poverty of Theory and Other Essays*. Merlin: London.
1979b. *The Poverty of Theory and Other Essays*. Merlin: London.
Tilly, C. 1964. *The Vendée*. London: Arnold.
Timmins, A. 2012. Review of *A History of History* (review no. 1356). *Reviews in History*. Downloaded at: www.history.ac.uk/reviews/ [Accessed January 8, 2013].
Trebitsch, M. 1998. "L'histoire comparée des intellectuels comme histoire expérimentale." In *Pour une histoire comparée des intellectuels*, ed. M.-C. Granjon and M. Trebitsch. Paris: Complexe, 61–78.

Tyrrell, I. 2011. "Historical Writing in the United States." In *The Oxford History of Historical Writing: Volume 5*, ed. A. Schneider and D. Woolf. Oxford: Oxford University Press, 199–219.

Welskopp, T, 2010. "Social History." In *Writing History: Theory and Practice*, ed. S. Berger, H. Feldner, and K. Passmore. London: Bloomsbury, 228–47.

Werner, M. and B. Zimmermann. 2004. *De la comparaison à l'histoire croisée*. Paris: Seuil.

2006. "Beyond Comparison: Histoire Croisée and the Challenge of Reflexivity," *History and Theory* 45.1:30–50.

Williams, G. A. 1980. *The Search for Beulah Land: The Welsh and the Atlantic Revolution*. London: Taylor & Francis.

Wood, A. 2001. "Poore Men Will Speak One Day": Plebeian Languages of Deference and Defiance in England, c. 1520–1640. In *The Politics of the Excluded*, ed. T. Harris. New York: Palgrave, 202–27.

Zambelli, P. 1985. From Menocchio to Piero Della Francesca: The Work of Carlo Ginzburg. *The Historical Journal* 28.4:983–99.

3

History of Anthropology

Henrika Kuklick

This essay is concerned primarily with the literature on the history of sociocultural anthropology, which is by far the largest of anthropology's subfields.[1] It also emphasizes anglophone anthropology, which dominated the entire discipline until relatively recently.[2] My aim will be to indicate how

1 My essay is largely based on my accumulated knowledge of the works that have been most influential among historians of anthropology. I supplemented my accumulated knowledge – as well as the works I was led to read by consulting works I had already read – by doing a JSTOR search. I entered the search term "history of anthropology" and read articles after reading their summaries to see whether reading them would be useful. The search "history of anthropology" turns up 8,633 pages of articles (at 25 items a page). I stopped at page 28. I did this for several reasons. One: The search algorithm seems to be "history and anthropology" not "history of anthropology"; many of the articles retrieved by such a search have nothing to do with the history of anthropology. Two: By page 28, I had seen citations to some articles several times over. Three, and most important: From reading the articles I got via JSTOR, I was able to work out several genres of history of anthropology that I had not identified prior to doing my JSTOR search. By page 28, I was not finding any new genres. The weakness of this method, as a comment of Nelia Dias's made me realize, is that there is no guarantee that articles identified by a search have any merit; Dias pointed out that I had cited an article that is not particularly good and reminded me that I knew of an article on the same subject that is better; personal communication, October 2, 2012.

2 Consider this telling example of the international dominance of anglophone anthropology. In his 1960 Inaugural Lecture of the Chair of Social Anthropology at the Collège de France, Claude Lévi-Strauss credited the anthropologist Bronislaw Malinowski with the methodological standard that sociocultural anthropologists still uphold today – the method of participant observation used during long periods of residence in the field. Born a citizen of the Austro-Hungarian Empire but trained in Britain, Malinowski began doing fieldwork in 1914. But Lévi-Strauss might have cited a homegrown example, Arnold van Gennep, who began doing fieldwork in 1911. I will discuss Malinowski and van Gennep later in this essay; see Lévi-Strauss (1967, p. 14). It is also notable that German anthropologists took to the field enthusiastically in the early years of the twentieth century, albeit largely in big expeditions mounted by museums rather than as individuals living alone for protracted periods; see Evans (2010, pp. 131–53).

the literature reflects – and has often been intended to shape – a particular disciplinary structure. To this end, I will examine what George Stocking termed "presentist" and "historicist" approaches, the diverse styles and viewpoints of scholars who have contributed to the literature, as well as the tendency to represent anthropologists as heroes and to rely on oral communications as much as on diverse sorts of written records. The United States has had a distinctive standard department structure, a union of four subfields – sociocultural anthropology, biological anthropology (formerly called physical anthropology), archaeology, and linguistic anthropology – a structure that is now becoming less than standard.[3] (The one exception to the generalization that there have been durable four-field departments only in North America – the department at University College, London (UCL) – represents a historical accident).[4] In the United States, the association of biological and sociocultural anthropology has grown increasingly problematic, however. Indeed, the percentage of anthropologists who do biological anthropology is very small; in 1998, for example, only 6.5 percent of the members of the American Anthropological Association were biological anthropologists (Calcano 2003, p. 6).[5] Moreover, despite the

3 Biological anthropology – originally described as the "new physical anthropology" – uses methods that differ considerably from those of its precursor and has a different objective; its basic problem is human evolution, not variation within the human species. Its emergence was heralded by the publication of Washburn (1951). For overviews of the field, see Strum, Lindburg, and Hamburg (1999). Biological anthropologists in the United States have their own learned society, the American Association of Physical Anthropologists (AAPA), and their own journal, the *American Journal of Physical Anthropology*. Archaeologists also have their own society, the Society for American Archaeology, which represents itself as an international society, as does the AAPA (see footnote 5).

4 The UCL department adopted the four-field structure structure under the leadership of C. Daryll Forde, who was appointed department chair in 1945, reviving a department that had been suspended during World War II. Forde was an anomaly in British anthropology. He earned his Ph.D. in prehistoric archaeology at UCL, where the diffusionists G. Elliot Smith and W. J. Perry reigned supreme. And he wrote a book with a diffusionist message, *Ancient Mariners*, published in 1927. He was the only person whose Ph.D. was earned at UCL during the interwar period who managed to find employment in Britain as an anthropologist – doubtless because he underwent an intellectual conversion after he had earned his degree. In 1928, Forde went to Berkeley to spend two years as a Commonwealth Fellow and became, in effect, an American anthropologist, to whom the four-field structure structure seemed reasonable.

5 The American Anthropological Association (AAA) now identifies a fifth subfield – applied anthropology. The AAA's current Web site says: "Rates of PhD production in each of anthropology's traditional subfields have been relatively stable since the mid-1970s.... For the past 20 years, cultural anthropology accounted for an average 50% of new PhDs awarded in the U.S.; archaeology = 30%; biological/physical = 10%; linguistic anthropology = 3%; applied/other = 7%. The figures for 1994–95 are, respectively, 52%, 24%, 10%, 1% and 12%. (*Note:* Fewer practicing anthropologists receive specific training

conventional expectation that practitioners of all of the discipline's subfields benefit from contact with one another, in reality there has been relatively little collaboration among practitioners of the subfields (Borofsky 2002). Some practitioners of archaeology belie this generalization, benefiting from research done in all three of the other subfields.[6] And biological and cultural anthropologists often collaborate in such fields as medical anthropology – a specialty that has so many practitioners that it has its own scholarly association.[7] Certainly, Franz Boas, who led American anthropologists to implement the four-field model of the discipline, himself worked in three of the four subfields (he did not do research in archaeology). His first Ph.D. student, Alexander Chamberlain, who earned his doctorate at Clark University in 1892 (the first Ph.D. in anthropology conferred in the United States), wrote a dissertation in linguistic anthropology and worked in cultural anthropology, as well as in folklore (Gilbertson 1914). (Chamberlain was appointed Boas's successor when Boas left Clark in the same year as Chamberlain earned his Ph.D.) One should note that folklore was virtually a fifth subfield in the early years of American anthropology. Boas was also active in folklore circles; this is not surprising, given the importance of folklore in Germany during the War II era.[8] Alfred Kroeber, Boas's first Ph.D.

in applied anthropology itself than in sociocultural.)" Available online at: http://www.aaanet.org/resources/departments/SurveyofPhDs95.cfm. Last accessed date: April 30, 2013.

The small percentage of AAA members who are physical anthropologists may be somewhat misleading as an index to the importance of physical anthropology in American academic circles, however; it seems highly probable that many American biological anthropologists do not belong to the AAA, but belong only to the American Association of Physical Anthropologists. That society's Web site says: "Physical anthropology is a biological science that deals with the adaptations, variability, and evolution of human beings and their living and fossil relatives. Because it studies human biology in the context of human culture and behavior, physical anthropology is also a social science. The AAPA is the world's leading professional organization for physical anthropologists. Formed by 83 charter members in 1930, the AAPA now has an international membership of over 1,700. The Association's annual meetings draw more than a thousand scientists and students from all over the world." Available online at http://www.physanth.org. Last accessed date April 30, 2013.

6 I am indebted to Joyce White for this observation; personal communication, September 30, 2012.

7 I am indebted to Joanna Radin for reminding me of this; personal communication, October 4, 2012.

8 After World War I, folklore became a separate discipline in Germany, and physical and cultural anthropology also became distinct. In the United States, folklore developed as a separate discipline after World War II and has now virtually disappeared from academe. On post–World War I Germany, see Gingrich (2010), p. 20. There is currently only one viable department of folklore in the United States – the Department of Folklore and Ethnomusicology at Indiana University. It is possible to do an M.A. in Folklore at the

student at Columbia University, worked primarily as a cultural anthropologist, but he also practiced archaeology and linguistic anthropology – and dabbled in physical anthropology.[9] When Kroeber went to Berkeley to teach in 1901 – in the year that both its anthropology department and its archaeology museum were founded – he worked in both the department and the museum until his retirement (and the museum's building would be named after him). Indeed, Kroeber preferred to write about phenomena that admitted of an approach that joined archaeological and cultural anthropological approaches, as his student Julian Steward (1960) wrote in an obituary notice.[10] Boas also had a museum career, but it was brief; he worked at the Field Museum in Chicago for two years, and then, when he moved to New York, worked at the American Museum of Natural History from 1896 to 1905.

But only early American anthropologists' careers crossed subdisciplinary boundaries, although all varieties of American anthropologists have generally shared fundamental values – and claimed Boas as a founding father (Marks 2008). In other parts of the English-speaking world – in Britain and Australia – there are anthropology departments that include biological anthropologists, but the two types of anthropologists in Britain and Australia may resemble their colleagues in the United States, who are engaged in an anthropological version of the "science wars" that broke out between scientists and practitioners of the hybrid academic discipline of science studies in the 1990s, primarily in the United States (Gusterson 2011).[11] The hostile camps are those who believe that the conduct of their enterprise

University of California at Berkeley. The once-outstanding Department of Folklore and Folklife at the University of Pennsylvania, founded in 1962, ceased to be a freestanding department in 1999. Today, there is once again an independent graduate program in folklore at the University of Pennsylvania – but at this time the program is not permitted to accept new graduate students.

9 During the time that Kroeber was a graduate student at Columbia, Franz Boas did virtually no teaching in physical anthropology. Given Boas's importance as a physical anthropologist during his early career, it is notable that he trained no Ph.D.s in physical anthropology between 1900 and 1925; see Frank Spencer (1981), p. 357. But notwithstanding his lack of training in physical anthropology, Kroeber published at least one article in physical anthropology; the selective bibliography in Julian Steward's biography of Kroeber includes an article on blood groups that he published in the *American Journal of Physical Anthropology* in 1934; Steward (1973), p. 135.

10 Available online at: http://www.americanethnography.com/article.php?id=10. Last accessed date April 30, 2013.

11 Practitioners of science studies include persons with degrees in science studies (departmental titles differ) and in the scientific fields they study as well as in history, sociology, and anthropology; occasionally, recruits are from psychology and political science.

fits the pattern characteristic of the natural sciences and those who do not, and there are anthropologists in the former camp who are not biological anthropologists. But many of those who consider themselves scientists and are biological anthropologists have been changing their departmental affiliations. The most conspicuous example of the changing structure of American anthropology was the constitution of a new Department of Human Evolutionary Biology at Harvard on July 1, 2009; most of its members (though not all of them) had been members of Harvard's anthropology department.[12] Likewise indicative of the increasing dissociation between biological anthropologists and the discipline of anthropology per se is the current editorial profile of the *American Journal of Physical Anthropology*; the journal's editor and a substantial portion of its editorial board are not based in anthropology departments.[13] The fissures in anthropology departments reflect long-standing divisions within the discipline, exacerbated by the political uses to which notions about physical variations within the human species were put in the era of World War II; sociocultural anthropologists distanced themselves from physical anthropologists because they were appalled by popular beliefs that physical and behavioral differences were linked – notwithstanding anthropologists' frequent assertions that they were not.[14]

[12] Harvard's anthropology department's official announcement read: "On July 1, 2009, the program of Biological Anthropology in the Department of Anthropology of Harvard University was reconstituted as the new Department of Human Evolutionary Biology. The Department of Anthropology will continue as the home of vibrant programs in Archaeology and Social Anthropology. Both Anthropology and Human Evolutionary Biology will continue their close collegial relationships in research, graduate student training, and undergraduate education." Not all members of the department had previously been biological anthropologists in the anthropology department. Among the interests their faculty profiles describe are evolutionary biology, evolutionary psychology, scientific archaeology, and infectious diseases.

[13] The current editor, Christopher Ruff, describes himself as having a Ph.D. in "biological anthropology" (although he earned it at the University of Pennsylvania, which has a four-field department), and is professor in the Center for Functional Anatomy and Evolution at the Johns Hopkins Medical School. Sixteen out of twenty-six members of the editorial board are based in anthropology departments, but a quarter of them also have appointments in science departments and/or health care schools; ten members of the editorial board are based in science departments or health care schools.

[14] On this general point see Barkan (1992). It is of some interest that during the 1930s Margaret Mead and Gregory Bateson believed that there was evidence of some sort of association between innate predispositions and social behavior but determined that the political uses to which their judgment might be put indicated that they must remain silent about it – at least for the time being; Mead (1972, pp. 254–259).

The History of Anthropology Becomes an Academic Specialty

In 1965, the *Journal of the History of the Behavioral Sciences* began publication. This event represents a benchmark: It was a formal indication that writing the history of the social sciences had become a collective scholarly endeavor (for which one might gain recognition in the academy), rather than an individual idiosyncrasy. The *JHBS*'s founding editorial board included George Stocking, and in its first volume he published what became a widely cited article – "On the Limits of 'Presentism' and 'Historicism' in the Historiography of the Behavioral Sciences" – a call to historians of the social sciences to consider the nature of their research (Stocking 1965). Stocking's importance to the creation of the history of anthropology as an academic specialty cannot be overestimated. When he began circulating the *History of Anthropology Newsletter* in 1983, he effectively created a network. And he edited a series in the history of anthropology, the first volume of which was published by the University of Wisconsin Press in 1983.[15] His efforts and others' made the subject a recognizable specialty within anthropology. The overwhelming majority of historians of anthropology are anthropologists. For example, disciplinary history figures in posts on the anthropology blog "Savage Minds," and a Web site maintained by the Cambridge anthropologist Alan MacFarlane is a major resource for historians, offering online videos of interviews with prominent anthropologists (many of them now deceased).[16] Andre Gingrich suggests that the current academic-demographic profile of historians of anthropology may be less than ideal, arguing that when anthropologists write their own histories they display their "inherent preference for 'local peculiarities,'" and that there is always "the danger of [adopting] national biases"; what should be written is the critical history that results from adoption of a transnational perspective.[17]

Histories written by anthropologists fit several genres. First, there is old-fashioned history of ideas: Ideas are analyzed in abstraction from any sort of social context, using the approach that historians of science used to

[15] That the last volume in the series was Stocking's autobiography, published in 2010, should not suggest that the field is moribund. As I indicate throughout this essay, there are many publication outlets for histories of anthropology, and there is an ongoing series published by the University of Nebraska Press and edited by Regna Darnell and Frederick Gleach, *Histories of Anthropology Annual*, first published in 2005.

[16] The Web address of "Savage Minds" is http://savageminds.org/. Last accessed date: April 30, 2013. The Web address of "Ancestors" is http://www.alanmacfarlane.com/ancestors/audiovisual.html. Last accessed date: April 30, 2013.

[17] Personal communication, October 1, 2012.

call "internalism," which identifies ideas worthy of our attention because they were produced by figures who were very influential, and their discussion in the abstract generated new ideas (see, e.g., Buckley 1988; Das 1998; Gailey 2003; Jacknis 2002; Lincoln 2001; Peletz 1995; Pratt and Du Ponceau 1971).[18] Such accounts may be qualified with pronouncements that contemporary anthropologists know more about certain things than their predecessors did (see, e.g., Buckley 1988). Then, there is the style that represents what historians of science used to call "externalism" (a style of analysis that is no longer fashionable among historians of science); that is, ideas are explained as products of patronage – as dutiful corroborations of patrons' preconceptions (see, e.g., Snead 1999).[19] The sorts of cases that have suited old-style externalists are exemplified by episodes in the history of the Rockefeller Foundation during the interwar period, when the foundation anointed the leaders of many disciplines, anthropologists among them. For example, when the foundation put its financial weight behind the functionalist anthropology program led by Bronislaw Malinowski at the London School of Economics and refused to support G. Elliot Smith's diffusionist anthropology program at University College, London (although it endorsed Smith's work as an anatomist and funded the construction of a new anatomy building), the success of Malinowski's professional progeny became a foregone conclusion. And there is no denying that Malinowski and his students learned that in order to secure Rockefeller patronage they had to phrase their grant applications in language that appealed to foundation officers; they routinely claimed that applied anthropology (if done properly) would resolve global social tensions – and, coincidentally, a peaceful world would be safe for commercial exchanges. But foundation officers were not merely agents of the Rockefeller brothers' commercial interests (and the brothers were also committed philanthropists). We cannot reduce anthropologists' motives and actions to their rhetoric, and the goal that foundation officers consistently set in their diverse programs – to "make the peaks higher" – meant that Rockefeller money went to persons their peers regarded highly. Evidently, patrons' directives are effective – but

[18] For a qualified effort to establish the intellectual significance of an anthropologist – Wilhelm Schmidt – published in the journal Schmidt founded, see Brandewie (1982).

[19] When historians of science divided themselves into "internalists" and "externalists," internalists claimed the moral high ground: because they were discussing the great ideas produced by great men, they were analyzing what was truly important about science; to analyze factors external to science per se – such as patterns of patronage – was to inquire into factors that became irrelevant to scientists once they acquired the wherewithal to do their science. Nowadays, historians of science whose primary concern is history of ideas know that patronage is important – but in varying degrees.

recipients of philanthropic largesse also command all manner of techniques of passive resistance (see Kuklick 1991, pp. 182–241). There is also a variety of externalism that focuses on work structures, demonstrating that the growth of anthropology has followed a pattern of institutionalization familiar to historians of all types of academic disciplines (see, e.g., Rogge 1976). A subcategory of this genre is the study of anthropology as a profession, an approach that can be applied to the study of any knowledge-based occupation. Using this approach, scholars have identified career patterns of individual anthropologists and routes to the discipline's institutionalization in different nations' university systems (see, e.g., Bernstein 2002; Darnell 1998; Hassler 1989; Hurlbert 1976; Mills 2003; Osterling and Martínez 1983; Thompson 2005). Finally there is what one might call the anthropology of anthropology: Anthropologists' ideas are explained as products of their cultural milieux (see, e.g., Frank 1999; Godina 2003; Guyer 2004; Piddington 1960; Jonathan Spencer 2000). A subcategory of this genre mixes intellectual history with the anthropology of anthropology (see, e.g., Modell 1988; Jules-Rosette 1991). Certainly, one could say that the anthropology of anthropology is a variety of historicism.

I stress that Stocking's practitioners do not fall into a dichotomous category based on their disciplinary affiliations; there are historians who are "presentists" as well as social scientists turned historians who are "historicists." Those historians who fit Stocking's category of "presentists," who have pursued inquires designed to improve current practices in human science disciplines, have almost invariably been trained in the fields they describe.[20] They have asked such questions as, Have notable figures been unjustifiably ignored? Do their ideas now deserve our attention? Among the most notable figures who have been rediscovered is Arnold van Gennep, a chronically underemployed student of Émile Durkheim's nephew and disciple, Marcel Mauss, who did his first field research in Algeria in 1911. He wrote a Ph.D. dissertation under Mauss's supervision, and for a brief period taught in Switzerland, but was unable to find a permanent position in France – both because he quarreled

[20] The conspicuous exception to this generalization is James Clifford, who earned his Ph.D. in history but whose audience is evidently largely composed of anthropologists. See, e.g., his *The Predicament of Culture* (1988). My own case exemplifies the phenomenon. Although I am a member of the faculty in the University of Pennsylvania's Department of History and Sociology of Science, I am the only member of the department with a Ph.D. in sociology (and I have arguably become more of a historian than a sociologist, adapting to the local intellectual ecology – an adaptation that was relatively easy, since my first degree was in history). I began writing the history of my discipline in the presentist spirit – trying to explain how sociology took what I believed to be a wrong turn when functionalists became the discipline's dominant theorists in the late 1930s; see Kuklick (1973).

with Mauss shortly after he finished his dissertation and because he had significant differences with Durkheim and his school, who dominated French sociocultural anthropology in his day.[21] Likewise, A. M. Hocart, who had aspirations to become an anthropologist but spent much of his career as archaeological commissioner of Ceylon (now Sri Lanka), has been celebrated as an original thinker who did not subscribe to any of the anthropological creeds of his day and held only one academic position, as E. E. Evans-Pritchard's successor as professor of sociology at the University of Cairo from 1934 to 1938, the year of his death (on Hocart, see Needham 1970). Related to questions about unjustifiably jettisoned heroes and ideas are questions about the merits of established practices. Typical anthropologist-historians have often agonized about whether anthropologists' long-established subject, the "primitive" (or the "other"), is a viable category, either conceptually or empirically (usual answer: "no"), or whether their long-established method, participant observation, is sufficiently distinctive to differentiate their enterprise from other varieties of social science (answer: Anthropologists have not had a monopoly on the use of this method, but they made its use a defining property of their discipline and have practiced it at the highest standard, recursively modifying it; see, e.g. Fortun 2009).

Presentist historians of the various social sciences have also worried about where in the academy their disciplines fit. Do they belong with the humanities, the social sciences, or the natural sciences? Few recent anthropologist-historians categorize their discipline as a member of the natural science family (not least because they have an oversimplified vision of the natural sciences and imagine that all types of science maintain the conventions of the laboratory sciences). The question about a discipline's appropriate place in the academy is generally beloved of historians who began their careers as practitioners of social science disciplines, who wonder both whether the social sciences *can* follow natural scientific models and whether they *should* do so. Historians of science have also asked the former question, but, unlike social scientists, they have no stake in the answer to the second.

To fit Stocking's "historicist" category, by contrast, means distancing oneself from the discipline's present, viewing social scientific ideas as products of their historical moments, using analyses of the social sciences as means to answer general historical questions. Scholarship of this sort has many varieties. For example, anthropological developments have often been (somehow) related to two basic arguments: about whether speculation about varieties of human behavior was prompted by imperialist encounters; and

[21] On van Gennep, see Sibeud (2008).

about how Europeans' movements over the globe (for whatever purposes) stimulated discussion of the significance of visible physical variations within the human species. Or one can come to the history of anthropology after having treated anthropologists' findings as historical records. The late Douglas Cole, a student of the cultural history of the Northwest Coast of British Columbia, may well have begun writing his masterful biography of the young Franz Boas because Boas's research concerned peoples of interest to Cole (Chaiken and Long 1999).

Historians of science have their own subculture of inquiry. They (or, I suppose, I should say we, since I became a historian of science after earning my Ph.D. in sociology) have classified anthropology variously and framed their analyses accordingly. Many (indeed, most) have classified anthropology as one of the variety of disciplines that the social sciences comprise, and their accounts may take the form of identifying generic properties of such enterprises. Relatively recently, I and others have employed a different classificatory scheme, judging that especially interesting insights are possible if one sees *any* sort of esoteric research as a form of work. If one identifies anthropology's work site as the field (as opposed to the laboratory), one understands it as a member of the family of field sciences – specialties that range from anthropology to zoology. In essence, field scientists are historians, not experimentalists. That is, they chronicle events and relationships; they do not provoke them. Their experiments can be only quasi-experiments; for example, those who study animal communication can play recordings of their subjects' calls to their subjects, who range from birds to primates, to see whether recorded sounds elicit anticipated responses (see, e.g., Kuklick and Kohler 1996; Kuklick 2011).[22]

Last but hardly least, the history of anthropology has been pursued by a congeries of others: literary critics, such as Michael North and Patrick Brantlinger, who have interpreted anthropological ideas in cultural contexts; students of American society, such as John Gilkeson and George Stocking in his original scholarly incarnation (Stocking earned his Ph.D. at a University of Pennsylvania department that no longer exists – American Civilization); and students of religious thought, such as Ivan Strenski. It seems intuitively obvious that virtually all such persons belong in the historicist camp – although they are interested in anthropology per se in different degrees. My paper will address a question that for which I have only a tentative answer: Does anthropology by its very nature inspire historical

[22] For discussion of experiments with recorded sounds, see Radick (2007). To see science as a form of work is to adopt a sociological way of thinking.

inquiry among practitioners of a wider range of academic disciplines than other varieties of social science? I suspect that the answer is "yes," and anticipate that others will agree when they read this essay in conjunction with other contributions to this volume. Moreover, anthropology is distinctive because it experienced a soul-wrenching crisis of confidence during the era in which former colonies became independent. At that time, many practitioners found their discipline's original sin in its history: It developed along with the establishment of colonialism. For British anthropologists, the crisis of confidence was heralded by the 1973 publication of Talal Asad's edited volume *Anthropology and the Colonial Encounter*. (Ironically, British government support for anthropological research was most generous during the decolonization era – when anthropologists were supposed to assist colonial subjects to develop viable development projects, so that their countries could become economically independent – although the professional leaders who guided the Colonial Social Science Research Council's Committee on Anthropology and Sociology subverted government intentions, assigning scholars they considered mediocre to practical projects and perceiving their most important task to be sponsorship of research of the highest academic significance; see Kuklick 1991, pp. 191–2.) At roughly the same time, American anthropologists displayed a range of anxieties; they worried both about their discipline's connections with internal and external colonialism and about their failure to sustain the Boasian legacy of critical commentary on their own society's defects, a matter to which I will return (see Hymes 1969).[23] Historians of French anthropology – in France and elsewhere – have likewise been disturbed by evidence that anthropologists provided instrumental guidance to colonial rulers (see, e.g., Conklin 1997; Salemink 2003; Sibeud 2012; Wilder 2005).

Indeed, some now argue that the sins of the fathers persist in the postcolonial era. Nowadays, many believe that anthropologists serve as handmaidens of neocolonialism, disguised as providers of benevolent action in aid of economic development in erstwhile colonies (see Pathy 1981).[24] Indeed, anthropologists in former colonies stand accused by some of their

[23] American anthropologists were late to recognize that Native Americans were subjects of internal colonialism, however; for example, when Solon Kimball commented in 1946 that all over the world subject peoples were revolting against the "domination of colonial overlords," the restive American subjects he identified were in the Philippines, observing that American Indians did not want independence from the United States – although they were demanding "greater self-government" (1946, p. 8; quotation on p. 16).

[24] For an analysis of the growth of the subspecialty of development anthropology, see Escobar (1991).

colleagues of a form of intellectual neocolonialism, of being preoccupied with the research problems their European and American counterparts set themselves, rather than attending to the need for practical research in their own countries (see Debnath 1999).[25] Various forms of navel gazing have followed the denunciation of anthropology as a tool of domination (see, e.g., Marcus and Fischer 1986 Kirby 1988). Scholars have provided a range of solutions to the problem of assessing anthropology's relation with colonialism. Some have exonerated anthropologists of blame. Some have lamented that the association of anthropology with colonialism means that anthropologists are viewed with such suspicion that their research subjects refuse to respond to their inquires. Others have argued that anthropologists were able to serve colonial regimes only if they assumed roles quite different from their academic ones.[26] The general debate is far from over.

Pre–World War II Histories of Anthropology

The very oldest histories of anthropology – formally outside the province of our deliberations – were concerned to establish the intellectual viability of anthropology and direct its future development (see also Boas 1904). By definition, then, they were presentist. It is worth considering them briefly because they represent the work that post–World War II historians reacted against. The oldest full-length study I know was written by an erstwhile zoologist, A. C. Haddon, whose entrepreneurial efforts, beginning with his organization of the 1898 Cambridge Anthropological Expedition to Torres Straits, did much to legitimate his new subject in British universities – although the institutionalization of anthropology at Cambridge was a protracted process.[27]

25 For a contrary view, see Wallace and Harris (1989); but note that Debnath is a local observer, whereas Wallace and Harris are Americans.

26 Taatgen (1988) makes the first argument; see also Gray (1997) and Brown (2003). Lewis (1973) makes the second argument. For the last, see Piddington (1960). Lewis's article is followed by comments by a number of anthropologists, some of whom were quite critical of her views, and some of whom endorsed them. In particular, David Brokenshaw emphasized that anthropologists of the colonial era were quite critical of colonialism (pp. 592–3), and Richard Frucht observed that Lewis's solution to anthropology's professional problem was inadequate (p. 593); see also Handelman (1994). See also Gray (2007). For an illustration of the capacity of an academic anthropologist to serve as a powerful advocate for indigenous peoples, see Pulla (2003).

27 When Haddon organized the Torres Straits Expedition, he was professor of zoology at the Royal College of Science in Dublin. Cambridge appointed him a lecturer in ethnology in 1900, but he did not gain the financial security to resign his Dublin post until 1901, when he was elected to a fellowship at Christ's College; he rose to the rank of reader, retiring

In his *History of Anthropology*, first published in 1910, Haddon (1910) was concerned to establish that anthropology was a science, finding its sources in various scientific ideas – Darwin's conspicuous among them. Indeed, that anthropology derived from Darwinian biology was the argument advanced by Alfred Russel Wallace – today best known as Darwin's codiscoverer of the mechanism of natural selection – who was among the most ecumenical of the persons active in British anthropological societies during the 1860s, a member of both the monogenist Ethnological Society of London and the polygenist Anthropological Society of London (Wallace 1864). Moreover, it is of some significance that at a time when virtually every discipline that might do so was engaged in claiming a Darwinian pedigree – during the various scholarly celebrations staged in 1909 and 1910 that commemorated the fiftieth anniversary of the publication of *On the Origin of Species* – Franz Boas insisted that Darwin's ideas about racial variation were consistent with his own.[28] Boas's position then was especially notable in the light of subsequent developments in American anthropology, since Boas's school would be associated with repudiation of all forms of evolutionist thinking. (I am not suggesting that Boas spoke approvingly of Darwin *only* because he hoped that some of Darwin's glory would rub off on him; the argument Boas made – that all varieties of the human species had some traits that seemed "primitive" and some that seemed "advanced," making it impossible to assign different races different places on an evolutionary ladder – was consistent both with Darwinian reasoning and with the antiracism that consistently informed Boas's thinking.) A quarter-century later, however, when Boas's student Robert Lowie (1937) undertook analysis of anthropology's past for presentist purposes, he was concerned to demonstrate the foolishness of evolutionist anthropology – lumping all of its varieties together – and thus wrote Darwin's contribution out of the history of the field. We should note, however, that the evolutionist anthropology Boasians despised was a homegrown variety founded in the ideas of Lewis Henry Morgan, which were quite different from Darwin's. And because early anthropologists had various intellectual pedigrees, they wrote rather different histories. The classicist-anthropologist John Linton Myres

in 1926. In 1932, Cambridge established the William Wyse Professorship, but it was not occupied by a credentialed anthropologist until 1950, however, when it was assumed by Meyer Fortes; its first occupants were T. C. Hodson and J. H. Hutton, both retired members of the Indian Civil Service.

[28] Franz Boas, "The Relation of Darwin to Anthropology," unpublished lecture, apparently delivered in 1910 in a course organized by John Dewey. The original is in the Boas Papers at the American Philosophical Society; it is also available online at: http://www.journals.uchicago.edu/CA/journal/issues/v42n3/013002/013002.text.html.

found anthropology's disciplinary ancestors among the ancient Greeks – the earliest precursors identified by any historian of the field. But Myres's *The Influence of Anthropology on the Course of Political Science* (1914) represented protoanthropologists' motivations in remarkably modern terms. When ancient Greeks ventured into the Mediterranean region in the seventh and sixth centuries B.C.E., Myres (1914, p. 4) said, they were provoked by their experiences to ask:

> Is there, for example, among all the various regions and aspects of the world, any real earthly paradise,... where, without let or hindrance the good man may lead the good life? Is there an ideal diet? an ideal social structure? or in general an ideal way of life for all men? Or are all the good things of this world wholly relative to the persons, the places, and the seasons where they occur?[29]

Contemporary Research

We thus come to the era that this volume treats. In John Burrow's *Evolution and Society*, published in 1966, one of the first works of serious scholarship in the history of anthropology written by a historian, Darwin's influence on anthropology became just one among many; Burrow pointed to pre-Darwinian ideas that shaped early anthropology, such as those of the eighteenth-century Scottish Enlightenment. This was a history that suited the sociocultural anthropologists who dominated the discipline in the anglophone world, concerned to establish their independence from biological anthropologists, then chronically suspect because any investigation of human physical variation was thought inextricable from racism; and a history of social thought with intellectual antecedents *only* in social thought (as opposed to past biological thought, which was not necessarily more genuinely *scientific* than social thought) was also more flattering to sociocultural anthropologists' self-image. I should add that Burrow had good reasons for his claim (see Berry 1997).

But Burrow could have paid more attention to Darwin's influence on anthropology. Indeed, as a close examination of Darwin's 1871 *The Descent of Man* in its unabridged form indicates, Darwin read broadly and deeply in the anthropological literature, and his anthropologist contemporaries learned a good deal from him. (Darwin's links to his anthropologist contemporaries

[29] Myres (1869–1954), whose final academic post was as Wykeham Professor of Ancient History at Oxford, was very active in anthropological circles. He served as president of the Royal Anthropological Institute (RAI), for example, and was the first editor of the RAI's lesser journal, *Man* (at the time when the RAI published two journals), from 1901 to 1903, editing it again from 1931 to 1946. See Kuklick (1991, p. 311).

are obscure in abridged versions of *Descent,* not least because they are clearly specified in the book's footnotes, which are cut severely in abridged versions.) Furthermore, one wonders how Darwin could have kept his distance from anthropology. His most important anthropological source in *Descent* was the scientific polymath (and Liberal Member of Parliament) John Lubbock, the son of Darwin's close neighbor and friend, whom Darwin had served as an informal tutor – and who became, in fact, a major target of Lowie's attack on evolutionist anthropology (see Kuklick 2012). The point of what may seem to have been a series of connected digressions is this: Even the most rigorously historicist historians are affected by the intellectual politics of the human sciences they study. The anthropological debate that informed Stocking's earliest work was whether Franz Boas and his students were guided by theory. Anthropologists' conventional wisdom was once that Boasian anthropology was atheoretical, and that American anthropologists were not introduced to theoretically grounded research until 1931, when the British anthropologist A. R. Radcliffe-Brown traveled to the United States to spend six years at the University of Chicago. Indeed, because Stocking has a large audience among anthropologists, his analyses have led American anthropologists to reconsider their assessment of the Boasians.

Varieties of Presentist History

At its most basic, presentist history of anthropology may best fit the genre of the history of heroism. Consider, for example, Michael Young's (2004) first volume of a planned two-volume biography treatment of Bronislaw Malinowski. Memorably described by Stocking (1992, p. 17) as the "mythic culture hero of anthropological method," Malinowski plays a major role in anthropology's folk tradition – its oral history. Anthropologists' folk-traditional narrative reports that Malinowski formulated the discipline's core method of participant observation through a historical accident: He traveled to Australia to attend the 1914 meetings of the British Association for the Advancement of Science; when World War I broke out, he was trapped in Australia because he was, as a citizen of the Austro-Hungarian Empire, officially an enemy alien; he escaped internment but spent a good portion of the war years doing fieldwork, first (for a relatively brief period) among a population of Papua New Guinea, and subsequently (during several visits) among the people of the Trobriand Islands. According to legend, Malinowski found himself with no option other than to pursue funding that allowed him to live in the field for an unprecedented period and retrospectively recognized the merits of his experience, realizing that he had inadvertently contrived an ideal research method – the practice of taking up sustained residence among a population sufficiently small that the anthropologist could have some sort of personal contact with each member of the group.[30] In fact, he had intended to spend two years in the field, and, thanks largely to his mentor at the London School of Economics, C. G. Seligman, had the wherewithal to do so; he was able to secure additional financial support from the Australian government by promising to identify information useful to Australia's colonial administrators (Young 2004, p. 245n).[31]

Young's biography closes the gap between anthropological legend and the reality of Malinowski's personal history – but tacitly sustains the discipline's view of Malinowski as a near-mythic hero, describing the events of his life in such detail that a reader sometimes feels as if she were experiencing them vicariously in real time. Of course, there are studies like Young's of other scientific figures – of different types. Other social scientific Founding Fathers have received similarly detailed biographical treatment; Steven Lukes's (1973) masterful biography of Durkheim is an obvious example.

A related genre to the biography of the hero is that of the celebrity – the individual whose personal life is seen as fascinating regardless of its relevance to the accomplishments that called the individual to public attention. The treatment of anthropologists as celebrities has taken various forms and has been produced by various types. Practitioner-historians such as Adam Kuper have written books that surely are widely read because they treat anthropologists as celebrities, focusing on anthropologists' personal lives and their relationships with one another. Kuper's *Anthropology and Anthropologists: The Modern British School*, first printed in 1973 and amended and reprinted many times subsequently, literally reproduced anthropological gossip; it was based on the tape recordings Kuper made when he organized a seminar in which anthropologists reminisced.[32] Likewise, Jack Goody's *The Expansive Moment* (1995) printed gossip that had long circulated within anthropology's elite circles, revealing the personalities behind notable ideas and exposing the alliances and feuds that, respectively, facilitated and hindered these ideas' dissemination (Goody's

[30] For one reiteration of anthropology's folk tradition, see Hoffman and Gardner (2006).

[31] See also Malinowski to Atlee Hunt, secretary, Department of External Affairs, April 28, 1915, and Hunt to Malinowski, May 4, 1915, Yale University Archives, MS 19, Box 4. For another example of interest in Malinowski as a form of hero worship, see Średniawa (1981); see also Paluch (1981).

[32] It seems fitting that I learned of Kuper's method from a discussion with the anthropologist Abner Cohen during a seminar I attended in 1978.

book has the *formal* appearance of scholarly research, being replete with footnoted references to anthropologists' correspondence, but the reader is unable to check Goody's reports, since they do not reveal where cited letters are archived). And one must note the apparently insatiable appetite for books about Margaret Mead and Ruth Benedict – together or separately – which reflect the celebrity status that both (and especially Mead) enjoyed during their lifetimes as public intellectuals. (They began as student and teacher, became close friends, and were briefly lovers.) Other social scientists have been public intellectuals, but Mead and Benedict seem to have been special variants of the type.

I argue that anthropologists' view of their discipline's past is distinctive, unlike other social scientists' views of their specialties' pasts. It inclines toward a history of celebrity because it is informed by oral tradition, which is, of course, one of the things anthropologists collect when they are doing research in the field; anthropological research depends heavily – if not exclusively – on information transmitted orally. (I cannot resist recalling the rejection letter I received for the very first article I submitted to an anthropology journal, which stated that I could not be believed because I had relied on written records; my response was laughter.) All of the anthropologists I know learned anecdotes about their intellectual forebears in the seminars they took as students. Oral tradition takes various forms, of course, and some of it may be reduced to gossip.

The routine transmission of gossip surely also reflects a disciplinary culture that has seen professional growth as a function of *character* rather than mastery of a set of skills that can be defined and taught. If witnesses can be considered reliable only if they are persons of good character, then knowledge of their personal traits is essential to judgments of the merits of their observations.[33] Qualities of character – other than good work habits – are irrelevant to judgments of evidence if reliable witnesses' skills are merely technical. Consider the contrast between the training of sociologists and anthropologists. Apprentice sociologists take required courses in statistics and methods; practitioners assume that their discipline has developed a set of useful analytic tools, which can be learned. Anthropologists are thrown into the field to "sink or swim," with the expectation that only the truly talented will survive.[34] Anthropology's history is also suffused with famous personal spats – Evans-Pritchard's with Malinowski, for example, or

[33] Unfortunately, confounding the personal and the professional makes judgments of controversial studies very difficult to resolve. See Eakin (2013).

[34] For an influential repudiation of the "sink or swim" approach, see Barrett (1996). For a comparison of sociology and anthropology, see Record (1981).

Edmund Leach's with Meyer Fortes – spats in which the personal and the intellectual were coincident. Certainly, tales of the dead are retailed in the seminars of other social sciences.[35] But anthropologists' pedagogy is different, and thus their view of their history is different. Their oral tradition is sustained not only in seminar rooms but also in published interviews with anthropologists, as well as in the memoirs that introduce each volume of the *Annual Review of Anthropology* (see, e.g., Comaroff and Comaroff 1988; Firth 1975; Leach 1984; Parkin 1988).[36] Moreover, that anthropologists' versions of their history are habitually conveyed orally is consistent with anthropologists' habit of relying heavily on information they collect orally while doing field research. Indeed, as Regna Darnell (1977, p. 399) observed, the required course in the history of anthropology that has long been a part of graduate training has been a course in oral tradition; often "taught by the eldest member of the department, who [was] presumably qualified to teach the history because he [had] lived through more of it than anyone else," it has provided "the fledgling anthropologist with a collection of anecdotes, later to prove useful in socializing his own students within the profession."

Other projects in presentist history written by anthropologists have evident relevance to anthropological practice. Evans-Pritchard (1981) used his forays into the history of the discipline to place it among the humanities (see also Record 1981). Marvin Harris's *The Rise of Anthropological Theory* represents a perfect realization of the presentist project to reform anthropology by reviving goals that recent practitioners have largely disavowed. In Harris's view, anthropologists ought not to have abandoned the goal of developing a science of humankind and a generally materialist orientation; indeed, the developments he decried were the very ones that Lowie had endorsed. Certainly, Harris allowed, anthropologists could not produce science resembling Newtonian physics, but they could follow the method – if not the objective – of Darwinian biology. But renouncing scientific standards had led them to embrace "a view of culture that exaggerated all the

35 I recall hearing only one such tale during my years of graduate study in sociology. I heard it from the professor who taught me sociological theory. At Harvard, where my professor had earned his Ph.D. in the department that Talcott Parsons founded, he was told that Parsons's writing became far less comprehensible when his father died. His father had been an English professor and had edited Parsons's prose. This story made no sense to me, since I could see little difference between the style of *The Structure of Social Action*, Parsons's first book, published in 1937, and that of *The Social System*, published in 1951.

36 It is of some interest that each volume of the *Annual Review of Sociology* is introduced by a memoir of a famous sociologist. None of the other annual reviews (which cover the sciences as well as the human sciences) is introduced in this way. See also Record (1981).

quixotic, irrational and inscrutable ingredients in human life" and to publishing analyses that revealed "more and more about less and less"; indeed, he argued, if anthropologists did not mend their ways, their discipline would disappear, since its practitioners would be unable to secure funding for their research (Harris 1968; quotations on pp. 2 and 3). Efforts similar to Harris's – attempts to change anthropology's core mission – need not be so sweeping in scope; Derek Freeman's infamous *Margaret Mead and Samoa* (1982) attempted to defend an allegedly scientific – anti-Boasian – approach to anthropological research by revealing that Freeman's own research in Samoa, done four decades after Mead had done hers, led to an account of Samoan society very different from hers. As Mead wrote in her preface to the 1973 edition of *Coming of Age in Samoa* (originally published in 1928), the Samoa she visited was a historical phenomenon and could not be revisited (Freeman 1983; Mead 1973). (She was surely anticipating Freeman's critique of her work, which he waited to publish until after her death.)

Consider a more recent account, Nancy Lutkehaus's addition to the substantial body of biographical studies of Margaret Mead. Lutkehaus's project is substantially different from other books about Mead because it is in essence arguing for Mead's *causes*, not the celebrity that gave her an audience for her causes – which is to say that it is a defense of a publicly engaged anthropology, committed to (implicitly liberal) social reform, a brand of anthropology advocated by Mead's teacher, Franz Boas, which Mead practiced more successfully than any of his other students (Lutkehaus 2008).[37] The best indicator of Boas's success in making himself a public figure may be the cover story that *Time*, a weekly American newsmagazine, ran in its May 11, 1936, issue on the occasion of Boas's retirement from Columbia University; the story published in the magazine highlighted Boas's longtime commitment to reform, emphasizing his concern to eradicate racism.

Nowadays, there is a new type of historian of anthropology, exemplified by the anthropologists Lise Dobrin and Ira Bashkow. Their analyses are both presentist and historicist. And because Dobrin and Bashkow are rigorous historians, both anthropologists and scholars who are not committed to reforming contemporary anthropology can find the pair's work congenial. For example, their analysis of the ill-fated anthropological (as well as marital) partnership of Reo Fortune and Margaret Mead shows how Fortune and Mead reached different conclusions while sharing a field site because their experiences there were different; she was immobilized by a foot injury,

[37] For a book that exemplifies the treatment of Mead and Benedict as celebrities, see Banner (2003).

confined to their campsite, and acquired much of her information from servants, whereas he hiked all over the area they were studying, gaining an appreciation of both individual and geographical variation. Dobrin and Bashkow have surely gained readers because there is an established audience for analyses of Mead's personal life (and the episode they describe is particularly sensational, since it led to Fortune's divorce from Mead, which had a devastating affect on his career). But their significant achievement has been a historicized epistemology. Dobrin and Bashkow's analysis assuages contemporary anthropologists' anxiety about the inevitable subjectivity of their findings by showing that varieties of subjectivity can be explained (Dobrin and Bashkow 2010).[38]

Varieties of Historicist History

I do not want to suggest that anthropologists have a trained incapacity to write fully historicist accounts. Gillian Feeley-Harnik (1999), for example, has brilliantly decoded Lewis Henry Morgan's understanding of kinship as commentary on the worldview of nineteenth-century Americans. Regardless, historicist accounts have many varieties, and I can only give a sense of their range in this paper.

Perhaps the most fully contextualized history of anthropological ideas is Philip Curtin's masterful *Image of Africa: British Ideas and Action, 1780–1850*, first published in 1964. Curtin's primary concern was to explain varieties of British engagement with Africa – commercial and political – as well as the politics of the eventually outlawed slave trade, but his narrative necessarily covers the emergence of formally organized anthropology (and the nascent discipline's factions). Other notable early works are William Cohen's *The French Encounter with Africans* (1980), a relatively modest replication of Curtin's work in a different national context, and Michael Osborne's *Nature, the Exotic, and the Science of French Colonialism* (1994), less ambitious in both substantive and temporal terms, which has the virtue of analyzing anthropology as a member of the family of natural history enterprises. Martin Staum's *Nature and Nurture in French Social Sciences, 1859–1914 and Beyond* (2011) is an exemplary survey. I should also mention Winthrop Jordon's *White over Black: American Attitudes toward the Negro, 1550–1812* (1968); although its reputation has suffered somewhat over time, it was regarded as an instant classic at the time of its publication. My own *The Savage Within: The Social History of British Anthropology,*

[38] For a similar type of analysis, see Chapoulie (2004).

1885–1945 (1991) began as an effort to explain anthropological ideas in the context of British imperialism, although my research led me to conclude that this was not the only relevant context. Before I cease surveying surveys, I should mention works that attempt to answer German anthropologists' most important question about their history: How could a fundamentally liberal enterprise – begotten by Boas's mentors Adolf Bastian (on the socio-cultural side) and Rudolf Virchow (on the physical side) – turn into "race science," an intellectual justification for Nazi crimes? Andrew Zimmerman's *Anthropology and Antihumanism in Imperial Germany* (2001) dismisses German liberalism as more apparent than real, finding an ineradicable anti-Semitic taint in German character (as have many German historians). Andre Gingrich (2007) argues to the contrary: Before World War I, liberalism was the dominant paradigm among anthropologists in Germany – as well as in Russia and in the Austro-Hungarian Empire. Andrew Evans (2010) shows that there were shifts in internal power structure of the anthropological community that were effected by a changed market for anthropologists' services during World War I; because physical anthropologists made themselves useful measuring (and diagnosing the defects of) those prisoners of war whom the Germans judged of inferior stocks, the appeal of race science rose after the war (and the economic fortunes of the anthropologists who had worked in prisoner of war camps improved considerably).[39] Gingrich has carried the story forward, describing anthropologists' behavior during the Nazi era and in the immediate post–World War II period. Race scientists (along with folklorists) were Nazi ideologues, while cultural anthropologists maintained contact with British and (to a lesser extent) American anthropologists until the outbreak of World War II, when contact became illegal; many German cultural anthropologists then found refuge elsewhere in Europe as well as the Americas; however, the most prominent of them – Richard Thurnwald – became a Nazi ideologue (Gingrich 2010).

For literary critics, the origin point of concern with anthropology's history was the publication in 1978 of Edward Said's *Orientalism*, a book that provoked stimulating analyses notwithstanding its many oversimplifications; sometimes, oversimplifications *are* insights. Patrick Brantlinger's *Dark Vanishings* (2003), for example, identified a political argument that had strong appeal in territories that were especially attractive to white settlers, particularly those who colonized Australia – the myth of the empty land or *terra nullius* (in Latin, "land belonging to no one"), empty *both*

[39] Evans has also produced the best survey of the prehistory of German anthropology I know.

because whatever indigenous inhabitants were found there were of such inferior quality that they were unable to settle on it and cultivate it properly *and* because resident indigenes belonged to types of human stock so low on the evolutionary scale that they were bound to become extinct when they had contact with superior humans; this narrative seemed accurate, but it was both because settlers introduced diseases to which indigenes had no immunities and because indigenous populations fell in large numbers to settlers who hunted them for sport.[40] Brantlinger's latest book, *Taming Cannibals* (2011), considers a hierarchy of peoples considered inferior – cannibals the most lowly among them – who were nonetheless able to survive exposure to Euroamericans, constituting social problems in settler societies as well as the European societies to which they traveled and settled. But he observes that traveling indigenes were not thought the only sources of social problems in Euroamerican societies; Europeans themselves were supposedly capable of degeneration to savage states in both physical and behavioral terms. What distinguishes the work of a literary critic such as Brantlinger from that of a historian – apart from the background material he provides – is his sources of information, who include (but are not limited to) Charles Dickens, Benjamin Disraeli (in his capacity as a novelist, not as a major political figure in late nineteenth-century Britain), H. Rider Haggard, and H. G. Wells.[41] In short, the approach many literary scholars use when they undertake what might be called history of anthropology is well described by Andrew Curran, a student of French literature, who (2011, p. 18) states that his approach to understanding eighteenth-century notions of blackness entailed writing a "book [that] replicates the reading practices of an imagined eighteenth-century reader." This reader is implicitly an upper-middle-brow reader.

By contrast, for Michael North, a professor of English, the distinction between high and low culture remains significant, and anthropology is a form of high culture, with affinities to other such forms.[42] Thus, he judges that Franz Boas and Bronislaw Malinowski conferred a sensibility like that of the literary avant-gardes on their analyses of language, and analogizes their attitudes toward language to the appropriation of motifs of so-called primitive art by experimental visual artists; indeed, North suggests, because

40 These issues were critical for Australian anthropology's intellectual ancestors. See Hiatt (1996).

41 For example, a historian, Russell McGregor (1997), based an argument very like Brantlinger's in *Dark Vanishings* on very different sources.

42 For an extremely influential argument that the distinction between high and low culture is socially constructed and historically contingent, see Levine (1988).

Malinowski's views derived from the same cultural matrix as the views of his fellow displaced Pole the novelist Joseph Conrad (whose books Malinowski took to the field with him), an understanding of Malinowski enhances appreciation of Conrad. (It is of interest that Malinowski sent his work to Conrad, although we do not know whether Conrad read it; North 1994, pp. 29, 44–6; see also North 1999, p. 50). And Malinowski must have been fully aware of the value of the various persuasive ploys he used in his narratives, including his representation of himself as a hero, not least because he contributed to another landmark effort associated with the University of Cambridge, C. K. Ogden and I. A. Richards's *The Meaning of Meaning*, published in 1923.[43] One should also note the recent literary turn in anthropology, heralded by George Marcus and Michael Fischer's *Anthropology as Cultural Critique* (1986).[44]

A number of scholars have concerned themselves with what might be called anthropology at the low end of the sociocultural scale – the exhibitions of exotic peoples staged during the late nineteenth and early twentieth centuries. For Eric Ames (2009, esp. pp. 63–102), a professor of German, they should be understood as one expression of a genre of popular entertainment, and need not be of special interest to historians of anthropology. To Sierra Bruckner and Sadiah Qureshi, who have studied these exhibitions in Germany and Great Britain, respectively, they figure in the history of anthropology, not least because persons active in anthropological circles availed themselves of opportunities to examine exotic peoples directly when these peoples visited their home countries – a form of direct exposure to unfamiliar human types that substituted for encounters with these peoples in their homelands when travel to these was or seemed (for whatever reason) impossible. Both Qureshi and Bruckner argue that the exhibits joined the esoteric world of scholarship and popular culture; Bruckner (2003, pp. 127–55) notes that such figures as Virchow patronized the exhibits, and Qureshi (2011, esp. pp. 137 and 279 respectively) says that they constituted the means by which "the lay public engaged with nineteenth-century anthropological debates."

Perhaps the most expansive form of historicist history of anthropology is that which virtually obliterates boundaries between specialist practitioners and society at large. John S. Gilkeson's recent book, *Anthropologists and the Rediscovery of America, 1886–1965* (2010), represents a limiting case.

[43] On Malinowski's relationship with Ogden and Richards and his general understanding of the relationship between language and worldview, see North (1999, pp. 9, 32, and 49).

[44] See also Aunger (1995), Clifford (1999), Handelman (1994), and Rabinow (1989. For a hostile response to the literary turn, see Debnath (1999), p. 3111.

In Gilkeson's narrative, the concept of culture that Franz Boas took from Germany to the United States had a special resonance with Americans, who were at the end of the nineteenth century contemplating the peculiar character of their country as it experienced dramatic social change. Gilkeson claims that Boas's socially engaged – and broadly influential – disciples had much to do with alterations in public opinion, with the emergence of a widespread sense of "American exceptionalism."[45]

A common theme of many histories of anthropology is the degree to which anthropologists have suffered (or enjoyed) so-called outsider status, which has conferred two disciplinary virtues. One, because they have cast critical eyes on the customary practices of the social world around them, they were able, in the time-worn phrase, to "make the familiar strange and the strange [other social worlds] familiar." Two, their outsider status made them likely to identify with the oppressed. Many anthropologists had Jewish backgrounds – especially in the United States, Great Britain, and South Africa. But outsider status had various bases. Many British anthropologists had dissenting backgrounds, E. B. Tylor (1832–1917) and A. C. Haddon (1855–1940) prominent among them; others, such as C. G. Seligman (1873–1940), were from secular Jewish families. In the United States, Franz Boas had a secular Jewish background, as did many of his students, such as Edward Sapir (1884–1941) and Melville Herskovits (1895–1963). In South Africa, many anthropologists, such as Isaac Schapera (1905–2003) and Max Gluckman (1911–75), were of Jewish extraction. Other South African anthropologists, many of whom were women, gravitated to the oppositional politics that characterized virtually all South African anthropologists from diverse backgrounds. Monica Hunter Wilson (1908–82), for example, was the child of crusading Scots Presbyterian missionaries.[46]

45 Once upon a time, "American exceptionalism" was a phrase that was uttered in scornful tones by professional historians, but it is now used without irony by political candidates; especially during the primary phase of the 2012 presidential campaign, which led to the nomination of Mitt Romney as the Republican Party candidate for the presidency, "American Exceptionalism" became a statement of putative fact – the greatness of America – and candidates were accused of having lost faith in it. Once upon a time, historians noted that every national history remarks upon the claims to exceptional features of the country it describes to explain national character; the citizens of both Britain and Japan, for example, supposedly have virtues that derived from their countries' island situations. Boas landed on the American scene around the time that Frederick Jackson Turner was bewailing the closing of the American frontier (in a speech he gave in 1893), which meant a diminution of opportunities for upward mobility and varieties of innovation – which had supposedly been greater on the frontier.

46 To be a Dissenter in Britain means to be a Protestant who belongs to a nonestablished church: Tylor was raised as a member of the Society of Friends, but became secular as an

And Gilkeson (2010, p. 7) argues that once fieldwork became essential to professional identity in anthropology, all anthropologists acquired an outsider's perspective, by virtue of being strangers among the peoples they studied (travel away from home ceased to be an obligatory *rite de passage* on the anthropologist's path toward recognition as a fully qualified anthropologist in the 1980s, but that is another matter).[47]

One More Type of Historicist Reasoning

As I suggested early in this chapter, there are two ways of thinking of anthropology as a member of a family of disciplines. One way is to classify it as a type of social science – as the editors of this volume do. Another way is to see it as one of a family of field sciences, derivatives of the subjects that were once collectively natural history – botany, geology, zoology, and so on. Unquestionably, the most important question for scientists – of whatever type – is how to justify belief in observers' reports; justification necessarily entails explaining failures to relevant audiences. The laboratory scientist whose experiments do not produce anticipated results can always fall back on what the sociologist Harry Collins (1981) has termed "the experimenter's regress," which explains failure as the product of factors external to the experiment per se: Experiments do not work in consequence of unforeseen factors, such as dirty glassware and unusually high humidity, which contaminate the laboratory. In contrast, the field scientist can deploy what the sociologist Amanda Rees calls "the fieldworker's regress": In the ordinary course of events, fieldworkers seek to observe natural situations, monitoring events beyond their control (if they naively interfere with the lives of their subjects, they open themselves to the charge that they have shifted from observing "nature" to demonstrating the behavioral effects of specific types of "nurture") (McGrew 2007). That is, field scientists must accept that their subjects are completely unpredictable – which means that many of

adult; Haddon was raised to be a Baptist, and also became secular as an adult. On Tylor, Haddon, and Seligman, see Kuklick (1991), pp. 303–4, 308–9, 312–13. On Boas's Jewish background, see Cole (1999). On the Jewish backgrounds of many American anthropologists, see Feldman (2004). On South African anthropologists see Comaroff and Comaroff (1988) and Bank and Bank (2013).

47 It is of some interest that at least as early as 1914, the British anthropologist/psychologist W. H. R. Rivers (1864–1922) argued that anthropologists gained perspective on their own societies – as well the strange societies they visited – through travel; leaving home liberated them from the conventional expectations of their own societies; see Rivers (1914), volume 2, p. 566. On the possibility of becoming an anthropologist at home, see Kirschner and Martin (2000), esp. pp. 249–59.

their most important findings are serendipitous.[48] Because the events they witness are transitory by definition, fieldworkers whose findings are challenged can always point out that reproducing them is impossible (Rees 2009). As the biologist Michael Canfield (2011, p. 1) observes, fieldworkers of every type experience "one-in-a-lifetime sightings," and the immediate products of their labors – their field notebooks – are, as the botanist James Revel (2011, p. 199) notes, "historical records." Thus, practitioners of all types of field science rely on judgments of observers' *characters* to assess observers' reports; reliable witnesses are persons whose characters are built as they work under difficult, hazardous, and uncomfortable conditions. For sustained analysis of this sort, I refer the reader to a recent article of mine (Kuklick 2011). The question that remains unanswered for me is why anthropologists differ from other sorts of field scientists in that instruction in proven techniques of field research is not a standard feature of graduate training – although teachers of applied anthropology, now considered a fifth subfield in many anthropological quarters, are relatively open to methods courses.[49] Methods courses – many sponsored by the National Science Foundation – are now becoming more common features of anthropologists' education in the United States, but resistance to them is fierce in many departments. The tendencies to see gossip about anthropologists as relevant to judgment of their reports and first fieldwork as a test of character are two aspects of the same mind-set.

What Have I Omitted?

One: There is a fairly substantial literature on the difficulties involved in the institutionalization of anthropology in various national contexts, which focuses on university systems reluctant to embrace new disciplines as well as governments reluctant to establish anthropological agencies either in the metropoles or in outposts of empire. I am not strongly engaged by

[48] For example, a fieldworker studying moose-wolf interactions asks, "Who knows where a moose will go next? Once you find moose tracks, it's anybody's guess – it might even be the moose's guess – where they'll go." John Vucetich, "Much to Learn from What Remains," a post from the *New York Times* "Scientist at Work" blog, posted February 6, 2012, http://www.nytimes.com/adx/bin/adx_click.html?type=cookie&pos=Position1B. For a discussion of the importance of serendipity, see Spyer (2011), who argues that anthropology is distinguished by its reliance on serendipity, but nonanthropological researchers might well disagree with her.

[49] Note that applied anthropologists work in many quarters, in corporate settings as well as social welfare settings. See Singer (2008), an applied anthropologist who works in medical settings.

this literature (although I have contributed to it), since it has a relatively standard – and not very interesting – plotline (i.e., parties with rather different interests are less than honest in their negotiations; resistance to the legitimation of new disciplines is dictated by such economic factors as the competition for large numbers of enrolled undergraduate student bodies, who justify hiring of additional personnel, rather than intellectual objections). Two: With the breakdown of the distinctly North American departmental organization of the four anthropological subfields of cultural anthropology, archaeology, linguistics, and biological anthropology – as much because biological anthropologists identify themselves as biological scientists and want to leave anthropology departments as because the other subtypes do not quite see the relevance of biological anthropology to their subjects – there has been some reflection on the history and legitimacy of the four field structure. The unanswered question is why divisions in anthropology have become so bitter. Contrast fissiparous tendencies in other social sciences: Experimental psychologists join separate cognitive science departments – as well as interdisciplinary programs in cognitive science that join people from various departments. Social psychologists take up lucrative positions in business schools. Sociologists can form separate criminology departments – or function as members of specialized units within sociology departments. Perhaps consideration of the reasons that psychology departments do *not* break up along subfield lines would help clarify the reasons that anthropology departments *do*.

General Trends

Over time, historical analyses of notable anthropologists and schools have grown less hagiographic – with the exception of some of the work done by those who worship at the intellectual feet of Émile Durkheim, notably some affiliates of Le Groupe d'études durkheimiennes, which was formed in Paris in 1975 in the Maison des Sciences de l'Homme, and affiliates of the British Centre for Durkheimian Studies, which is a special group within the University of Oxford's Institute of Social and Cultural Anthropology and began operating in 1991. There have been flash points in anthropologists' understanding of their history, moments when the discipline's major questions changed – flash points that have been associated with changes in the world outside academe. In the recent past, the most notable change affecting anthropologists' historical understanding was, of course, the era of decolonization, which stimulated a variety of intellectual responses (see, e.g., Wolf 1982; Fabian 1983). But anthropologists' anxieties that their discipline has an insecure place in the academy because it cannot throw off the burden of its past have surely been exacerbated by the declining economic prospects that young academics have faced since the 1970s. It is worth noting that during the 1970s American and British sociologists also declared that their disciplines were in crisis and decried functionalist theory as a justification for perpetuation of the status quo – which for most practitioners meant failure to criticize many features of contemporary society, not just practices somehow associated with colonialism (see, e.g., Gouldner 1970; Bottomore 1974). The history of applied sociology is rather different from the history of applied anthropology, but the key to the mind-set shared by practitioners of both disciplines may well have been their shared pessimism about their professional futures. It is worth recalling that functionalist theory became dominant in American sociology during the Great Depression, when the young repudiated the previously dominant school of thought, that was associated with the sociology department at the University of Chicago – the first department of sociology in the world, founded in 1892 (Kuklick 1973). Whatever relationships obtain between theoretical orientation and practical action, they are indubitably complex.

The first serious writers of the history of anthropology – those whose writing was not intended to address matters of critical importance to practitioners of anthropology, which included persuading the public that anthropological knowledge per se was valuable – were historians, the likes of John Burrow, Philip Curtin, and George Stocking (of course, only Stocking made his career as a historian of anthropology). As I observed earlier, the subject then attracted a broad range of scholars. When I began writing this essay, I expected to find that in the decades following the 1960s, when writing about anthropology's past became a serious academic subject, the scholars who wrote the history of anthropology would be drawn from an increasingly narrow professional pool. I was wrong. Although most historians of anthropology are anthropologists, the specialty's disciplinary catchment area has grown.

The State of the Art

What have historians of anthropology accomplished to date? George Stocking's (1987, 1995) two books on British anthropology are indispensible for any historian who writes about the historical developments he has described. Historians of French anthropology who work in North America have expanded their intellectual networks to incorporate French historians; Martin Staum (2011, p. xi), for example, clearly the leading light of his intellectual sphere in North America, is linked to the French historian of anthropology Claude Blanckaert, who has trained many French historians of French anthropology. When we look beyond anthropology as practiced in Europe and the Americas, we see analyses of the two anthropological cultures that developed in South Africa – that of the English speakers and of the Afrikaans speakers (see Gordon 1988, 1989). It would be fascinating to know, however, what differences obtained between the South African English-speaking anthropologists who worked in South Africa and those whose pilgrimage to Britain was permanent, apart from the obvious one – that those who made their careers in Britain were of Jewish extraction. Andrew Bank (2008) has established two distinguishing features of those who remained in South Africa: Many of them were women and many of them were politically radical. (Some of those who migrated to Britain were also radical – such as Gluckman – but a left-wing orientation did not distinguish the migrants as a group.)[50] The history of anthropology in Australia has received considerable attention from anthropologists who work there, many of whom, like Geoffrey Gray, whose works I have cited in this paper, have focused on anthropologists' role in Australia's poor treatment of Aborigines. When one reads about the treatment of indigenes in other white settler societies, such as those of Canada and the United States, and the sorts of roles anthropologists have played in them, one yearns for comparative analysis.

The shortcomings of the literature on the history of anthropology become clearer when one considers works produced by historians of the other social sciences. No historian of anthropology has matched Kurt Danziger's accomplishment in his *Constructing the Subject* (1990). Trained as a social psychologist and raised in South Africa, Danzinger wrote a book that can be read with profit by any sort of historian of psychology, whether she is a novice or a specialist in psychology's history. No historian of anthropology has produced the functional equivalent of Quentin Skinner's masterful two-volume *The Foundations of Modern Political Thought* (1978), which is compulsory reading not only for political theorists but also for historians of the times and places in which Skinner's characters figured. No historian of anthropology has matched the sociologist Marian Fourcade's synthetic work in the history of economics. Her *Economists and Societies* (2009) is truly comparative, showing variations in the discipline across national boundaries. There have been edited collections that treat anthropology as it has been written in many places – not

[50] See also Comaroff and Comaroff (1988) and Dubow (1995).

only in Britain, France, Germany, and the United States, but also in China, the Netherlands, Russia, Scandinavia, and other places – but editorial oversight is of necessity limited by the limits of editors' substantive knowledge (see, e.g., Bošković 2008; Johler, Marchetti, and Scheer 2010; Kuklick 2008). The history of anthropology is arguably the most difficult to write. As a discipline, anthropology is more complex than any of the other social sciences. Writing its history requires attention to a broader range of contexts than does writing the history of any other discipline; these contexts include not only contexts of the discipline and of scholars' lives but also those of the worlds they studied. Arguably, this is reflected in the diversity of approaches reviewed here.

Acknowledgments

For their comments on this paper, I am grateful to Ira Bashkow, Andrew Bank, Joshua Berson, Brian Daniels, Nelia Dias, Martha Farah, Andre Gingrich, Anna Grimshaw, Jerry Jacobs, Ira Jacknis, Matthew Hoffarth, Jonathan Marx, Howard Morphy, Alicia Puglionese, Joanna Radin, Richard Staley, Hannah Voorhees, and Joyce White.

References

Ames, Eric. 2009. *Carl Hagenbeck's Empire of Entertainments*. Seattle: University of Washington Press.

Asad, Talal, ed. 1973. *Anthropology and the Colonial Encounter*. London: Ithaca Press.

Aunger, Robert. 1995. "On Ethnography: Storytelling or Science?" *Current Anthropology* 36.1:97–130.

Bank, Andrew. 2008. "'The Intimate Politics' of Fieldwork: Monica Hunter and her African Assistants, Pondoland and the Eastern Cape, 1931–1932," *Journal of Southern African Studies* 34.3:557–75.

Bank, Andrew, and Leslie J. Bank, eds. 2013. *Inside African Anthropology: Monica Wilson and Her Interpreters*. Cambridge and Capetown: Cambridge University Press.

Banner, Lois W. 2003. *Intertwined Lives: Margaret Mead, Ruth Benedict, and Their Circle*. New York: Knopf.

Barkan, Elazar. 1992. *The Retreat of Scientific Racism: Changing Concepts of Race in Britain and the United States Between the World Wars*. New York: Cambridge University Press.

Barrett, Stanley R. 1996. *A Student's Guide to Theory and Method*. Toronto: University of Toronto Press.

Bernstein, Jay H. 2002. "First Recipients of Anthropological Doctorates in the United States, 1891–1930," *American Anthropologist* n.s. 104.2:551–64.

Berry, Christopher J. 1997. *The Social Theory of the Scottish Enlightenment*. Edinburgh: Edinburgh University Press.

Boas, Franz. 1904. "History of Anthropology," *Science* 20:513–24.

Borofsky, Robert. 2002. "The Four Subfields: Anthropologists as Mythmakers," *American Anthropologist* 104.2:463–80.

Bošković, Aleksandar, ed. 2008. *Other People's Anthropologies: Ethnographic Practice on the Margins*. New York: Berghahn Books.

Bottomore, T. B. 1974. *Sociology as Social Criticism*. New York: Pantheon Books.

Brandewie, Ernest. 1982. "Wilhelm Schmidt: A Closer Look," *Anthropos* 77.1–2:151–62.

Brantlinger, Patrick. 2003. *Dark Vanishings: Discourse on the Extinction of Primitive Races, 1800–1930*. Ithaca, NY: Cornell University Press.

2011. *Taming Cannibals: Race and the Victorians*. Ithaca, NY: Cornell University Press.

Brown, Mark. 2003. "Ethnology and Colonial Administration in Nineteenth-Century British India: The Question of Native Crime and Criminality," *British Journal for the History of Science* 36.2:201–19.

Bruckner, Sierra. 2003. "Spectacles of (Human) Nature: Commercial Ethnography between Leisure, Learning, and *Schaulust*." In *Worldly Provincialism in the Age of Empire*, ed. H. Glenn Penny and Matti Bunzl Ann Arbor: University of Michigan Press, 127–55.

Buckley, Thomas. 1988. "Kroeber's Theory of Culture Areas and the Ethnology of Northwestern California," *Anthropological Quarterly* 61.1:15–16.

Burrow, John. 1966. *Evolution and Society: A Study in Victorian Social Theory*. Cambridge: Cambridge University Press.

Calcano, James M. 2003. "Keeping Biological Anthropology in Anthropology, and Anthropology in Biology," *Current Anthropology* 105.1:6–15.

Canfield, Michael R. 2011. "Introduction." In *Field Notes on Nature and Science*, ed. Michael Camfield. Cambridge, MA: Harvard University Press.

Chaiken, Ira, and Alex Long, 1999. "Foreword." In Douglas Cole, *Franz Boas: The Early Years. 1859–1906*. Seattle: University of Washington Press, vii–viii.

Chapoulie, Jean-Michel. 2004. "Using the History of the Chicago Tradition of Sociology for Empirical Research," *Annals of the American Academy of Political and Social Sciences* 595:157–67.

Clifford, James. 1988. *The Predicament of Culture: Twentieth-Century Ethnography, Literature and Art*. Cambridge, MA: Harvard University Press.

1999. "After *Writing Culture*," *American Anthropologist* n.s. 101.3:643–5.

Cohen, William B. 1980. *The French Encounter with Africans: White Responses to Blacks, 1530–1880*. Bloomington: Indiana University Press.

Collins, Harry M. 1981. "Son of Seven Sexes: The Social Destruction of a Physical Phenomenon," *Social Studies of Science* 11.1:33–62.

Comaroff, Jean, and John Comaroff. 1988. "On the Founding Fathers, Fieldwork and Functionalism: A Conversation with Isaac Schapera," *American Ethnologist* 15.3:554–65.

Conklin, Alice C. 1997. *A Mission to Civilize: The Republican Idea of Empire in France and West Africa, 1895–1930*. Stanford, CA: Stanford University Press.

Curran, Andrew S. 2011. *The Anatomy of Blackness: Science and Slavery in an Age of Enlightenment*. Baltimore: Johns Hopkins University Press.

Curtin, Phillip D. 1964. *Image of Africa: British Ideas and Action, 1780–1850*. Madison: University of Wisconsin Press.

Danzinger, Kurt. 1990. *Constructing the Subject*. Cambridge and New York: Cambridge University Press.

Darnell, Regna. 1977. "History of Anthropology in Historical Perspective," *Annual Review of Anthropology* 6:399–417.

1998. "Toward a History of Canadian Departments of Anthropology: Retrospect, Prospect, and Common Cause," *Anthropologica* 40.2:153–68.

Das, Veena. 1998. "Wittgenstein and Anthropology," *Annual Review of Anthropology* 22:171–95.

Davis, Kingsley, and Wilbert E. Moore. 1944. "Some Principles of Stratification," *American Sociological Review* 10:242–49.

Debnath, Biswanath. 1999. "Crisis of Indian Anthropology," *Economic and Political Weekly* 34.44:3110–16.

Dobrin, Lise M., and Ira Bashkow. 2010. "'The Truth in Anthropology Does Not Travel First Class': Reo Fortune's Fateful Encounter with Margaret Mead," *Histories of Anthropology Annual* 6:66–128.

Dubow, Saul. 1995. *Scientific Racism in Modern South Africa*. Cambridge and New York: Cambridge University Press.

Eakin, Emily. 2013. "How Napoleon Chagnon Became Our Most Controversial Anthropologist," *New York Times Magazine*, February 13.

Escobar, Arturo. 1991. "Anthropology and the Development Encounter," *American Ethnologist* 18.4:658–82.

Evans, Andrew D. 2010. *Anthropology at War: World War I and the Science of Race in Germany*. Chicago: University of Chicago Press.

Evans-Pritchard, E. E. 1981. *A History of Anthropological Thought*, ed. André Singer. London: Faber and Faber.

Fabian, Johannes. 1983. *Time and the Other: How Anthropology Makes Its Object*. New York: Columbia University Press.

Feely-Harnik, Gillian. 1999. "'Communities of Blood': The Natural History of Kinship in Nineteenth-Century America," *Comparative Studies in Society and History* 41.2:215–62.

Feldman, Jeffrey D. 2004. "The Jewish Roots and Routes of Anthropology," *Anthropological Quarterly* 77.1:107–25.

Firth, Raymond. 1975. "An Appraisal of Modern Social Anthropology," *Annual Review of Anthropology* 4:1–25.

Fortun, Kim. 2009. "Figuring Out Ethnography." In *Fieldwork Is Not What It Used To Be*, ed. James D. Faubion and George E. Marcus. Ithaca, NY: Cornell University Press, 167–83.

Fourcade, Marion. 2009. *Economists and Societies: Discipline and Profession in the United States, Britain, and France, 1890s to 1990s*. Princeton, NJ, and Oxford: Princeton University Press.

Frank, Gelya. 1999. "Jews, Multiculturalism, and Boasian Anthropology," *American Anthropologist* n.s. 101.4:731–45.

Freeman, Derek. 1883. *Margaret Mead and Samoa: The Making and Unmaking of an Anthropological Myth*. Cambridge, MA: Harvard University Press.

Gailey, Christine Ward. 2003. "Richard Lee: The Politics, Art and Science of Anthropology," *Anthropologica* 45.1:19–26.

Gilbertson, Albert N. 1914. "In Memoriam: Alexander Francis Chamberlain," *American Anthropologist* n.s. 16.2:337–48.

Gilkeson, John S. 2010. *Anthropologists and the Rediscovery of America, 1886–1965*. New York: Cambridge University Press.

Gingrich, Andre. 2007. "Liberalism in Imperial Anthropology: Notes on an Implicit Paradigm in Continental European Anthropology before World War I," *Ab Imperio* 1.7:224–39.

2010. "Alliances and Avoidance: British Interactions with German-speaking Anthropologists' Accounts." In *Culture Wars: Context, Models and Anthropologists*. ed. Deborah James, Evie Plaice, and Christina Toren. Oxford/New York: Berghahn, 19–31

Godina, Vesna V. 2003. "Anthropological Fieldwork at the Beginning of the Twenty-First Century. Crisis and Location of Knowledge," *Anthropos* 98.2:473–87.

Goody, Jack. 1995. *The Expansive Moment: The Rise of Social Anthropology in Britain and Africa, 1918–1970*. Cambridge: Cambridge University Press.

Gordon, Robert B. 1988. "Apartheid's Anthropologists: The Genealogy of Afrikaner Anthropology," *American Ethnologist* 15.3:535–53.

1989. "The White Man's Burden: *Ersatz* Customary Law and Internal Pacification in South Africa," *Journal of Historical Sociology* 2.1:41–65.

Gouldner, Alvin W. 1970. *The Coming Crisis of Western Sociology*. New York: Basic Books.

Gray, Geoffrey. 1997. " 'Mr. Neville Did All in [His] Power to Assist Me': A. P. Elkin, A. O. Neville and Anthropological Research in Northwestern Australia, 1927–1928," *Oceania* 68.1:27–46

2007. *A Cautious Silence: The Politics of Australian Anthropology*. Canberra: Aboriginal Studies Press.

Gray, Geoffrey and Doug Munro. 2011. "Establishing Anthropology and Maori Language (Studies), Auckland University College: The Appointment of Ralph Piddington, 1949." *Histories of Anthropology Annual* 7:49–82.

Gusterson, Hugh. January 9, 2011. "What If They Gave a Science War and Only One Side Came? Ask the American Anthropological Association," *The Chronicle of Higher Education*. downloaded from http://chronicle.com/article/What-if-They-Had-a-Science-War/125828/.

Guyer, Jane I. 2004. "Anthropology in Area Studies," *Annual Review of Anthropology* 33:499–523.

Haddon, A. C., with the assistance of A. Hingston Quiggin. 1910. *History of Anthopology*. New York and London: G. Putnam's Sons.

Handelman, Don. 1994. "Critiques of Anthropology: Literary Turns, Slippery Bends," *Poetics Today* 15.3:341–81.

Harris, Marvin. 1968. *The Rise of Anthropological Theory: A History of Theories of Culture*. New York: Crowell.

Hassler, Robert. 1989. "The Effects of CRM: A Sociohistorical Perspective of the Department of Anthropology, University of Nebraska at Lincoln," *The Plains Anthropologist* 34.124 (Part 1):111–28.

Hiatt, L. R. 1996. *Arguments about Aborigines*. Cambridge: Cambridge University Press.

Hoffman, David M., and Andrew M. Gardner. 2006. "Fieldwork and Writing from the Field." In *Dispatches from the Field*, ed. Andrew M. Gardner and David M. Hoffman. Long Grove, IL: Waveland Press, 1–13.

Hurlbert, Beverly McElligott. 1976. "Status and Exchange in the Profession of Anthropology," *American Anthropologist* n.s. 78.2:272–84.
Hymes, Dell, ed. 1969. *Reinventing Anthropology*. New York: Random House.
Jacknis, Ira. 2002. "The First Boasian: Alfred Kroeber and Franz Boas, 1896–1905," *American Anthropologist* n.s. 104.2:520–32.
Johler, Reinhard, Christian Marchetti, and Monique Scheer, eds. 2010. *Doing Anthropology in Wartime and War Zones: World War I and the Cultural Sciences in Europe*. Bielefeld: transcript.
Jordon, Winthrop D. 1968. *White over Black: American Attitudes toward the Negro, 1550–1812*. Chapel Hill: University of North Carolina Press.
Jules-Rosette, Benetta. 1991. "Speaking about Hidden Times: The Anthropology of V. Y. Mudimbe," *Callaloo* 14.4:944–60.
Kimball, Solon T. 1946. "The Crisis in Colonial Administration," *Human Organization* 5:8–16.
Kirby, Vicky. 1988. "Review of *Writing Culture*," *Oceania* 58.4:315–16.
Kirschner, Suzanne R. and Emily Martin. 2000. "From Flexible Bodies to Fluid Minds: An Interview with Emily Martin," *Ethnos* 27.2:247–82.
Kuklick, Henrika. 1973. "A 'Scientific Revolution': Sociological Theory in the United States, 1930–1945," *Sociological Inquiry* 43.1:3–22.
1991. *The Savage Within: The Social Context of British Anthropology, 1885–1945*. Cambridge and New York: Cambridge University Press.
2008. *A New History of Anthropology*. Oxford and Malden, MA: Blackwell.
2011. "Personal Equations: Reflections on the History of Fieldwork, with Special Reference to Sociocultural Anthropology," *Isis* 102.1:1–33.
2012. "The Theory of Evolution and Cultural Anthropology." In *The Theory of Evolution and Its Impact*, ed. Aldo Fasolo. Heidelberg and New York: Springer Verlag, 83–102.
Kuklick, Henrika, and Robert Kohler, eds. 1996. *Science in the Field*, a special issue of *Osiris* n.s. 11.
Kuper, Adam. 1973. *Anthropology and Anthropologists: The Modern British School*. London: Routledge & Kegan Paul.
Leach, Edmund R. 1984. "Glimpses of the Unmentionable in the History of British Social Anthropology," *Annual Review of Anthropology* 13:1–23.
Levine, Lawrence W. 1988. *Highbrow/Lowbrow: The Emergence of Cultural Hierarchy in America*. Cambridge, MA: Harvard University Press.
Lévi-Strauss, Claude. 1967. *The Scope of Anthropology*. London: Jonathan Cape.
Lewis, Diane. 1973. "Anthropology and Colonialism," *Current Anthropology* 14.3:581–602.
Lincoln, Bruce. 2001. "Revisiting Magical Fright," *American Ethnologist* 28.4:778–802.
Lowie, Robert H. 1937. *The History of Ethnological Theory*. New York: Holt, Reinhardt, & Winston.
Lukes, Steven. 1973. *Émile Durkheim: His Life and Work*. London: Allen Lane.
Lutkehaus, Nancy C. 2008. *Margaret Mead: The Making of an American Icon*. Princeton, NJ: Princeton University Press.
Marcus, George E., and Michael M. J. Fischer. 1986. *Anthropology as Cultural Critique: An Experimental Moment in the Human Sciences*. Chicago: University of Chicago Press.
Marks, Jonathan. 2008. "Race across the Physical Cultural Divide in American Anthropology." In *A New History of Anthropology*, ed. Henrika Kuklick. Oxford/Malden, MA: Blackwell Publishing, 242–58.

McGregor, Russell. 1997. *Imagined Destinies: Aboriginal Australians and the Doomed Race Theory, 1880–1939*. Carlton, Victoria: Melbourne University Press.

McGrew, W. C. 2007. "New Wine in New Bottles: Prospects and Pitfalls of Cultural Primatology," *Journal of Anthropological Research* 63.2:167–83.

Mead, Margaret. 1972. *Blackberry Winter: My Earlier Years*. New York: Simon & Schuster.

1973. "Preface." In Margaret Mead, *Coming of Age in Samoa*. New York: Harper Collins, xxiii–xxviii.

Mills, David. 2003. "Quantifying the Discipline: Some Anthropology Statistics from the UK," *Anthropology Today* 19.3:19–22.

Modell, Judith. 1988. "'It Is Besides a Pleasant English Word': Ruth Benedict's Concept of Patterns," *Anthropological Quarterly* 61.1:27–40.

Myres, John Linton. 1914. *The Influence of Anthropology on the Course of Political Science*. Berkeley: University of California Press.

Needham, Rodney. 1970. "Editor's Introduction." In, *Kings and Councillors: An Essay in the Comparative Anatomy of Human Society* [originally published in 1936], ed. A. M. Hocart Chicago: University of Chicago Press, xiii–xcix

North, Michael. 1994. *The Dialectic of Modernism*. Cambridge, MA: Harvard University Press.

1999. *Reading 1922: A Return to the Scene of the Modern*. New York: Oxford University Press.

Osbourne, Michael A. 1994. *Nature, the Exotic, and the Science of French Colonialism*. Bloomington: Indiana University Press.

Osterling, Jorge P., and Héctor Martínez. 1983. "Notes for a History of Peruvian Anthropology, 1940–1980," *Current Anthropology* 24.3:343–60.

Paluch, Andrzej K. 1981. "The Polish Background to Malinowski's Work," *Man* n.s. 16.2:276–85.

Parkin, David. 1988. "An Interview with Raymond Firth," *Current Anthropology* 29.2:327–41.

Pathy, Jaganath. 1981. "Imperialism, Anthropology, and the Third World," *Economic and Political Weekly*, April 4:623–7.

Peletz, Michael G. 1995. "Kinship Studies in Late Twentieth-Century Anthropology," *Annual Review of Anthropology* 24:343–72.

Piddington, R. O. 1960. "Action Anthropology," *The Journal of the Polynesian Society* 69.3:199–214.

Pratt. Peter P., and Peter Du Ponceau. 1971. "Peter Du Ponceau's Contributions to Anthropology," *Ethnohistory* 18.2:147–58.

Pulla, Siomann P. 2003. "Frank Speck and the Moisie River Incident: Anthropological Advocacy and the Question of Aboriginal Fishing Rights in Quebec," *Anthropologica* 45.1:129–45.

Qureshi, Sadiah. 2011. *Peoples on Parade: Exhibitions, Empire, Empire and Anthropology in Nineteenth-Century Britain*. Chicago: University of Chicago Press.

Rabinow, Paul. 1989. Untitled review of *The Anthropologist as Author* by Clifford Geertz and *Tales of the Field. On Writing Ethnography* by John Van Maanen, *Symbolic Interaction* 12.1:171–3.

Radick, Gregory. 2007. *The Simian Tongue: The Long Debate about Animal Language*. Chicago: University of Chicago Press.

Record, Wilson. 1981. "Anthropology and Sociology: Three Common Problems," *Anthropological Quarterly* 54.1:28–35.

Rees, Amanda. 2009. *The Infanticide Controversy. Primatology and the Art of Field Science*. Chicago: University of Chicago Press.

Revel, James L. "The Evolution and Fate of Botanical Field Books." In *Field Notes on Nature and Science*, ed. Michael Camfield. Cambridge, MA: Harvard University Press, 187–200.

Rogge, A. E. 1976. "A Look at Academic Anthropology: Through a Graph Darkly," *American Anthropologist* n.s. 78.2:829–43.

Said, Edward. 1978. *Orientalism*. New York: Pantheon.

Salemink, Oscar. 2003. *The Ethnography of Vietnam's Central Highlanders: A Historical Contextualization, 1850–1990*. Honolulu: University of Hawaii Press.

Sibeud, Emmanuelle. 2008. "The Metamorphosis of Ethnology in France, 1839–1930." In *A New History of Anthropology*, ed. Henrika Kuklick. Oxford/Malden, MA: Blackwell, 98–110

2012. "'A Useless Colonial Science'? Practicing Anthropology in the French Colonial Empire, circa 1880–1960," *Current Anthropology* 53.4:583–94.

Singer, Merrill. 2008. "Applied Anthropology." In *A New History of Anthropology*, ed. Henrika Kuklick. Oxford/Malden, MA: Blackwell, 326–40.

Skinner, Quentin. 1978. *The Foundations of Modern Political Thought*, 2 Vols. Cambridge and New York: Cambridge University Press.

Snead, James E. 1999. "Science, Commerce, and Control: Patronage and the Development of Anthropological Archaeology in the Americas," *American Anthroplogist*, New Series 101.2:256–71.

Spencer, Frank. 1981. "The Rise of Academic Physical Anthropology in the United States (1880–1980): A Historical Overview," *American Journal of Physical Anthropology* 56.4:353–64.

Spencer, Jonathan. 1989. "Anthropology as a Kind of Writing," *Man n.s.* 24:145–64.

2000. "British Social Anthropology. A Retrospective," *Annual Review of Anthropology* 29:1–24.

Spyer, Patricia. 2011. "What Ends with the End of Anthropology?" In *The End of Anthropology?* Ed. Holger Jebens and Karl-Heinz Kohl. Wantage, UK: Sean Kingston, 61–80.

Średniawa, Bronislaw. 1981. "The Anthropologist as a Young Physicist: Bronislaw Malinowski's Apprenticeship," *Isis* 72.4:613.620.

Staum, Martin S. 2011. *Nature and Nurture in French Social Sciences, 1859–1914 and Beyond*. Montreal: McGill-Queens University Press.

Steward, Julian H. 1960. "Obituary: Alfred Louis Kroeber 1876–1960," *American Ethnography Quasimonthly*. Downloaded from http://www.americanethnography.com/article.php?id=10.

1973. *Alfred Kroeber*. New York: Columbia University Press.

Stocking, George W., Jr. 1965. "On the Limits of 'Presentism' and 'Historicism' in the Historiography of the Behavioral Sciences," *Journal of the History of the Behavioral Sciences* 1.3:211–18.

1987. *Victorian Anthropology*. New York: The Free Press.

1992. *The Ethnographer's Magic and Other Essays*. Madison: University of Wisconsin Press.

1995. *Victorian Anthropology*. Madison: University of Wisconsin Press.
2010. *Glimpses into My Own Black Box: An Exercise in Self-Deconstruction*. Madison: University of Wisconsin Press.
Strum, Shirley C., Donald G. Lindburg, and David Hamburg, eds. 1999. *The New Physical Anthropology*. Upper Saddle River, NJ: Prentice Hall.
Taatgen, H. A. 1988. "Anthropological Involution." The Legacy of S. F. Nadel," *Anthropos* 83.1:87–99.
Thompson, Raymond H. 2005. "Anthropology at the University of Arizona, 1893–2005," *Journal of the Southwest* 47.3:327–74.
Wallace, Alfred Russel. 1864. "The Origins of Human Races and the Antiquity of Man Deduced from the Theory of Natural Selection," *Journal of the Anthropological Society of London* 2:clviii–clxxxvii.
Wallace, Ben J. and Michael Harris. 1989. "Anthropology and Development in Bangladesh," *Urban Anthropology* 18.3–4:241–64.
Washburn, Sherwood L. 1951. "The New Physical Anthropology," *Transactions of the New York Academy of Sciences* 13 series II.7:298–304.
Wilder, Garry. 2005. *The French Imperial Nation-State: Negritude and Colonial Humanism between the Two World Wars*. Chicago: The University of Chicago Press.
Wolf, Eric R. 1982. *Europe and the People without History*, Berkeley: University of California Press.
Young, Michael. 2004. *Malinowski: Odyssey of an Anthropologist, 1864–1920*. New Haven, CT: Yale University Press.
Zimmerman, Andrew. 2001. *Anthropology and Antihumanism in Imperial Germany*. Chicago: University of Chicago Press.

4

Periphery toward Center and Back

Scholarship on the History of Sociology, 1945–2012

Charles Camic

Inescapably, birth order casts a long shadow over a child's later development and interests, as social scientists who study family dynamics have often observed. Among other effects, siblings born late into large families exhibit a strong ambivalence about the history of their family: disdaining, in their resolve to chart their own path forward, dusty stories about the group's past and yet curious, occasionally at least, about their own place in the saga of their tribe.

As latecomers to the family of the social sciences, entering a household already full of the brothers and sisters discussed in other chapters of this volume – historians, political theorists, economists, psychologists, and even anthropologists – sociologists have long shown a similar ambivalence. Typically, they have been impatient spending hours around the family hearth listening to tales about their forebears, even as their collective ancestry now and then piques their interest – especially when it appears to hold treasures that might help them on their forward journey.

From the immediate post–World War II years to the present day, sociologists' deeply rooted ambivalence about their history has been a fact of disciplinary life, particularly among sociologists in the United States. The two component attitudes that constitute this ambivalence toward sociology's past have crested, however, at different historical moments, or so I seek to document in this chapter. Dividing the postwar era into three periods, the chapter describes the changing nature of scholarship on the history of sociology and the changing position of this scholarship in the discipline of sociology at large. To facilitate this description, the first two sections introduce the period divisions, data sources, and terminology that I will use in this analysis. The following sections examine the practice and location of scholarship on the history of sociology in each of the periods identified.

Note on Period Divisions and Data Sources

As the other chapters in this volume make evident, the disciplinary historiography produced from the end of World War II up to the present time subdivides this sixty-nine-year era, rather naturally, into three periods. With regard to sociology in particular, these three periods correspond to shifts in the incidence of published scholarship on topics relating to the history of sociology: to a noticeable pendulum swing from years of comparatively lean scholarly output, to an interval of considerably greater activity, back to another relatively quiescent phase. Because the transition between these phases was gradual rather than abrupt, there is some arbitrariness in attaching specific calendar dates to the phases, although to avoid doing so would only unnecessarily complicate the historical narrative of this chapter.

For this reason, I divide the following account into three loosely distinguishable periods: 1945 to 1969, 1970 to 1999, and 2000 to 2012. In this periodization, the two outside dates, 1945 and 2012, fit with the specific temporal focus of this book, while the two internal points of demarcation – 1969/1970 and 1999/2000 – coincide with two temporally bounded events that, while not decisive in themselves, were part and parcel of broader developments that came to a head *around* these dates with regard to the historiography of sociology.[1] Described more fully in the sections that follow, these events were, first, the appearance in 1970 of two widely noticed books that breathed life in the previously fairly moribund subject of the history of sociology and, second, the termination in 1999 of the book series that had provided the primary publication outlet for scholarship on the historiography of sociology during the good times that were now winding down. To these considerations, I might add[2] that these period break-points are roughly consistent with the pattern that one sees in word-search databases such as the Google Books Ngram program.[3]

This pendulum movement from relatively sparse times (1945–1969), to relatively abundant times (1970–1999), and then back to sparse times (2000–2012) bears comparison with the patterns described in others chapters in this

[1] I use of "around" here to underscore that a calendar date within a few years on either side of 1970 and 2000 would serve as well to mark the temporal divisions I describe. I have opted for 1970 and 2000 not only because events I will now mention occurred, but also because these dates conveniently correspond with familiar decennial divisions.

[2] I want to acknowledge that the idea for this addition was suggested by Jennifer Platt, whom I wish to thank for valuable advice here (as well as elsewhere in this chapter)

[3] At an early stage of my research (November 2012), I used of the "Google Books Ngram Viewer" to construct a graph of the percentage of books in the database on the "history of sociology" which appeared between 1945 and 2012. At that point, the years included

volume. In his chapter, for, example, Capshew documents how research on the history of psychology has increasingly moved away from the margins of the discipline of psychology over the course of the period from World War II to the present; in contrast, Backhouse and Fontaine report that scholarship on the history of economics has become more and more marginal to the discipline of economics during the same period. When examining work on the history of sociology, however, one finds a more oscillating pattern: disciplinary marginality, followed by greater centrality, followed by a return to the margins.

In order to sustain this interpretation of the historiography of sociology, my focus in the following analysis will be on the character of scholarship on the history of sociology in each of the three periods that I have distinguished. For evidence about this I build to some degree on my personal understanding of the relevant historiographic literature. During the last thirty-five years, my own research has involved several projects dealing with the history of the social sciences, in most cases with intellectual or institutional developments that took place in the United States. To make use of this background for the purpose of this chapter, my focus here will be on the English language, principally the American, historiography of sociology. This is a body of scholarship that consists, on the one hand, of a modest number of books, most of which were familiar to me prior working on this chapter, and, on the other hand, of a somewhat larger number of articles, about which my previous knowledge was spottier, but which I wanted to include in order to anchor my examination of the postwar era in something more than my own impressions, while also providing a wider angle than books alone can offer onto the work of historians of sociology and the location of this work on the larger map of the discipline of sociology.

in the database stopped with 2008. With this restriction, the resulting graph (which indicated a slow rise after the 1945 start date) showed a sharp upward movement around 1970, a trend that crested in the late 1980s and then began a gradual decline (punctuated with upward bounces) until around 2000, after which the downturn was deeper and more continuous.

This said, however, there are good reasons for skepticism about Google ngrams. For one thing, they are case sensitive, so that switching the search term from "history of sociology" to "History of sociology" to "History of Sociology" (etc.) all produce graphs with somewhat different shapes – simply as an artefact of the different capitalization practices of different authors and copyeditors. (Readers can easily re-create these graphs at https://books.google.com/ngrams) Further, because Google continually scans additional books to its database, its contents are constantly changing. For these (and other) reasons, I decided not to include ngrams in this chapter, nor to base my argument on this evidence. Even so, these data are suggestive of trends which broadly correspond to those described above.

To accomplish this analysis of articles, I enlisted the help of a research assistant[4] and the two of us entered the expression "history of sociology" as a search term into JSTOR for the years 1945 to 2012. Our objective was to devise, in an efficient and economical manner, a rough index of the volume and content of scholarship on the history of sociology by assuming *a broad correspondence* between articles containing the "history of sociology" during the periods under study and the contemporaneous state of the literature on the subject: by assuming, in other words, that a historical era that saw the appearance of many, rather than fewer, articles containing the term "history of sociology" was an era that produced a greater, rather than a lesser, volume of historiographic scholarship related to sociology. Admittedly, there are other expressions that might have served the same purpose. Not only this, but any and all search terms presented the problem of being both too inclusive, likely to pick up articles containing the search term but *not* concerned with the history of sociology, as well as too exclusive, likely to omit articles concerned with the history of sociology but *not* containing the search term – and only the first of these two problems allowed for a feasible correction (see next paragraph). Arguably, however, these limitations were less consequential than relying exclusively on my preformed impressions about the literature on the history of sociology.

For the sixty-nine-year period examined here, the JSTOR search produced 753 hits, which the JSTOR sorting function then arranged as a randomly ordered list. Using this list, our initial plan was to take the first 20 percent of these randomly ordered hits and subject these 151 articles to closer examination and content analysis. Because of one of the problems just described, however, using "history of sociology" as the search term did prove overly inclusive, since approximately 4.6 of the every 10 articles (346/753) that mentioned the expression did so for a reason that was idiosyncratic and *not* an indicator of an article actually about the history of sociology. To correct for this problem, we eliminated articles of this type when we encountered them on our list as we worked toward the target of 151 usable articles – a number that, by the end of this process of elimination, constituted a 37 percent sample of the surviving articles (c. 407) that contained the "history of sociology" and were published between 1945 and 2012. The Appendix lists the 151 sampled articles, grouping these into three panels, according to the historical period in which they appeared.

[4] Iga Kozlowski of the Department of Sociology, Northwestern University, took on this role. Along the way, she and I received advice from my colleague Jeremy Freese. I thank both of them for their help.

To facilitate a comparison across the three historical periods, we read and coded each of the 151 articles for several features: (A) the main topic treated in the article: whether a recognized figure in the history of sociology, an academic department or school of thought, a concept, a neglected figure, or "other"; (B) the methodological basis of the article; and (C) the relation between the article and previous scholarship on the history of sociology: that is, whether the article builds upon, criticizes, or is "not classifiable" in relation to previous scholarship. The results of this analysis are shown in Table 4.1. In constructing this table, articles that overlap more than one subcategory under categories A, B, and C appear only once in each of these three categories, counted under the subcategory that seemed the best fit for the article. The lack of a precise metric for "best fit" poses no serious problem in terms of the following discussion since the central concern here is with overall similarities and differences across periods – matters largely unaffected by small judgment calls about subcategory placement. For inter-period comparisons, columns i, ii, and iii of Table 4.1 provide the most relevant data from the JSTOR sample.

One additional caveat about these data. In the sections that follow, the primary unit of analysis is the published article or book referred to, not the backstory behind any particular publication. In this way, this chapter differs from several of the others in this volume. This point is noteworthy because not every publication relevant to the historiography of sociology was a publication that came into being at the initiative of an author whose own purpose was to address questions about the history of sociology. Rather, some articles and book chapters that belong to the historiography of sociology were publications originally commissioned by other scholars: that is, publications invited for a "special issue" of a sociological journal, or for an edited collection of essays, by an editor who may have given the author specific instructions about his or her topic – as in the case of volumes designed to commemorate events like milestones in the lives of major sociologists, the publication date of influential books, or the anniversary of particular institutions for sociological training and research. Still further, some publications that retrospectively fall within the bounds of the historiography of sociology began life as projects on the sociology of sociology, or as autobiographical sketches by prominent sociologists in other areas of the discipline. Tracing the diverse early life histories of the publications examined in the following, however, exceeds the purview of this chapter.[5]

[5] This said, my sense, nevertheless, is that editors would not invite articles and chapters of the sort just described, nor publish the autobiographies of sociologists or historically

Table 4.1. *Summary characteristics of JSTOR articles on the history of sociology, 1945–2012*

	1945–1969 (i)	*1970–1999 (ii)*	*2000–2012 (iii)*
A. Topic			
Recognized figure			
Bourdieu, Pierre			1
Comte, Auguste	1		
Durkheim, Émile	1	7	1
Gouldner, Alvin W.			1
Lynd, Robert		1	
Marx, Karl		3	
Mills, C. Wright		1	
Pareto, Vilfredo		1	
Park, Robert		1	
Parsons, Talcott	1	4	2
Simmel, Georg		3	
Spencer, Herbert		1	
Tönnies, Ferdinand, Werner Sombart, and Robert Michels	1		
Weber, Max	1	3	
Subtotal	**5**	**25**	**5**
University departments/schools of thought			
Berkeley		1	
Chicago		2	1
Columbia			1
Harvard		1	
Minnesota		1	
North Dakota		1	
Marxism/Historical Materialism/ Critical Sociology		2	1
Phenomenology	1		
Symbolic interactionism		1	
Subtotal	**1**	**9**	**3**
Theory or concept			
Anomie		2	2
Authority		1	
Game theory			1
Integrationist and conflict theories	1		
"Interest"			1
Looking glass self		1	
Marxism			1
Microsociology		1	
Normal science		1	

	1945–1969 (i)	*1970–1999 (ii)*	*2000–2012 (iii)*
Protestant ethic thesis/ rationalization	1		
Religious transcendence		1	
Secularization		1	
Social control		1	
Social justice		1	
Systems theory			1
Value neutrality/Objectivity	1	1	
Subtotal	**3**	**11**	**6**
Neglected figure			
Breckinridge, Sophonisba			1
Clark, S. D.		1	
Crane, Caroline Bartlett		1	1
Dawson, Carl		1	
DuBois, W. E. B.		2	
Frazier, E. Franklin		1	
Gabel, Joseph		1	
Geiger, Theodor			1
George, Henry		1	
Hobhouse, L. T.		1	
Hughes, Everett C.		2	
Katz, Elihu, and Paul Lazarsfeld			1
Myrdal, Alva			2
Myrdal, Gunnar			1
Ogburn, William Fielding		2	
Parmelee, Maurice		1	
Porter, John			1
Richards, Ellen Swallow			1
Schutz, Alfred		1	
Thomas, Dorothy Swaine		1	
Thomas, W. I.	1		
Ward, Lester Frank		1	
Westermarck, Edvard		2	1
Women sociologists		2	2
Subtotal	**1**	**21**	**12**
Other			
Archives/journals/textbooks		5	5
Relation to other disciplines	1	1	1
Specific historical era/location	3	15	3
Specific subfield	3	10	2
Subtotal	**7**	**31**	**11**
Grand total	**17**	**97**	**37**

(Continued)

Table 4.1. (*Continued*)

	1945–1969 (i)	1970–1999 (ii)	2000–2012 (iii)
B. Method			
Analysis/discussion of text(s) by a single figure	7	21	8
Analysis/discussion of text(s) by multiple separate figures	8	25	7
Analysis/discussion of text(s) by multiple connected figures	1	5	3
Analysis of historical context(s)		6	2
Institutional analysis		12	6
Analysis of archival materials		8	2
Textbooks		6	2
Secondary sources	1	10	7
Autobiography		3	
Biography		1	
Grand Total	**17**	**97**	**37**
C. Relation of article to previous scholarship			
Building on past scholarship			
Nebulous		6	4
Existing theory	2	5	
Existing subfield	3	8	4
Previous scholar		12	3
Subtotal	**5**	**31**	**11**
Criticism of past scholarship			
Nebulous	1	6	3
Existing theory	3	9	3
Existing subfield		12	3
Previous scholar		15	8
Subtotal	**4**	**42**	**17**
Not classifiable	**8**	**24**	**9**
Grand total	**17**	**97**	**37**

Note on Terminology

In describing the historiography of sociology in the post–World War II era, my account will make use of some terms that warrant a little brief

focused studies on the sociology of sociology, in the absence of an assumed sociological audience interested in writings relating to the history of sociology. Whether or not this impression is empirically correct, however, does not affect the following analysis.

clarification. This clarification is necessary because – as the other chapters of this volume illustrate – although these expressions are recurrent ones in the literature of the social sciences and in writings on the history of these fields, their usage is not standardized across disciplines. Particularly as regards sociology and the study of its history, these terms have tended to assume somewhat specific connotations to which I want to call attention briefly. The terms at issue here have occurred in four pairs.

The first of these is the distinction between "theory" and "empirical research." Here it is the first term that is the troublemaker for the reason that not only do sociologists use "theory" in ways that often depart from the conventions of other social scientists, but sociologists differ among themselves – across periods and even within particular periods – in how they conceive of theory (see Abend 2008; Camic and Gross 1998). To the extent that a common denominator runs across their different conceptions (during the last half-century, at any rate), it is that theory is *something more general than* the subject matter of any specific empirical study. Now what this "something more general" consists of may be a more general set of propositions about – or model of – the structure or dynamics of the social world (or some slice of the social world, or some historical era in its development); or a more general explanatory or interpretive approach or framework; or a more general perspective, thesis, or argument; or a more general set of analytical tools or concepts; or a more general program of inquiry, and so on – although sociologists further disagree as to what constitutes such a model, framework, thesis, or set of concepts. What is more, most of these usages presuppose a distinction between "theory" and "empirical research," inasmuch as the latter expression denotes the quantitative or qualitative investigation of some particular facet of social life – that is, particular social processes, spheres, groups, institutions, and so forth. Still further, the linkage between theory and research is, by and large, one of fairly loose coupling: for while empirical studies by sociologists *may* consist of more-or-less rigorous tests or applications of a given model or bundle of propositions, postwar sociologists have more typically cast their empirical projects as simply drawing upon available conceptual vocabularies or perspectives, instantiating certain explanations or interpretations, or producing "findings" that support, amend, or contest the adequacy of some model, framework, thesis, or set of analytical tools. Indeed, some critics of sociology have gone so far as to claim that there is much empirical research in the discipline that has virtually no connection to sociological theory in any of its forms, though the accuracy of this claim is also the subject of dispute.

The second pairing that I will refer to is the contrast between "idealist" and "materialist" points of view. In regard to the nineteenth century, this contrast is a shorthand for the intellectual differences between Hegel and Marx, and much the same distinction has long echoed – and, indeed, continues to echo – in the work of sociologists. Over time, the expressions themselves have changed, and for most of the sixty-nine postwar years sociologists have resurrected the Hegel/Marx divide using the same terms that Kevin Passmore refers to in his chapter: namely, "cultural" versus "social" (or "socioeconomic," or "social-structural"). Regardless of the specific words chosen, however, postwar sociological theory and research have both generally taken *as their main objects of analysis* structures and processes that lie within the "material" sphere of social life: that is to say, within economic and political (and kindred) institutions, such as capitalist and socialist economic systems, business organizations, social movements, communities, private and public places of work, and so on, particularly as these institutions are stratified by divisions of social class, race, and gender (see the chapters on postwar sociology in Calhoun 2007). To call attention to this emphasis is not to deny that various "ideal" factors – cultural practices, ideas, ideologies, values, beliefs, attitudes, opinions, and sentiments – have frequently been included in sociological studies from this era among the causes and the effects of material forces, but sociological writings that focus primarily on this idealist realm have been far more atypical. For reasons having to do (inter alia) with the interests of the kinds of young scholars who are recruited into sociology and with the distribution of employment opportunities within the profession, sociologists' gravitational pull has been strongly in the materialist direction. This state of affairs has created a situation in which scholarship dealing with the history of sociology – and, therefore, very frequently (though not exclusively) with the *ideas* of sociologists from the past – runs sharply against the disciplinary grain.

The third pair of terms relevant to the following account is "presentist" and "historicist." Unlike the concepts in the first two couplets, "presentist" and "historicist" refer not to features of the literature of sociology at large, but to scholarship on the history of sociology and, more specifically still, to the different purposes that may motivate and justify historical inquiries into sociology's past. The terms originate outside sociology in historiographic writings on some of the other social sciences (the classic statement here is Stocking 1968, pp. 1–12, but see as well the chapters in this volume by Adcock, Capshew, and Kuklick); and they have been used as well in scholarship on the history of sociology (see Jones 1977; Camic 1979).

Applied to the historiography of sociology, "presentist" refers to historical investigations whose *raison d'être* is to contribute to sociological theory and (or) empirical research as these stand at the moment in real time when the historian of sociology is engaged in his or her particular study. In contrast, "historicist" describes historical writings that seek, first and foremost, to depict and understand the historical figure, episode, or development under investigation with reference to the specific time and place – the context – in which that figure, episode, or development was situated. From the point of view of historians of the latter persuasion, although studies of the history of sociology may have implications for the discipline's present-day agenda, identifying such implications is secondary to the task of comprehending sociology's past in its own terms.

The fourth set of terms, "internalist" and "externalist," also applies to the historiography of sociology (as well as to the historiography of other intellectual fields, as the other chapters of this volume all illustrate). Rather than describing the reason for investigating sociology's history, however, "internalist" and "externalist" typically refer – as they will in this chapter – to different means of conducting historical research: that is, to whether the historian of sociology adopts an "internal" mode of analysis, which concerns itself primarily with written texts from the past (particularly with the exposition and interpretation of the writings of earlier sociological thinkers), or an "external" mode of inquiry, which locates sociological thinkers and intellectual trends in the discipline's history in relation to a configuration of the broader cultural, political, and economic (and other) conditions that furnished the social context in which the focal sociological texts were written. As Capshew, Kuklick, and Passmore make clear in their accounts, however, these different styles of research are not inherently opposed to each other, and, in recent years, historians of sociology have sometimes sought intentionally to combine internalist and externalist styles of historiography.[6]

In speaking of intentionality here, I do not mean to suggest that scholars studying the history of sociology typically announce their stance regarding any of the four divisions that I have just drawn, because that has not been the case.[7] For this reason, the extent to which any particular text in the

6 Throughout this section I have obviously treated the four couplets as if they are independent of one another. They sometimes stand, however, in more complex relations, such that historical researchers of an idealist bent may incline (to take one example) to internalist accounts – although this is not inevitably the case. For the purpose of this chapter, it will not be necessary to enter into these more subtle interrelationships.

7 For the record, however, I would acknowledge that, within its very tight space constraints, the present chapter itself is a modest effort to make use of both internalist and externalist tools and to take account of both idealist and materialist aspects of the historiography

historiography of sociology is internalist or externalist, presentist or historicist, idealist or materialist (or lies at some point along the continua that these terms anchor) is an issue that researchers analyzing these texts have to determine inferentially. This is what I have done in the following discussion.

Period I, 1945 to 1969

In the quarter-century following the conclusion of World War II, scholarship on the history of sociology was both relatively light in volume and marginal to the mainstream of the discipline.

In the background to this situation lay the discipline's demography in the United States during this era. Short in its supply of Ph.D. holders before the war, American sociology had contracted further in size by 1945, at which point it stood in need of major rebuilding in all its core subfields – social stratification, political sociology, complex organizations, urban sociology, criminology, sociology of the family, sociology of religion, social psychology, and so on (Turner and Turner 1990). At the time, the majority of these subfields – with the partial exception of the sociology of religion and social psychology – were broadly "materialist" in their focus, and the majority of them were also heavily reliant on research methods devised for the study of the societies of the postwar era rather than for more historical kinds of inquiry. This combination of features served effectively to divert sociologists from looking inward and backward to the history of sociological ideas, instead of outward toward the investigation of contemporary social conditions and forward to working out and advancing the agenda of contemporary research and theory.

In this context, the historical appetite of American sociologists who were at all interested in their discipline's past was easily satisfied by a scattering of volumes that had appeared before and during the war and that, in the early postwar years, were supplemented by a modest number of publications that were similar in form and content. Before the war, two genres of historiography had been predominant. The first consisted of encyclopedic reference works that broadly surveyed – for sociologists who did not specialize in the study of the discipline's history and for other curious readers – numerous older schools of social thought along with the contributions of various protosociologists from the past (e.g., Auguste Comte, Herbert Spencer).

of sociology – while adopting a historicist, rather than a presentist, stance toward the past. (My reasons for preferring these positions are elaborated in a number of previous publications.)

The model for books in this genre was a massive (twelve-hundred-page) two-volume collaboration between the intellectual historian Harry Elmer Barnes and the sociologist Howard Becker, aptly titled *Social Thought from Lore to Science* (1938); but other compendia also appeared occasionally (Small 1905, 1924; Bogardus 1922; Odum 1927; Sorokin 1928; House 1936; Bernard and Bernard 1943; and the first edition of the *Encyclopaedia of the Social Sciences*, Seligman 1930–5). Aside from these eclectic historiographic writings, which tended to mix presentist and historicist thinking, there was a second, more insistently presentist genre, strongly on display in seminal works by Park and Burgess (1921) and Parsons (1937), which put forth triumphalist, teleological narratives that portrayed earlier social thinkers and schools of social thought as moments in a grand historical process of immanent intellectual development that just so happened to be reaching its (variously conceived) culmination in the (supposedly) more highly advanced social-theoretical framework, or method of social research, that was crystallizing at the present time – in whatever fashion these narratives depicted the present moment.

In the postwar years, writings on the history of sociology consisted chiefly of accretions to these same two genres: as found, on the one hand, in the encyclopedia projects of Barnes (1948) and Martindale (1960), and, on the other hand, in a smattering of more overtly presentist articles that sought to cull bits and pieces from earlier texts in the sociological tradition in order to push forward one or another item on the generally agreed upon agenda of contemporary mainstream sociology (see the following discussion). That the later, presentist objective was, indeed, the principal reason for sociologists to examine their past was the central message of the vastly influential opening chapters of all three editions of Robert Merton's *Social Theory and Social Structure* (1949, 1957, 1968), which applauded efforts at the "selective accumulation of those small parts of earlier theory which … survived the tests of empirical research," even as Merton deplored the time sociologists spent revisiting "the false starts, the archaic doctrines and the fruitless errors of the past" (1949, pp. 4–5). (That the "false starts" and "archaic doctrines" of the past were topics that actually roused Merton's attention when they occurred in the *natural sciences* and served to illuminate the historical processes by which the natural sciences were socially *institutionalized* is a discrepancy that Merton and other early sociologists of science would not emphasize for some years.)[8]

[8] In associating Merton, here and throughout this chapter, with a presentist point of view, I am aware that I am offering a one-sided characterization of his thinking. The rationale

Against this backdrop, the historiography of sociology occupied a peripheral place in the larger discipline of sociology. Indicative of its marginal position is the telling fact that, in the postwar period, "the history of sociology" did not yet exist as an organized and recognized subfield of research in its own right, that is, as a subject of investigation carried out on a continuing basis by an identifiable and respected group of scholars focused on a set of relatively autonomous historical questions that merited study by specialized methods of historical research. Scholarship on the history of sociology remained, rather, a sporadic activity on the part of a shifting subset of sociologists who either were presenting overviews of the past for general readers inside and outside sociology or were combing through earlier sociological writings for theoretical concepts, empirical insights, and other "finds" that might benefit mainstream projects in other areas of sociology. That the appeal of work along either of these lines was severely limited is suggested by the fact that, for the entire 1945 to 1969 period, only seventeen articles – each one by a different author – appear in my sample, for an average of less than .7 article per year. Revealing as well of the still-unorganized nature of the history of sociology as a scholarly subfield are the heterogeneity of topics treated in the sampled articles (Table 4.1, column i, category A) and the rarity with which the writers of these articles situate their work in relation to any previous historiography on the subject (Table 4.1, column i, category C).

What is more, in all but one of the articles listed for this period in the Appendix (panel i) – the article by Hinkle and Hinkle (1952) – the author's principal reason for examining some feature of sociology's earlier history was to address a then-contemporary issue outside the history of sociology per se – whether it was the methodology of modern sociology (Znaniecki 1945; Timasheff 1952; Tiryakian 1965), the appropriate theoretical framework for the sociology of religion (O'Dea 1954), the adequacy of structural functionalism (Bennett and Wolff 1955; Habenstein 1955), or the nature and origins of modern society (Kolegar 1964; Mitzman 1966; Wertheim 1967; Forcese 1968). Still further, in every article, the method of historical research consisted primarily in an internalist analysis of one or more published sociological texts from the past (Table 4.1, column i, category

Merton articulates in *Social Theory and Social Structure* for research on the history of sociology warrants emphasis because of the book's enormous readership and far-reaching impact. As I have shown elsewhere (Camic 2010), however, in a number of his other writings, especially in his later work on sociological semantics, Merton strongly embraces a historicist orientation toward the study of the sociology's past (see also Zuckerman 2010). Unfortunately, this current in his work remains, as of yet, virtually unknown among historians of sociology.

B). During these years, scholars writing on the history of sociology rarely made use of archival sources or examined either the broader historical contexts or the specific institutional settings from which past sociological ideas emerged – though, on the latter subjects, Hinkle and Hinkle (1954) offered a striking exception with their pioneering study of the early institutional development of American sociology (cf. Hughes 1958).

This picture that one observes throughout much of the quarter-century that followed the end of World War II grew more complex, however, as the last decade of the period set in. The shifting choice of which foreign-language writings to translate, particularly from the oeuvres of the Continental thinkers who had by this time come to constitute the sociological canon,[9] provides a useful measure of sociologists' gradually expanding interests in their own history. For whereas English translations of canonical authors like Émile Durkheim and Max Weber had, in the immediate postwar years, focused on texts – such as Weber's essays on bureaucracy and authority, Durkheim's writings on the problems of modern society – that related directly to American sociologists' contemporary concerns, the 1960s saw the translation of texts such as Durkheim's *Montesquieu and Rousseau: Forerunners of Sociology* (1960; translation by Manheim) and Weber's *Economy and Society* in its entirety (1968; translation by Roth and Wittich), along with the appearance of Bendix's (1960) full-dress intellectual-historical biography of Weber and of Lukes's (1968; published 1973) monumental intellectual-historical account of Durkheim.

The late 1960s produced as well a raft of entries in the new *International Encyclopedia of the Social Sciences* (Sills 1968) on a broad range of earlier social thinkers, schools of thought, and other developments in the past history of sociology in Europe and America. There also appeared two ambitious books designed to integrate the new historical scholarship (on thinkers like Durkheim, Weber, Marx, and others) into master narratives – divergent from each other, to be sure – about the development of sociology from the mid-eighteenth to the early twentieth century. These were Robert Nisbet's *The Sociological Tradition* (1966) and Raymond Aron's *Main Currents in Sociological Thought* (1965–7).[10] Written by well-regarded figures within the discipline of sociology and widely noticed at the time of

[9] How the sociological canon emerged, when it did so, and how its boundaries changed over time are themselves complex questions for historians of sociology. Addressing these questions falls, however, beyond the purview of this chapter.

[10] At the time, Aron held the chair of sociology at the Sorbonne, and the title given here was the English translation of a two-volume work that appeared nearly concurrently in French.

their publication, these studies signaled the rising prominence of the historiography of sociology. Both studies were notable as well for their efforts to combine internalist and external modes of inquiry into the history of sociology.

Period II, 1970 to 1999

The second period of the post–War World II era began very differently from the first period. Where peacetime conditions, the challenges of university rebuilding, and a shortage of sociologists were the facts of life in 1945 (and would remain so into the early 1950s), the 1970s was the era of the Vietnam War, of widespread antiwar protests and vocal movements for racial and gender equality, of American academic institutions thriving after their rapid expansion during the 1960s, and of sociology itself in a unusual phase of prosperity, more abundantly furnished with faculty, students, and institutional resources than at any previous time in the discipline's history (Turner and Turner 1990).[11] Surrounded by these and accompanying social changes, the emerging generation of scholars, as well as many already established figures throughout the humanities and the social sciences, were increasingly attracted to a reflective engagement with a wide range of historical questions (Adams et al. 2005; McDonald 1996; Sica and Turner 2005). Among these were critical questions that sought to plumb the historical character of human knowledge and to problematize the *historicity of disciplinary knowledge*. The increasing salience of these questions represented a major shift in emphasis that was traceable, in part, to the revival of the Marxist concept of ideology and to two newer developments that Capshew and Passmore also stress in their chapters: namely, dissemination of the early writings of the French philosopher Michel Foucault and, perhaps above all, the powerful influence of the historian of science Thomas Kuhn's assault on narratives of scientific progress through his analysis of paradigms, crises, and revolutions in *The Structure of Scientific Revolutions* (1962/1970).[12]

[11] For this reason, one should be cautious in accepting Kuklick's claim about the "declining economic prospects" faced by American academics during this period.

[12] These developments were mutually reinforcing, and they stimulated ancillary trends that further augmented their combined effect. Among these ancillary trends was social scientists' growing capacity to pursue library-based research projects, of which historical projects constitute a principal subtype. For, as Abbott (2008) has argued, library-based projects entail a very different style of research from that involved in quantitative projects; and the more social scientists engaged in the library investigations with respect to any one

In sociology, this broad-scale transformation in outlook reverberated, over the course of the next three decades, so as to give greater disciplinary centrality to scholarship on the history of sociology,[13] while also increasing the quantity of work in the area.[14] Portents of these changes were evident already by 1970 in two books explicitly concerned with the history of sociology, both of them a blend of externalist and internalist analysis: Alvin Gouldner's popular best seller *The Coming Crisis of Western Sociology* (1970), which presented a historical examination of the discipline's long-term development as the basis for critiquing the destination at which the field had arrived, and Robert Friedrichs's *A Sociology of Sociology* (1970) – the recipient in 1971 of the American Sociological Association's highest annual award for distinguished scholarship – which depicted sociology's recent past as a series of paradigm changes that pointed forward to a revolutionary transformation for the better just over the horizon.

In the two decades that followed, writings of a similar kind became increasingly conspicuous in American as well as European sociology. These years witnessed, in fact, such major English-language publications as Giddens (1971, 1976), Collins (1975, 1985), Eisenstadt (1976), Hawthorn (1976), Alexander (1982–3), and Seidman (1983), as well as comparable works – all of them quickly translated into English – by leading Continental figures

historical topic, the more inclined and better equipped they were, on the whole, to undertake historical inquiries on other topics.

[13] To say this is not to imply that sociologists flocked by the dozen to the study of knowledge and other intellectual products and institutions. Although more receptive to these subjects than in the past – when they had widely scorned Mannheimian proposals for a "sociology of knowledge" – American sociologists remained on the whole more materialist than idealist in their intellectual proclivities. As a result, even as their interests became increasingly historical in this second period under consideration, these interests flowed more heavily toward research on class formations, state structures, and related topics than toward inquiries into the historical development of knowledge and other ideational forms (with the partial exception of religion). This materialist inclination persisted even among sociologists of science, for scholarship on the sociology of science continued in this period to center chiefly on the study of institutional patterns and rarely concerned the content of knowledge, let alone the historically changing content of sociological knowledge (see Camic et al. 2011).

[14] Because this period was (as noted previously) an era when the ranks of sociologists were expanding numerically, some part of the increasing quantity of scholarship on the history of sociology that I will now describe further might well be attributed simply to the growing number of sociologists. In studies like the current one, disentangling the separate role of multiple causal factors is always problematic. Even so, I would caution against assigning too much weight to the expanding number of sociologists alone since, as the next section will show, during the following historical period, while the number of sociologists held steady at a high level, the volume of research on the history of sociology sharply declined.

including Bourdieu (1977), Habermas (1984–7), and Joas (1985). Differing in their specifics, these works had in common the strong presentist ambition to advance contemporary sociological theory by reappropriating sociology's historical legacy. To this end, each of the theorists named came forth with a detailed exposition of the ideas of past sociological theorists – chiefly Marx, Durkheim, and Weber, with Georg Simmel, G. H. Mead, and Talcott Parsons occasionally appended to the recognized canonical trio – in order to construct from these sources what each author proffered as a superior paradigm (tellingly, a *different* paradigm in each instance) for sociology in the next stages of its historical development.

Accompanied by a new generation of encyclopedic volumes (e.g., Bottomore and Nisbet 1978; Ritzer 1983; Turner 1974)[15] – volumes that surveyed a wide range of traditions in the history of sociological research and theory and then linked these traditions forward to ongoing disputes among later twentieth-century sociologists – the efflorescence of these various theoretical reconstructions had the pronounced effect of propelling the historiography of sociology away from the discipline's periphery and repositioning it at the core of some of the most lively mainstream debates.[16] By so doing, this rearrangement overcame (to some degree) the subfield's previous marginal position and raised its overall status among sociologists. In taking notice of this relocation, however, it is important to appreciate that it carried along with it, and indeed perpetuated, the established premise that the historiography of sociology is a subordinate activity, an activity justified – much as Merton had earlier proposed, in terms only slightly more restrictive – mainly by what research on sociology's past could contribute to the present-day work of sociologists who were *not* historians of sociology. In this sense, scholarship on the history of sociology in the period that commenced around 1970 had somewhat more in common with the immediate postwar years than would initially appear to be the case.

By no means was this the full story, however. Instead, in bodies of scholarship less visible than those just described, a less presentist view of the historiography of sociology was gradually emerging during the same period from three directions. While these three lines of work all exhibited a more

[15] The texts by Ritzer and by Turner proved extremely popular and appeared in many later editions.

[16] Significantly enhancing this effect was the dramatic rise of interest in and research on historical questions throughout the discipline of sociology at large, as evidenced by the successful movement to establish "comparative-historical sociology" as one of the discipline's largest, most active, and most intellectually vibrant subfields.

antipresentist viewpoint, however, in other respects the three were largely independent of one another, and it is instructive to differentiate them.

First, with regard to the historiography on sociological *ideas* – the "idealist" subject matter of most scholarship on the history of sociology up to this point in time – there appeared in sociology a growing number of studies that disregarded in practice, if not always in precept, the presumption that the historical researcher's purpose was to ransack the past for propositions, arguments, concepts, and other items useful to contemporary sociological projects. Here, Lewis Coser's *Masters of Sociological Thought* (1971), with its nonchalant attitude toward what earlier sociological thinkers could contribute to the present-day agenda and its commitment to the close internalist exposition of their writings as totalities, combined with an externalist analysis that situated these thinkers in their biographical, institutional, and wider social contexts, provided a new model, as did the meticulous historical works of Bierstedt (1981) and Hinkle (1980, 1994).[17] Also highly consequential in this regard was the University of Chicago Press's Heritage of Sociology series, which (under the general editorship of Morris Janowitz and later Donald Levine) published between 1964 and 1999 more than thirty volumes that, while inclusive of such household names as Marx, Durkheim, Weber, Simmel, Mead, and Parsons,[18] also resurrected the writings of such then noncanonical figures as Martin Buber, Kenneth Burke, W. E. B. Dubois, Maurice Halbwachs, L. J. Henderson, Everett Hughes, Harold Lasswell, Paul Lazarsfeld, Alfred Schutz, Max Scheler, Hermann Schmalenbach, Gabriel Tarde, and Willard Waller, and carefully located these writings in their respective intellectual and social contexts. To be sure, the editors of several of these volumes – aiming for a broad contemporary readership – still labored to identify the present-day contributions of the authors being examined, but doing so was now rather less incumbent on the historian of sociology. Indeed, it was in this period that Robert Alun Jones (writing in the lead article in the *American Journal of Sociology*, 1977; see also Jones 1983) issued a compelling call to liberate sociologists from Merton's presentist criterion for studying the past and to replace that criterion with historicist principles that would license and encourage historians of sociology to investigate sociological ideas in reference primarily to the

[17] Relevant here as well were several of the entries in the two later supplementary volumes to the *International Encyclopedia of the Social Sciences*, Sills (1979) and Sills and Merton (1990).

[18] During the period under examination, the thinkers named here were the subjects also of a wide range of interpretive monographs and historical accounts. These works are too numerous to include in this overview.

intellectual-historical contexts in which those ideas arose – a call that, for some years, attracted considerable notice within the field (see the discussion of the debate over Jones's work in Baehr 2002). Facilitating scholarship in this historicist vein was the increasing willingness of historians of sociology to conduct archival research, as they started to do using collections at universities that were early centers of American sociology, such as the University of Chicago, Columbia University, and Harvard University, as well as a number of less elite institutions.[19]

Side by side with this first line of scholarship emerged a second. This second cluster of work represented a turn in focus from the history of sociological ideas to the investigation of more "material" aspects of the history of sociology: that is, to the social structures and processes by which the activities of sociologists were organized, maintained, and transformed in different times and locations. Research on these features of the discipline had not previously weighed into discussions of the purposes for studying sociology's past, and they were not elements that had entered into the calculus that Merton, writing in his capacity as a sociological theorist, had used to build his case for a presentist historiography of sociology.

The more material features of intellectual fields were, however, topics of primary concern in work that Merton produced when he donned his hat as a sociologist of science; and during the second postwar period, historians of sociology, inspired by the example of the Mertonian sociology of science, as well as by literatures in the sociology of organizations, the sociology of higher education, and the sociology of the professions, began to venture into these territories. Important historiographic scholarship in this vein included several studies of the social conditions that made possible the emergence and institutionalization of sociology as an academic discipline in the United States, Britain, France, and Germany (Shils 1970; Vidich and Lyman 1985; Abrams 1968; Clark 1973; Besnard 1983; Oberschall 1972); research on the institutional origins and development of sociology departments at

[19] This period also witnessed strenuous efforts to create an official archive for the records of the American Sociological Association, efforts that in 2000 bore fruit in the establishment of the ASA Archives at Pennsylvania State University, which also houses – thanks to the dedicated work of Alan Sica – collections of many major players in twentieth-century American sociology. These materials include the Luther Lee Bernard and Jessie Bernard Collection, which Sica has described as "almost surely, after Chicago's and perhaps Harvard's, the most useful and interesting archive on the history of sociology in the United States" (1995, p. 73). That the correspondence and papers of other important figures in the discipline's history are still dispersed haphazardly across a number of universities, however, remains a serious problem to which Sica has drawn attention.

particular American universities (Abbott 1999; Bulmer 1984; Camic and Xie 1994; Deegan 1979, 1983; Fine 1995; Fine and Severance 1985; Galliher 1995; Johnson 1995; Martindale 1980; Matthews 1977; McGuire and Dawes 1983; Miller 1986; Nichols 1992; Sica 1983; Turner 1991); an institutional history of American sociology at large (Turner and Turner 1990); a history of the American Sociological Association (Rhoades 1981); and a history of the International Sociological Association (Platt 1998). Significant here as well were historical studies of sociologists' changing research practices, a trend of inquiry exemplified by Bulmer et al.'s (1991) analysis of the "social survey" in the United States and Europe, Converse's (1987) examination of the history of survey research in the United States, Johnson and Johnson's (1980) study of the first half-century of the Institute for Research in Social Science, and Platt's path-breaking *History of Sociological Research Methods in America, 1920–1960* (1999).

The two preceding numbered points both deal with bodies of scholarship that were produced by sociologists engaged in studying the history of sociology. As such, these two bodies of work are distinguishable from a third stream that also took shape during Period II: research relating to the history of sociology by scholars whose professional location (and/or area of investigation) lay outside sociology itself – and who, as a result, were even more indifferent to using historiographic inquiry to address issues on the agenda of contemporary sociological theory and empirical research. This third stream was, in turn, composed of two currents: (a) research by historians studying the history of the social sciences en bloc; and (b) research by scholars concerned with the history of another of the social sciences, one whose development intertwined with – and thus shed light on – developments in the history of sociology. Important examples of stream (a) included Baker (1975), Bannister (1979, 1987, 1992), Cravens (1978), Curti (1980), Furner (1975), Haskell (1977), Jay (1973), Kloppenberg (1986), Lewis and Smith (1980), Mandelbaum (1971), Pels (1973), Pickering (1993), and, perhaps above all, Lepenies's *Between Literature and Science: The Rise of Sociology* (1988) and Ross's *The Origins of American Social Science* (1991). Regarding stream (b), understanding of the history of sociology was augmented also by complementary research by historians of anthropology (e.g., Kuklick 1991; Kuper 1973, 1988; and Stocking 1968, 1987, 1995); economics (Backhouse 1985; Mirowski 1989; Morgan 1990; Swedberg 1991; and Yonay 1998); history (Novick 1988); political philosophy and political science (Ball et al. 1989; Collini 1979; Collini et al. 1983; Ricci 1984; Seidelman 1985; and Westbrook 1991); psychology (Capshew 1999; Chapman 1988; Danziger 1990; Hacking 1995; O'Donnell 1985; Ross 1972; and Smith 1986); and statistics (Desrosieres 1998; Gigerenzer et al. 1989; Hacking 1990; Porter 1986, 1995; and Stigler 1986).

Several of these studies appeared as volumes in the prestigious Ideas in Context series, which Cambridge University Press launched in 1977 (under the editorship of Richard Rorty, J. B. Schneewind, Quentin Skinner, and Wolf Lepenies) and that served – along with the Chicago's Heritage of Sociology series – significantly to promote scholarship on the history of sociology. Additional infrastructural support arose from the International Sociological Association's Research Committee on the History of Sociology, established in 1974, and, for a time, from the *Journal of the History of Sociology*, which ran from 1978 to 1987. When the latter lost financial footing and ceased publication, historians of sociology during this period could still find outlets for their work in periodicals such as the *Journal of the History of the Behavioral Sciences* (1965–), *Human Studies* (1978–), *History of European Ideas* (1980–), and the *American Sociologist* (particularly under the editorship of L. T. Nichols, 1998–), although none of these journals catered exclusively to research on the history of sociology. This was especially true of the *Journal of the History of the Behavioral Sciences*, which, as Capshew and Kuklick discuss in their chapters, was principally a beacon for scholars studying the history of psychology and the history of anthropology.

Even so, in conjunction with the overall improvement in infrastructure, the "history of sociology" became a more continuous and organized – a more institutionalized – pursuit than it had been in Period I, creating the possibility, for some scholars at least, of devoting a career to research in the area, rather than dipping into it only occasionally. Even at their most effective, however, the new infrastructural mechanisms proved incapable of reining in the intellectual dispersion that had been a nascent feature of the historiography of sociology during the previous period. As a result, at the same time that sociological theorists were giving the historiography of sociology a vigorous centripetal push toward the center of some of the major debates in contemporary sociology, the writings of the scholars whom I have classified under the latter three points previously were exerting strong centrifugal effects. What is more, these centrifugal effects were themselves heterogeneous, for the reason that these three additional sets of scholars tended to work unaware of one another and to pursue very different historical questions, their sole point of overlap – though it was, admittedly, no small matter – lying (as I have indicated) in their concern with probing the history of sociology in its own right, rather than for the sake of some extrahistorical purpose. Still further, these groupings themselves are little more than categories imposed retrospectively; on the ground during the period, none of the three exhibited much internal topical or methodological unity, but rather a wide variety of research activity – with each scholar marching to his or her own tune, out of step with one another and with the scores then on offer from many of the discipline's theorists. In this fractured context, it is not surprising that – insofar as one sets aside the theorists' (varied) historical depictions of where sociology had been and of where it was heading – these decades produced from within sociology few cohesive master narratives as to the character and direction of the field's long-term historical development. Tellingly, the major synthetic work on the history of sociology from this era, Donald Levine's magisterial *Visions of the Sociological Tradition* (1995), consisted not in an account of sociology's own course of intellectual and institutional development, but in an anatomy of the contrasting ways in which historians of sociology had heretofore constructed their narratives of the discipline's history.

The evidence from my sample of articles confirms this overall picture.[20] On the one side, the data for the 1970–99 period (Table 4.1, column ii) show a definite increase in the volume of scholarship on the history of sociology – an upswing to an average of 3.2 articles per year (in the JSOTR sample alone), as compared with .7 during the first postwar period. Notable, also, is the growth in the number of repeat authors (Appendix, panel ii), a further indicator that writing about the history of sociology had become, for some scholars at any rate, an ongoing career practice, not simply a one-time undertaking.

On the other side, however, articles from the period show little in the way of central historiographical tendencies, but, rather, a wide scattering across the different modes of historical research that I have been distinguishing. Of the 97 sampled articles (Appendix, panel ii), nearly a quarter (among them, Kienzle 1971; Goodwin 1973; Garrett 1974; Janowitz 1975; Hilbert 1986; Levine 1989; and Emirbayer 1996) continued to quarry texts from the past in order to uncover their present-day contributions either to theory or to particular areas of empirical research (e.g., the sociology of religion, the sociology of organizations, ethnomethodology). In an increasing proportion of articles, however, these various presentist approaches gave way to more historicist studies of past thinkers and schools of thought (Gibbons

[20] Because the articles in the sample were selected randomly, sampled articles and articles that I purposely intended to include in this chapter (because of their substantive importance) were sometimes exactly the same articles. It is for that reason that there is a degree of overlap between the articles that I have already referred to in this subsection and those that I cite in the following three paragraphs.

1974; Pipping 1982; Turner and Maryanski 1988), past concepts and practices (Laslett 1990; Platt 1995), and past institutional changes (Lengermann 1979; Deegan 1981; Soffer 1982; Henking 1993): studies that situated these focal developments in relation to various aspects of their intellectual and/or social context. For its part, moreover, even this latter type of research exhibited little in the way of cohesiveness (Table 4.1, column ii, category A), as the scholars in question focused their studies on an ever-expanding list of different historical figures, schools of thought, theories and concepts, and institutional developments, while enlarging the geographical scope of their projects (Bryant 1972; Sulek and Pomorska 1992; Weinberg 1992; Quah 1995) *and* significantly broadening their own repertoire of research methods (Table 4.1, column ii, category B), moving beyond the earlier near-exclusive reliance on printed texts to the use of archival materials, biographies and autobiographies, and various other kinds of internalist and externalist inquiry.

Fragmenting scholarship on the history of sociology still further, many of the sampled articles make minimal efforts to situate their inquiries against the backdrop of previous research in the area, contenting themselves (insofar as they are even classifiable in relation to past scholarship) with nebulous implied connections to some faceless prior literature or with unelaborated claims to be either building upon or departing from the historiographic claims associated with one or more existing theoretical perspectives, sociological subfields, or other bodies of scholarship (Table 4.1, column ii, category C). That more than 40 percent of sampled articles (42/97) adopt a critical stance toward prior historical work– most often by faulting previous studies for omitting figures, theories, times, or places that arguably formed parts of the history of sociology – accords with the critical tenor of American academic discourse at large in the years from 1970 onward. And this critical stance accords also with the single significant point of concurrence in this otherwise splintered disciplinary historiography – a concurrence point laden with irony. For the issue on which historians of sociology converged was in their tacit *agreement to disagree* over fundamentals: to disagree over the very boundaries of sociology's past – over the "who," the "what," the "when," and the "where" the history of sociology comprised – and therefore to disagree over how best to encompass the discipline's historical diversity. These fraught concerns move to the fore in several articles in the sample (Green and Driver 1976; Laslett 1992; Smith, 1995) as well as in major works by Lemert (1993) and Calhoun (1995) that appeared in the last decade of Period II.

Period III, 2000 to 2012

No sharp divide separates the second and third periods in this account, although one may for convenience take the millennium as marking a bend in the road for the history of sociology, which had already begun to experience shifting conditions – conditions that would grow in import during the ensuing decade as part of a process that is still ongoing. This process has entailed the subfield's return to the more purely peripheral intellectual and institutional position that it occupied in the discipline of sociology during the immediate postwar era and, correspondingly, a drop-off in the quantity of new research in the area. Indeed, barely half a decade into this third period, informed observers within the subfield were decrying the "marginality" of the history of sociology and the widespread inattention given "by practicing sociologists" to the historiographic scholarship that had been published up to this point (Sica 2007, p. 716; Phillips and VanAntwerpen 2007, p. 738; cf. Blasi 2005; Platt 2010).

Part and parcel of this transformation was the eroding infrastructure of support for additional scholarship in this vein. Most consequential in this respect was probably the decision of the University of Chicago Press to terminate its long-running Heritage of Sociology series as of 1999 due to insufficient readership for volumes on the subject. Significant, too, was the simultaneous disappearance from Cambridge's Ideas in Context series of new titles – aside from volumes on the canonical trio, Marx, Durkheim, and Weber – dealing with topics related to the history of sociology.[21] What is more, only by the persistent efforts of a small band of historians of sociology was strong opposition to the subfield inside the American Sociological Association overcome with the formal establishment in 2000 of a History of Sociology Section, a section that has since remained among the smallest in the ASA and, as such, annually at risk of elimination.[22]

21 Like its two predecessor editions, the new *International Encyclopedia of the Social and Behavioral Sciences* (Smelser and Baltes 2001) did contain a wider range of offerings relating to the history of sociology (as well as to the history of the social sciences more generally). Unlike the well-read previous editions, however, the 2001 edition attracted relatively slight notice either from professional scholars or from advanced students. As such, it did little to stimulate more research on the history of sociology (at least as far as I am aware).

22 According to the figures for 2011, membership in the largest sections of the ASA averaged slightly more than a thousand, with the breakdown running as follows: Sociology of Culture, 1,228 members; Sex and Gender, 1,190; Medical Sociology, 1,034; Race, Gender, and Class, 999; Political Sociology, 884; Economic Sociology, 882. At 199 members, the History of Sociology Section was only a fifth the size of these sections, slightly ahead of the Section on Animals and Society, 172.

While the sources of a change that is still under way are uncertain, among the conditions that appear to underlie the recent remarginalization of the history of sociology have been the demographics of generational transition and its intellectual correlates: viz., the aging and gradual exit from the discipline of cohorts that had entered sociology in a climate relatively favorable to disciplinary historiography and their replacement by cohorts whose members did not experience that same climate and whose interests developed in other directions. That is to say: Whereas trends outside and inside the university in the post-1970 period galvanized an interest in the historicity of knowledge among scholars who were then at the start of their careers, by the first decade of the twenty-first century these same trends had largely expired. Particularly was this the case with regard to the sharp spur that these trends had previously given to the study of the history of sociology. For, to the extent that historical questions continued to command attention among sociologists of the millennial generation – which they often did not (see Adams et al. 2005) – these questions now generally tilted away from topics with idealist connotations and again veered toward issues pertaining to the materialist realm of class, race, and gender stratification; economic and political institutions; and so forth.[23] Concomitantly, there occurred at this time a steep decline of interest in sociological theory itself, particularly in those forms of theorizing that aimed to construct from the writings of the past a better paradigm for the future – precisely the kind of theorizing that had been prevalent and popular during Period II and had then provided so forceful a stimulus to scholarship on the history of sociology.

To be sure, many members of the cohorts that attained professional maturity during Period II remained active scholars who were – and are – still engaged in the kinds of scholarship on the history of sociology described in the previous section. Prominent sociological theorists, Alexander (2001) and Joas (2003; Joas and Knobl 2009), for example, continued to bring forth accounts of sociology's past that were intended as interventions into contemporary mainstream debates; and encyclopedia historiographic

[23] Where they had somewhat more idealist interests, sociologists were likely to turn not to inward-looking studies on the history of sociology but to research in the sociology of culture, the sociology of religion, and the sociology of science – though "idealist" here is somewhat a misnomer, since the tendency in these subfields in recent decades has been to focus more on institutional patterns and practices than on the beliefs, values, and ideas of the women and men under study. As such, these subfields, the sociology of science in particular, have tended to absorb the modest materialist current that emerged during Period II in the historiography of sociology.

volumes – likewise designed to distill contributions to present-day debates from canonical and other writings from the earlier periods in the history of sociology – also continued to appear (Kivisto 1988, 1997; Ritzer 2003; see also footnote 15, this chapter). The same statement applies to more specialized studies – similar in their presentist aspirations, but too numerous to list individually – of the work of figures ranging from the well established (Durkheim, Weber, Simmel, Mead) to the previously unappreciated (Jane Addams, W. E. B. Dubois, Charlotte Perkins Gilman, Harriett Martineau). As had been true during Period II, moreover, less presentist-motivated scholarship also remained in evidence, as demonstrated by the appearance of several major studies that placed into context – social as well as intellectual context – the ideas of a range of earlier sociological thinkers *and* the institutions and research practices of earlier periods. These studies included Calhoun's *Sociology in America: A History* (2007), Igo's *Averaged American: Surveys, Citizens, and the Making of a Mass Public* (2007), Platt's *The British Sociological Association: A Sociological History* (2003), and Blasi's *Diverse Histories of American Sociology* (2005), the last a groundbreaking collection of historical essays on various neglected figures, topics, schools of thought, academic institutions, and nonacademic sites of sociological work (see also Keys and Galliher 2009; McGonigal and Galliher 2005; and, on neglected departments, Hill 2005).

Inside sociology, Period III has also witnessed a crystalizing interest in the study – in some instances, the comparative cross-national study – of the history of particular subfields of the discipline and of sociological journals (see Camic 2008–9; Crothers 2007; Platt 2009, 2010), plus the occasional return of grand-narrative accounts (some externalist, some internalist) of the processes by which the field of sociology emerged and subsequently developed (Abbott 2001; Bourdieu 2004; Platt 2010; Steinmetz 2005, 2007). In addition, from historical scholars whose professional location was outside sociology were *The Modern Social Sciences* (2003), Porter and Ross's massive, discipline-spanning volume in the Cambridge History of Science series, plus contributions concerned specifically with the historical connection between sociology and economics (Hodgson 2001, 2004; Sklansky 2002) and with the transfer of European social-scientific ideas to the American context (Grimmer-Solem 2003; Rodgers 1998; Schafer 2000).

As this précis will suggest, the intellectual dispersion that marked the literature of the history of sociology during the second period following World War II persisted into the third period in the face of the subfield's return to the discipline's fringes. Again, the JSTOR data corroborate these impressions, showing a gradual decrease in the annual production of articles on the history of sociology (down to 2.8 per year) yet no signs of any increase in their topical or methodical unity. To the contrary, with the slight exceptions of Talcott Parsons, Alva Myrdal, and anomie, no figure (previously recognized or neglected), no department or school of thought, nor any concept or theory serves to classify more than one of the sampled articles. Not only this, but viewed as a set, the articles continue to diverge in their research methods and to relate to previous historiographic scholarship in ways that are tenuous at best (see Table 4.1, column iii, categories A, B, and C).

That articles sampled from this era range from an internalist effort to use Durkheim and Parsons to construct "an alternative to the contemporary version of utilitarianism" (Tiryakian 2000); to a proposal to appropriate Theodor Geiger's theory of revolutions as an intervention into present-day debates about imperialism (Borch 2006); to a contextualized account of writings by women in the early issues of the *American Journal of Sociology* (Grant, Stalp, and Ward 2002); and still further to an historicist analysis of the early twentieth-century attempt of sociologists and psychiatrists to understand urban life and mental illness (Pols 2003). This wide diversity reinforces the picture that emerged in the previous section of this chapter; it demonstrates that in Period III, as in Period II, the majority of scholars who studied the history of sociology worked as solo practitioners, linked with other past and present contributors to the historiography of sociology by few, if any, ties of strong intellectual commonality – everyone operating more or less as his or her own historian. Not surprisingly, this situation brought no end to the disputes that had arisen in the previous era over what and who belonged within the boundaries of the history of sociology.

Looking forward, moreover, prospects seem dim that this situation will change in the direction of greater topical and methodological congruity and integration as the generational transition from Period II to Period III continues to play itself out. Among the reasons for this is that historians of sociology from the second postwar period have left a void whose ramifications are likely to persist long into the future. This void is a pedagogic one. Productive as many of these Period II historians have remained as scholars, they have generally been far less active in regard to graduate education in their area: that is, in transmitting knowledge about the history and the historiography of sociology to new cohorts of graduate students and in encouraging some of number of them to take up the torch (Phillips and VanAntwerpen 2007, p. 738; Sica 2007, p. 715).

To observe this circumstance is not to fault senior historians of sociology inasmuch as the paucity of courses and seminars on the history of sociology has been chiefly due to the curricular decisions of sociology department chairpersons and higher-level university administrators mindful of the job market for new Ph.Ds. and of the limited employment opportunities for graduates specializing in the history of sociology. While there presently exists no systematic information on the teaching of graduate courses on the history of sociology in American universities during the first four decades of the postwar era, anecdotal evidence suggests that such teaching did, at least occasionally, take place in Period I and in the earlier years of Period II – thereby imparting to graduate students (those studying in same department, at any rate) a certain uniform exposure to their professors' views of the current state of knowledge about the history of sociology, of the literature of the field, of promising topics for further research, and of appropriate research methods.[24] At the time of this writing, however, this training process appears to have come to a full-scale halt. Indeed, insofar as the Web sites of the top fifty graduate programs in American sociology (as of 2012) can be trusted on the matter – and in some instances the Web sites are somewhat unclear in this regard – not only are there no programs that currently offer a course specifically on the history of sociology, but not one program so much as includes a course of this type on its listing of occasionally offered graduate courses.[25] On the reasonable assumption that this evidence is more than a misleading artifact of departmental Web sites, this pronounced curricular lacuna in the intergenerational transmission of knowledge about the history of sociology directly accords with the ongoing intellectual fragmentation seen in the recent literature of the area, with the dwindling interest in the historiography of sociology among members of recent cohorts, and with the nearly total exile of scholarship on the history of sociology back to the periphery of the discipline.

Conclusion

An implication of this analysis is that one can appraise scholarship on the history of sociology during the post–World War II years from different angles.

[24] As a sociology graduate student at the University of Chicago in the mid-1970s, I was among those who had privilege of taking a (heavily subscribed) seminar, The History of Sociology, conducted by Morris Janowitz.

[25] In the interest of full disclosure, I would acknowledge that I have never offered, nor even proposed to offer, a course on the history of sociology (although I have taught occasional seminars on particular theorists from the past).

A historian of sociology comparing his or her subfield as it was in 1945 with conditions in 2012 would be struck, almost inevitably, by the prodigious growth and rich variegation of scholarship on the history of sociology. In the course of a relatively brief time span, the literature on the history of sociology has expanded from a small stack of encyclopedic surveys and triumphalist accounts of sociology's development to bookshelf after bookshelf of historical works examining thinkers, concepts, institutions, eras, and locations that were not even on the scholarly horizon at the conclusion of World War II. Still further, whereas scholarship at the beginning of the postwar period was limited principally to publications that were presentist in motivation, internalist in method, and idealist in subject matter, the following decades generated, alongside additional writings of these types, an outcropping of studies that were historicist in purpose, externalist in method, and (now and then) materialist in focus. Accompanying this intellectual efflorescence, moreover, was the emergence of "the history of sociology" as a professionally recognized area of research, underpinned by its own institutional infrastructure.

However, a fellow historian of sociology, considering the state of the subfield at the beginning and end of this sixty-nine-year era but also tracking its shifting fortunes across the periods into which the era divides, would chronicle a different historical arc. This is especially so insofar as she or he would take into account the location of the historiography of sociology on the map of the larger discipline whose history it seeks to examine. Seen from this standpoint, the post–World War II years decompose: first into an early period, when studying the history of sociology was an undertaking peripheral to the larger discipline, justified almost exclusively on presentist grounds in terms of its miscellaneous contributions toward advancing the agenda of mainstream sociological theory and research; next into a middle period, during which scholarship on the history of sociology rose to greater disciplinary centrality insofar as it underwrote an upsurge of interventions into contemporary debates, at the same time as counterforces inside the subfield held back from the center to pursue more historicist research and inadvertently fragmented the area into an unorganized diversity topics and methods; and, finally, into a third period, when the subfield returned to the periphery, now harboring both presentist and historicist orientations, still splintered across diverse topical and methodological fault lines, newly facing an erosion of institutional infrastructure, and slowly reckoning with atrophy in the pedagogical mechanisms that might otherwise enable veteran historians of sociology to enlist new recruits to carry the cause forward.

That appraisals as different as these by two observant historians of sociology can both find support in the evidence from the post–World War II era attests to a situation likely only to reinforce the sometimes stultifying ambivalence that sociologists at large have often felt about the historiography of their family – an ambivalence likely, perhaps, to bedevil historians of sociology until they find their own center.

References

Abbott, Andrew. 1999. *Department and Discipline: Chicago Sociology at One Hundred.* Chicago: University of Chicago Press.

2001. *Chaos of Disciplines.* Chicago: University of Chicago Press.

2008. "The Traditional Future: A Computational Theory of Library Research." *College and Research Libraries* 69:524–545.

Abend, Gabriel. 2008. "The Meaning of 'Theory'." *Sociological Theory* 26:173–199.

Abrams, Philip. 1968. *The Origins of British Sociology.* Chicago: University of Chicago Press.

Adams, Julia, Elizabeth Clemens, and Ann Orloff, eds. 2005. *Remaking Modernity: Politics, History, and Sociology.* Durham, NC: Duke University Press.

Alexander, Jeffrey C. 1982–83. *Theoretical Logic in Sociology,* 4 Vols. Berkeley: University of California Press.

Alexander, Jeffrey C., ed. 2001. *Mainstream and Critical Social Theory: Classical, Modern, and Contemporary,* 8 Vols. London: Sage.

Aron, Raymond. 1965–67. *Main Currents in Sociological Thought,* 2 Vols. Garden City, NY: Anchor.

Baehr, Peter. 2002. *Founders, Classics, Canons: Modern Disputes over the Origins and Appraisal of Sociology's Heritage.* New Brunswick, NJ: Transaction.

Baker, Keith Michael. 1975. *Condorcet: From Natural Philosophy to Social Mathematics.* Chicago: University of Chicago Press.

Ball, Terence, James Farr, and Russell L. Hanson, eds. 1989. *Political Innovation and Conceptual Change.* New York: Cambridge University Press.

Bannister, Robert C. 1979. *Social Darwinism.* Philadelphia: Temple University Press.

1987. *Sociology and Scientism: The American Quest for Objectivity, 1880–1940.* Chapel Hill: University of North Carolina Press.

1992. "Principle, Politics, and Profession." In *Sociology Responds to Fascism,* ed. Stephen P. Turner and Dirk Kasler. London: Routledge, 172–213.

Backhouse, Roger E. 1985. *A History of Modern Economic Analysis.* Oxford: Blackwell.

Barnes, Harry Elmer, ed. 1948. *An Introduction to the History of Sociology.* Chicago: University of Chicago Press.

Besnard, Philippe, ed. 1983. *The Sociological Domain the Durkheimians and the Founding of French Sociology.* Cambridge: Cambridge University Press.

Bendix, Reinhard. 1960. *Max Weber: An Intellectual Portrait.* Garden City, NY: Doubleday.

Bernard, Luther, and Jessie Bernard. 1943. *The Origins of American Sociology: The Social Science Movement in the United States.* New York: Crowell.

Bierstedt, Robert. 1981. *American Sociology Theory: A Critical History.* New York: Academic Press.

Blasi, Anthony, ed. 2005. *Diverse Histories of American Sociology.* Leiden, Netherlands: Brill.

Bogardus, Emory S. 1922. *A History of Social Thought.* Los Angeles: University of Southern California Press.

Bottomore, Tom, and Robert Nisbet, eds. *A History of Sociology Analysis.* New York: Basic Books.

Bourdieu, Pierre. 1977. *Outline of a Theory of Practice,* Trans. by Richard Nice. Cambridge: Cambridge University Press.

2004. *Science of Science and Reflexivity,* trans. Richard Nice. Chicago: University of Chicago Press.

Bourdieu, Pierre, and Loic Wacquant. 1992. *An Invitation to Reflexive Sociology.* Chicago: University of Chicago Press.

Bulmer, Martin. 1984. *The Chicago School of Sociology: Institutionalization, Diversity, and the Rise of Sociological Research.* Chicago: University of Chicago Press.

Bulmer, Martin, Kevin Bales, and Kathryn Kish Sklar, eds. 1991. *The Social Survey in Historical Perspective, 1880–1940.* Cambridge, MA.: Cambridge University Press.

Burrow, J. W. 1966. *Evolution and Society: A Study of Victorian Social Theory.* Cambridge: Cambridge University Press.

Calhoun, Craig. 1995. *Critical Social Theory.* Oxford: Blackwell.

Calhoun, Craig, ed. 2007. *Sociology in America: A History.* Chicago: University of Chicago Press.

Camic, Charles. 1979. "The Utilitarians Revisited." *American Journal of Sociology* 85:515–50.

2008–9. "The History of Sociology as a Bifocal Project." *Timelines* (Newsletter of the History of Sociology Section of the American Sociological Association) 12:1–3; 14:1, 9.

2010. "How Merton Sociologizes the History of Ideas." In *Robert K. Merton: Sociology of Science and Sociology as Science,* ed. Craig Calhoun. New York: Columbia University Press, 273–296.

Camic, Charles, and Neil Gross. 1998. "Contemporary Developments in Sociological Theory: Current Projects and Conditions of Possibility." *Annual Review of Sociology* 24:413–476.

Camic, Charles, Neil Gross, and Michèle Lamont, eds. 2011. *Social Knowledge in the Making.* Chicago: University of Chicago Press.

Camic, Charles, and Yu Xie. 1994. "The Statistical Turn in American Social Science: Columbia University, 1890–1915." *American Sociological Review* 59:773–805.

Capshew, James J. 1999. *Psychologists on the March: Science, Practice and Professional Identity in America, 1929–1969.* Cambridge: Cambridge University Press.

Chapman, Paul D. 1988. *Schools as Sorters: Lewis M. Terman, Applied Psychology and the Intelligence Testing Movement, 1890–1930.* New York: New York University Press.

Clark, Terry N. 1973. *Prophets and Patrons: The French University and the Emergence of the Social Sciences.* Cambridge, MA: Harvard University Press.

Collini, Stefan. 1979. *Liberalism and Sociology: L. T. Hobhouse and Political Argument in England, 1880–1914.* Cambridge: Cambridge University Press.

Collini, Stefan, Donald Winch, and J. W. Burrow. 1983. *That Noble Science of Politics*. Cambridge: Cambridge University Press.
Collins, Randall. 1975. *Conflict Sociology*. New York: Academic Press.
1985. *Three Sociological Traditions*. New York: Oxford University Press.
Converse, Jean M. 1987. *Survey Research in the United States: Roots and Emergence, 1890 1960*. Berkeley: University of California Press.
Coser, Lewis A. (1971) 1977. *Masters of Sociological Thought: Ideal in Historical and Social Context*. New York: Harcourt Brace Javanovich.
Cravens, Hamilton. 1978. *The Triumph of Evolution*. Philadelphia: University of Pennsylvania Press.
Crothers, Charles. 2007. "The Changing Profile of Core Publication in the Discipline of Sociology." Unpublished Paper.
Curti, Merle. 1980. *Human Nature in American Thought*. Madison: University of Wisconsin Press.
Danziger, Kurt. 1990. *Constructing the Subject: Historical Origins of Psychological Research*. Cambridge: Cambridge University Press.
Deegan, Mary Jo. 1979. "Sociology at Nebraska: 1884–1929." *Journal of the History of Sociology* 1:40–41.
1983. "Sociology at Wellesley College: 1900–1919." *Journal of the History of Sociology* 5:91.
Desrosières, Alain. 1998. *The Politics of Large Numbers*. Cambridge, MA: Harvard University Press.
Durkheim, Émile. 1960. *Montesquieu and Rousseau: Forerunners of Sociology*, trans. Ralf Manheim. Ann Arbor: University of Michigan Press.
Eisenstadt, S. N., with M. Curelaru. 1976. *The Form of Sociology: Paradigms and Crises*. New York: Wiley.
Fine, Gary Alan. 1995. *A Second Chicago School? The Development of a Postwar American Sociology*. Chicago: University of Chicago Press.
Fine, Gary Alan, and Janet S. Severance. 1985. "Great Men and Hard Times: Sociology at the University of Minnesota." *Sociological Quarterly* 26:117–134.
Friedrichs, Robert W. 1970. *A Sociology of Sociology*. New York: Free Press.
Furner, Mary O. 1975. *Advocacy and Objectivity: A Crisis in the Professionalization of American Social Science, 1865–1905*. Lexington: University Press of Kentucky.
Galliher, John F. 1995. *Marginality and Dissent in Twentieth-Century American Sociology: The Case of Elizabeth Briant Lee and Alfred McClung Lee*. Albany: State University of New York Press.
Giddens, Anthony. 1971. *Capitalism and Modern Social Theory*. Cambridge: Cambridge University Press.
1976. *New Rules of Sociological Method*. New York: Basic Books.
Gigerenzer, Gerd, Zeno Swijtink, Theodore Porter, Lorraine Daston, John Betty, and Lorenz Kruger. 1989. *The Empire of Change: How Probability Changes Science and Everyday Life*. Cambridge, MA: Harvard University Press.
Gouldner, Alvin W. 1970. *The Coming Crisis of Western Sociology*. New York: Basic Books.
Grimmer-Solem, Erik. 2003. *The Rise of Historical Economics and Social Reform in Germany, 1864–1894*. Oxford: Clarendon.

Habermas, Jurgen. 1984–1987. *The Theory of Communicative Action*, 2 Vols., trans. Thomas McCarthy. Boston: Beacon.

Hacking, Ian. 1990. *The Taming of Chance*. Cambridge, MA: Harvard University Press.

1995. *Rewriting the Soul: Multiple Personality and the Science of Memory*. Princeton, NJ: Princeton University Press.

Haskell, Thomas L. 1977. *The Emergence of Professional Social Science*. Baltimore: Johns Hopkins University Press.

Hawthorn, Geoffrey. 1976. *Enlightenment and Despair: A History of Sociology*. Cambridge: Cambridge University Press.

Hill, Michael R. 2005. *Centennial Bibliography on the History of American Sociology*. Washington, DC: American Sociological Association.

Hinkle, Roscoe C. 1980. *Founding Theory of American Sociology, 1881–1915*. Boston: Routledge.

1994. *Developments in American Sociology Theory, 1915–1950*. Albany: State University of New York Press.

Hinkle, Roscoe C., and Gisela J. Hinkle. 1954. *The Development of Modern Sociology, Its Nature and Growth in the United States*. New York: Random House.

Hodgson, Geoffrey. 2001. *How Economics Forgot History: The Problem of Historical Specificity in Social Science*. London: Routledge.

2004. *The Evolution of Institutional Economics*. London: Routledge.

House, Floyd Nelson. 1936. *The Development of Sociology*. New York: McGraw-Hill.

Hughes, H. Stuart. 1958. *Consciousness and Society: The Reorientation of European Social Thought, 1890–1930*. New York: Vintage.

Igo, Sarah E. 2007. *The Averaged American: Surveys, Citizens, and the Making of a Mass Public*. Cambridge, MA: Harvard University Press.

Jay, Martin. 1973. *The Dialectical Imagination: A History of the Frankfurt School and the Institute of Social Research, 1923–1950*. Boston: Little, Brown.

Joas, Hans. 1985. *G. H. Mead: A Contemporary Re-examination of His Thought*. Cambridge, MA: MIT Press.

2003. *War and Modernity*. Cambridge, MA: Polity Press.

Joas, Hans, and Wolfgang Knobl. 2009. *Social Theory: Twenty Introductory Lectures*. Cambridge: Cambridge University Press.

Johnson, Guy Benton, and Guron Griffs Johnson. 1980. *Research in Service to Society: The First Fifty Years of the Institute for Research in Social Science at the University of North Carolina*. Chapel Hill: University of North Carolina Press.

Johnston, Barry V. 1995. *Pitirim A. Sorokin: An Intellectual Biography*. Lawrence: University of Kansas Press.

Jones, Robert Alun. 1977. "On Understanding a Sociological Classic." *American Journal of Sociology* 83:279–319.

1983. "The New History of Sociology." *Annual Review of Sociology* 9:447–469.

Keys, David Patrick, and John F. Galliher. 2000. *Confronting the Drug Control Establishment: Alfred Lindesmith as a Public Intellectual*. Albany: State University of New York Press.

Kivisto, Peter, ed. 1988. *Illuminating Social Life: Classical and Contemporary Theory Revisited*. Thousand Oaks, CA: Pine Forge Press.

1997. *Social Theory: Roots and Branches*. New York: Oxford.

Kloppenberg, James T. 1986. *Uncertain Victory: Social Democracy and Progressivism in European and American Thought, 1870–1920*. New York: Oxford University Press.

Kuhn, Thomas S. (1962) 1970. *The Structure of Scientific Revolutions*, 2nd. ed. Chicago: University of Chicago Press.

Kuklick, Henrika. 1991. *The Savage Within: The Social History of British Anthropology*. New York: Cambridge University Press.

Kuper, Adam. 1973. *Anthropologists and Anthropology: The British School, 1922–1972*. London: Allan Lane.

1988. *The Invention of Primitive Society*. London: Routledge.

Laslett, Barbara. 1990. "Unfeeling Knowledge: Emotion and Objectivity in the History of Sociology." *Sociological Forum* 5:413–433.

Lemert, Charles, ed. 1993. *Social Theory: The Multicultural and Classical Readings*. Boulder, CO: Westview.

Lengermann, Patricia Madoo. 1979. "The Founding of the *American Sociological Review*: The Anatomy of a Rebellion." *American Sociology Review* 44:185–198.

Lepenics, Wolf. 1988. *Between Literature and Science: The Rise of Sociology*. Cambridge: Cambridge University Press.

Levine, Donald N. 1995. *Visions of the Sociology Tradition*. Chicago: University of Chicago Press.

Lewis, J. David, and Richard L. Smith. 1980. *American Sociology and Pragmatism: Mead, Chicago Sociology, and Symbolic Interaction*. Chicago: University of Chicago Press.

Lukes, Stephen. 1973. *Emile Durkheim: His Life and Work*. London: Harper & Row.

Mandelbaum, Maurice. 1971. *History, Man, and Reason*. Baltimore: Johns Hopkins University Press.

Martindale, Don. 1960. *The Nature and Types of Sociological Theory*. Boston: Houghton Mifflin.

1980. "The Golden Age of Minnesota Sociology, 1921–1930." *Journal of the History of Sociology* 2:35–60.

Matthews, Fred H. 1977. *Quest for an American Sociology: Robert E. Park and the Chicago School*. Montreal: McGill-Queen's University Press.

McDonald, Terrence J., ed. 1996. *The Historic Turn in the Human Sciences*. Ann Arbor: University of Michigan Press.

McGonigal, Kathryn, and John F. Galliher. 2005. *Mabel Agnes Elliott: Pioneering Feminist, Pacifist Sociologist*. Lanham, MD: Lexington Books.

McGuire, Patrick, and Denneth Dawes. 1983. "Sociology as Social Contribution: University of North Dakota as a Case Study of the Contradiction of American Sociology." *Sociology Quarterly* 24:589–603.

Merton, Robert K. (1949/1957) 1968. *Social Theory and Social Structure*, enlarged ed. New York: Free Press.

Mirowski, Philip. 1989. *More Heat than Light: Economics as Social Physics, Physics as Nature's Economics*. Cambridge: Cambridge University Press.

Morgan, Mary S. 1990. *The History of Econometric Ideas*. Cambridge: Cambridge University Press.

Miller, Delbert C. *One Hundred Years: The History of Sociology at Indiana University, 1885–1995*. Bloomington: Department of Sociology, Indiana University.

Nichols, Lawrence T. 1992. "The Establishment of Sociology at Harvard." In *Science at Harvard University*, ed. Clark A. Elliott and Margaret W. Rossiter. Bethlehem, PA: Lehigh University Press, 191–222.

Nisbet, Robert A. 1966. *The Sociological Tradition*. New York: Basic Books.

Novick, Peter. 1988. *That Noble Dream: The 'Objectivity Question' and the American Historical Professions*. Cambridge: Cambridge University Press.

Oberschall, Anthony, ed. 1972. *The Establishment of Empirical Sociology*. New York: Harper & Row.

O'Donnell, John M. 1985. *The Origins of Behaviorism: American Psychology, 1870–1920*. New York: New York University Press.

Odum, Howard W., ed. 1927. *American Masters of Social Science*. New York: Henry Holt.

Park, Robert E., and Ernest Burgess. (1921) 1969. *An Introduction to the Science of Sociology*. Chicago: University of Chicago Press.

Parsons, Talcott. 1937. *The Structure of Social Action*. New York: McGraw-Hill.

Pels, Richard H. 1973. *Radical Visions and American Dreams*. Middletown, CT: Wesleyan University Press.

Phillips, Alton, and Jonathan VanAntwerpen. 2007. "Histories of American Sociology: Readings and Resources." In *Sociology in America: A History*, ed. Craig Calhoun. Chicago: University of Chicago Press, 733–738.

Pickering, Mary. 1993. *Auguste Comte: An Intellectual Biography*. Cambridge: Cambridge University Press.

Platt, Jennifer. 1996. *A History of Sociological Research Methods in America, 1920–1960*. New York: Cambridge University Press.

1998. *History of ISA, 1948–1997*. International Sociological Association.

2003. *The British Sociological Association: A Sociological History*. Durham, UK: Sociologypress.

2009. "Work on the History of Subfields." *Timelines* (Newsletter of the History of Sociology Section of the American Sociological Association) 16:7–9.

2010. "Sociology." In *The History of the Social Sciences since 1945*, ed. Roger E. Backhouse and Philippe Fontaine. Cambridge: Cambridge University Press, 102–135.

Porter, Theodore M. 1986. *The Rise of Statistical Thinking, 1820–1900*. Princeton, NJ: Princeton University Press.

1995. *Trust in Numbers: The Pursuit of Objectivity in Science and Public Life*. Princeton, NJ: Princeton University Press.

Porter, Theodore, and Dorothy Ross, eds. 2003. *The Modern Social Sciences*. Vol. 7 of *The Cambridge History of Science*. Cambridge: Cambridge University Press.

Rhoades, Lawrence J. 1981. *A History of the American Sociology Association, 1905–1980*. Washington, DC: American Sociological Association.

Ricci, David M. 1984. *The Tragedy of Policy Science*. New Haven, CT: Yale University Press.

Ritzer, George. 1983. *Sociological Theory*. New York: Knopf.

Ritzer, George, ed. 2003. *The Blackwell Companion to Major Classical Social Theorists*. Malden, MA: Blackwell.

Rodgers, Daniel T. 1998. *Atlantic Crossings: Social Politics in a Progressive Age*. Cambridge, MA: Harvard University Press.

Ross, Dorothy. 1972. *G. Stanley Hall: The Psychologist as Prophet*. Chicago: University of Chicago Press.
1991. *The Origins of American Social Science*. Cambridge: Cambridge University Press.
Schafer, Axel R. 2000. *American Progressives and German Social Reform, 1875–1920*. Stuttgart: Franz Steiner Verlag.
Seidelman, Raymond. 1985. *Disenchanted Realists: Political Science and the American Crisis, 1884–1984*. Albany: State University of New York Press.
Seidman, Steven. 1983. *Liberalism and the Origins of European Social Theory*. Berkeley, CA: University of California Press.
Seligman, Edwin R. A., ed. 1930–35. *Encyclopaedia of the Social Sciences*. New York: Macmillan.
Shils, Edward. 1970. "Tradition, Ecology, and Institution in the History of Sociology." *Daedalus* 99:760–825.
Sica, Alan. 1983. "Sociology at the University of Kansas, 1889–1993." *Sociological Quarterly* 24:605–623.
2007. "Defining Disciplinary Identity: The Historiography of U.S. Sociology." In *Sociology in America: A History*, ed. Craig Calhoun. Chicago: University of Chicago Press, 713–731.
Sica, Alan, and Stephen Turner, eds. 2005. *A Disobedient Generation: Social Theorists in the Sixties*. Chicago: University of Chicago Press.
Sills, David, ed. 1968. *International Encyclopedia of the Social Sciences*, 17 Vols. New York: Macmillan.
1979. *Biographical Supplement*. Vol. 18 of the *International Encyclopedia of the Social Sciences*. New York: Macmillan.
Sills, David, and Robert K. Merton, eds. 1990. *Social Science Quotations: Who Said What, When, and Where*. Vol. 19 of the *International Encyclopedia of the Social Sciences*. New York: Macmillan.
Sklansky, Jeffrey P. 2002. *The Soul's Economy: Market Society and Selfhood in American Thought, 1820–1920*. Chapel Hill: University of North Carolina Press.
Small, Albion. 1905. *General Sociology: An Exposition of the Main Development in Sociological Theory from Spencer to Ratzenhofer*. Chicago: University of Chicago Press.
1924. *Origins of Sociology*. Chicago: University of Chicago Press.
Smelser, Neil J., and Paul B. Baltes. 2001. *International Encyclopedia of the Social and Behavioral Sciences*, 26 Vols. New York: Elsevier.
Smith, Laurence. 1986. *Behaviorism and Logical Positivism*. Stanford, CA: Stanford University Press.
Smith, Mark C. 1994. *Social Science in the Crucible: The American Debate over Objectivity and Purpose, 1918–1941*. Durham, NC: Duke University Press.
Sorokin, Pitirim. 1928. *Contemporary Sociological Theories*. New York: Harper.
Steinmetz, George. 2005. "Scientific Authority and the Transition to Post-Fordism: The Plausibility of Positivism in U.S. Sociology since 1945." In *The Politics of Method in the Human Sciences*, ed. George Steinmetz. Durham, NC: Duke University Press, 275–323.
2007. "American Sociology before and after World War II: The (Temporary) Settling of a Disciplinary Field." In *Sociology in America: A History*, ed. Craig Calhoun. Chicago: University of Chicago Press, 314–366.

Stigler, Stephen. 1986. *The History of Statistics: The Measurement of Uncertainty before 1900*. Cambridge, MA: Harvard University Press.
Stocking, George W. 1968. *Race, Culture, and Evolution*. London: Free Press.
1987. *Victorian Anthropology*. New York: Free Press.
1995. *After Tylor*. Madison: University of Wisconsin Press.
Swedberg, Richard. 1991. *Schumpeter: A Biography*. Princeton, NJ: Princeton University Press.
Turner, Jonathan H. 1974. *The Structure of Sociological Theory*. Homewood, IL: Dorsey.
Turner, Stephen P. 1991. "The World of Academic Quantifiers: The Columbia University Family and its Connections." In *The Social Survey in Historical Perspective, 1880–1940*, ed. Martin Bulmer, Kevin Bales, and Kathryn Kish Sklar. Cambridge, MA: Cambridge University Press, 291–315.
Turner, Stephen P., and Jonathan H. Turner. 1990. *The Impossible Science: An Institutional Analysis of American Sociology*. Newbury Park, CA: Sage.
Vidich, Authur J., and Stanford M. Lyman. 1985. *American Sociology: Worldly Rejections of Religions and Their Directions*. New Haven, CT: Yale University Press.
Wagner, Peter. 2001. *A History and Theory of the Social Sciences*. London: Sage.
Weber, Max. 1968. *Economy and Society*, trans. Guenther Roth and Claus Wittich. New York: Bedminister Press.
Westbrook, Robert B. 1991. *John Dewey and American Democracy*. Ithaca, NY: Cornell University Press.
Yonay, Yuval P. 1998. *The Struggle over the Soul of Economics: Institutionalist and Neoclassical Economics in America between the Wars*. Princeton, NJ: Princeton University Press.
Zuckerman, Harriet. 2010. "On Sociological Semantics as an Evolving Research Program," In *Robert K. Merton: Sociology of Science and Sociology as Science*, ed. Craig Calhoun. New York: Columbia University Press, 253–275.

APPENDIX: SAMPLE JSTOR ARTICLES ON THE HISTORY OF SOCIOLOGY, 1945–2012

Panel i: 1945–1969

Znaniecki, Florian. 1945. "Controversies in Doctrine and Method," *American Journal of Sociology* 6:515–521.

Boran, Behice. 1947. "Sociology in Retrospect," *American Journal of Sociology* 52:312–320.

Hinkle, Gisela. 1952. "The 'Four Wishes' In Thomas' Theory Of Social Change," *Social Research* 19:464–484.

Timasheff, N. S. 1952. "Comte in Retrospect," *The American Catholic Sociological Review* 13:224–234.

O'Dea, Thomas F. 1954. "The Sociology of Religion," *The American Catholic Sociological Review* 15:73–103.

Bennett, John W. and Kurt H. Wolff. 1955. "Toward Communication between Sociology and Anthropology," *Yearbook of Anthropology*: 329–351.

Habenstein, Robert W. 1955. "From Secular to Sectarian? Some Reflections on the Theory of Talcott Parsons," *The Midwest Sociologist* 17:19–27.

Jeffery, Clarence Ray. 1956. "Crime, Law and Social Structure. Part I: Methodology," *The Journal of Criminal Law, Criminology, and Police Science* 47:423–435.

Alpert, Harry. 1959. "Emile Durkheim: A Perspective and Appreciation," *American Sociological Review* 24:464–465.

Hauser, Philip M. 1959. "Demography in Relation to Sociology," *American Journal of Sociology* 65:169–173.

Freedman, Maurice. 1962. "Sociology in and of China," *The British Journal of Sociology* 13:106–116.

Benet, Francisco. 1963. "Sociology Uncertain: The Ideology of the Rural-Urban Continuum," *Comparative Studies in Society and History* 6:1–23.

Kolegar, Ferdinand. 1964. The Concept of 'Rationalization' and Cultural Pessimism in Max Weber's Sociology," *The Sociological Quarterly* 5:366–373.

Tiryakian, Edward A. 1965. "Existential Phenomenology and the Sociological Tradition," *American Sociological Review* 30:674–688.

Mitzman, Arthur. 1966. "Anti-Progress: A Study in the Romantic Roots Of German Sociology," *Social Research* 33:65–85.

Wertheim, W. F. 1967. "Sociology between Yesterday and Tomorrow," *Comparative Studies in Society and History* 9:180–189.

Forcese, Dennis P. 1968. "Calvinism, Capitalism and Confusion: The Weberian Thesis Revisited," *Sociological Analysis* 29:193–201.

Panel ii: 1970–1999

Shils, Edward. 1970. "Tradition, Ecology, and Institution in the History of Sociology," *Daedalus* 99:760–825.

Kienzle, Harry J. 1971. "The History of Social Thought and the History of Sociology," *Sociological Focus* 4:78–87.

Sibley, Elbridge. 1971. "Scientific Sociology at Bay?" *The American Sociologist* 6:13–17.
Bryant, C. G. A. 1972. "Sociology and Socialism in Poland—a View from the West." *Social Research* 39:102–133.
Curtis, James E., and John W. Petras. 1972. "The Sociology of Sociology: Some Lines of Inquiry in the Study of the Discipline." *The Sociological Quarterly* 13:197–209.
Goodwin, Glenn A. 1973. "The Emergence of Various Theoretical Trends and Their Prospects in Sociology," *Sociological Focus* 6:1–9.
Mullins, Nicholas. 1973. "The Development of Specialties in Social Science: The Case of Ethnomethodology," *Science Studies* 3:245–273.
Dynes, Russell R. 1974. "Sociology as a Religious Movement: Thoughts on Its Institutionalization in the United States," *The American Sociologist* 9:169–176.
Etzkorn, K. Peter. 1974. "On Music, Social Structure and Sociology," *International Review of The Aesthetics and Sociology of Music* 5:43–49.
Garrett, William R. 1974. "Troublesome Transcendence: The Supernatural in the Scientific Study of Religion," *Sociological Analysis* 35:167–180.
Gibbons, Don C. 1974. "Say, Whatever Became of Maurice Parmelee, Anyway?" *The Sociological Quarterly* 15:405–416.
Griffin, C. M. 1974. "L. T. Hobhouse and the Idea of Harmony," *Journal of the History of Ideas* 35:647–661.
Mariz, George. 1974. "L. T. Hobhouse as a Theoretical Sociologist," *Albion: A Quarterly Journal Concerned with British Studies* 6:307–319.
Allcock, J. B. 1975. "Sociology and History: The Yugoslav Experience and Its Implications," *The British Journal of Sociology* 26:486–500.
Janowitz, Morris. 1975. "Sociological Theory and Social Control," *American Journal of Sociology* 81:82–108.
Ferrarotti, Franco. 1976. "Preliminary Remarks on the Interaction between American and European Social Science," *Social Research* 43:25–45.
Green, Dan S., and Edwin D. Driver. 1976. "W. E. B. DuBois: A Case in the Sociology of Sociological Negation," 1976. *Phylon (1960–)* 37:308–333.
Levine, Donald N., Ellwood B. Carter, and Eleanor Miller Gorman. 1976. "Simmel's Influence on American Sociology. I," *American Journal of Sociology* 81:1112–1132.
Lammers, Cornelis J. 1978. "The Comparative Sociology of Organizations," *Annual Review of Sociology* 4:485–510.
Lengermann, Patricia Madoo. 1979. "The Founding of the American Sociological Review: The Anatomy of a Rebellion," *The American Sociologist* 44:185–198.
Reitzes, Donald C. 1980. "Beyond the Looking Glass Self: Cooley's Social Self and Its Treatment in Introductory Textbooks," *Contemporary Sociology* 9:631–640.
Bottomore, Tom. 1981. "A Marxist Consideration of Durkheim," *Social Forces* 59:902–917.
Coenen, Herman. 1981. "Developments in the Phenomenological Reading of Durkheim's Work," *Social Forces* 59:951–965.
Deegan, Mary Jo. 1981. "Early Women Sociologists and the American Sociological Society: The Patterns of Exclusion and Participation," *The American Sociologist* 16:14–24.
Hunt, Alan. 1981. "Dichotomy and Contradiction in the Sociology of Law," *British Journal of Law and Society* 8:47–77.
Lemert, Charles C. "Literary Politics and the 'Champ' of French Sociology," *Theory and Society* 10:393–410.

Honneth, Axel, and Mitchell G. Ash. 1982. "Work and Instrumental Action," *New German Critique* 26:31–54.
Noble, Trevor. 1982. "Recent Sociology, Capitalism and the Coming Crisis," *The British Journal of Sociology* 33:238–53.
Pipping, Knut. 1982. "The First Finnish Sociologist: A Reappraisal of Edward Westermarck's Work," *Acta Sociologica* 25:347–357.
Segre, Sandro. 1982. "Pareto and Weber a Tentative Reconstruction of Their Intellectual Relationship with an Excursus on Pareto and the German Language," *Revue europeenne des sciences sociales* 20:247–271.
Soffer, Reba N. 1982. "Why Do Disciplines Fail? The Strange Case of British Sociology," *The English Historical Review* 97:767–802.
Harvey, Charles E. 1983. "Robert S. Lynd, John D. Rockefeller, Jr., and Middletown," *Indiana Magazine of History* 79:330–354.
McGuire, Patrick, and Kenneth Dawes. 1983. "Sociology as Social Contribution: University of North Dakota as a Case Study of the Contradictions of Academic Sociology," *The Sociological Quarterly* 24:589–603.
Orru, Marco. 1983. "The Ethics of Anomie: Jean Marie Guyau and Émile Durkheim," *The British Journal of Sociology* 34:499–518.
Gabel, Joseph. 1984. "Durkheimianism and Political Alienation: Durkheim and Marx," *The Canadian Journal of Sociology* 9:179–189.
Oliver, Ivan. 1984. "Current Revivals of Interest in Religion: Some Sociological Observations," *Archives de sciences sociales des religions* 29:159–174.
Pipping, Knut. 1984. "Who Reads Westermarck Today?" *The British Journal of Sociology* 35:315–332.
Fine, Gary Alan, and Janet S. Severance. 1985. "Great Men and Hard Times: Sociology at the University of Minnesota," *The Sociological Quarterly* 26:117–134.
Ritzer, George. 1985. "The Rise of Micro-Sociological Theory," *Sociological Theory* 3:89–98.
Hilbert, Richard A. 1986. "Anomie and the Moral Regulation of Reality: The Durkheimian Tradition in Modern Relief," *Sociological Theory* 4:1–19.
Winter, Michael F. and Ellen R. Robert. 1986. "A Swift Backward Glance: Thirty Years of the BJS," *Berkeley Journal of Sociology* 31:201–214.
Bisztray, George. 1987. "The Controversy over Value Neutrality in Sociology and Literature," *Comparative Literature Studies* 24:40–57.
Hadden, Jeffrey K. 1987. "Toward Desacralizing Secularization Theory," *Social Forces* 65:587–611.
Schwartz, Mildred A. 1987. "Historical Sociology in the History of American Sociology," *Social Science History* 11:1–16.
Alexander, Jeffrey C. 1988. "Parsons' 'Structure' in American Sociology," *Sociological Theory* 6:96–102.
Baker, Paul J. 1988. "Sociology Textbooks: Managing Clones or Writing Works of Distinction," *Teaching Sociology* 16:381–383.
Boudon, Raymond. 1988. "Will Sociology Ever be a 'Normal Science'?" *Theory and Society* 17:747–771.
Dahme, Heinz-Jurgen. 1988. "On Georg Simmel's Sociology of the Sexes," *International Journal of Politics, Culture, and Society* 1:412–430.
Deegan, Mary Jo. 1988. "W. E. B. Du Bois and the Women of Hull-House, 1895–1899," *The American Sociologist* 19:301–311.

Farber, Bernard. 1988. "The Human Element: Sociology at Chicago," *Sociological Perspectives* 31:339–359.

Helmes-Hayes, Richard C. 1988. "The Image of Inequality in S. D. Clark's Writings on Pioneer Canadian Society," *The Canadian Journal of Sociology* 13:211–233.

Restivo, Sal. 1988" Modern Science as a Social Problem," *Social Problems* 35:206–225.

Turner, Jonathan H., and Alexandra R. Maryanski. 1988. "Sociology's Lost Human Relations Subfield Files," *Sociological Perspectives* 31:19–34.

Agger, Ben. 1989. "Do Books Write Authors? A Study of Disciplinary Hegemony," *Teaching Sociology* 17:365–369.

Bulmer, Martin. 1989. "Theory and Method in Recent British Sociology: Whither the Empirical Impulse?" *The British Journal of Sociology* 40:393–417.

Levine, Donald N. 1989. "Simmel as a Resource for Sociological Metatheory." *Sociological Theory* 7:161–174.

Platt, Tony. 1989. "E. Franklin Frazier Reconsidered," *Social Justice* 16:198–195.

Sica, Alan. 1989. "Social Theory's 'Constituency,'" *The American Sociologist* 20:227–241.

Swatos Jr., William H. 1989. "Religious Sociology and the Sociology of Religion in America at the Turn of the Twentieth Century: Divergences from a Common Theme," *Sociological Analysis* 50:363–375.

Busino Giovanni. 1990. "Sociology in Crisis," *Revue européenne des sciences sociales* 88:55–75.

Jaworski, Gary Dean. 1990. "Robert K. Merton's Extension of Simmel's Ubersehbar," *Sociological Theory* 8:99–105.

Laslett, Barbara. 1990. "Unfeeling Knowledge: Emotion and Objectivity in the History of Sociology," *Sociological Forum* 5:413–433.

Nemedi, Denes. 1990. "Durkheim and the 'Strong Programme' in the Philosophy of Science," *Revue européenne des sciences sociales* 28:55–75.

Hall, Robert T. 1991. "Communitarian Ethics and the Sociology of Morals: Alasdair MacIntyre and Emile Durkheim," *Sociological Focus* 24:93–104.

Laslett, Barbara. 1991. "Biography as Historical Sociology: The Case of William Fielding Ogburn," *Theory and Society* 20:511–538.

Peters, Barbara J. 1991. "Disparate Voices: The Magic Show of Sociology," *The American Sociologist* 22:246–260.

Laslett, Barbara. 1992. "Gender in/and Social Science History," *Social Science History* 16:177–195.

Nishihara, Kazuhisa. 1992. "Schutz in Japan: A Brief History," *Human Studies* 15:17–34.

Straus, Murray A. 1992. "Sociological Research and Social Policy: The Case of Family Violence," *Sociological Forum* 7:211–237.

Sulek, Antoni, and Barbara Mlynarz-Pomorska. 1992. "The Rise And Decline of Survey Sociology in Poland," *Social Research* 59:365–384.

Weinberg, Elizabeth A. 1992. "Perestroika and Soviet Sociology," *The British Journal of Sociology* 43:1–10.

Fine, Gary Alan. 1993. "The Sad Demise, Mysterious Disappearance, and Glorious Triumph of Symbolic Interactionism," *Annual Review of Sociology* 19:61–87.

Henking, Susan E. 1993. "Sociological Christianity and Christian Sociology: The Paradox of Early American Sociology," *Religion and American Culture: A Journal of Interpretation* 3:49–67.

Keen, Mike F. 1993. "No One above Suspicion: Talcott Parsons under Surveillance," *The American Sociologist* 24:37–54.
Nielson, Donald A. 1993. "A Gothic Sociology of Modern Civilization," *International Journal of Politics, Culture, and Society* 7:109–120.
Helmes-Hayes, Richard C. 1994. "Canadian Sociology's First Textbook: C. A. Dawson and W. E. Gettys's An Introduction to Sociology (1929)," *The Canadian Journal of Sociology* 19:461–497.
Birnbaum, Pierre. 1995. "French Jewish Sociologists between Reason and Faith: The Impact of the Dreyfus Affair," *Jewish Social Studies* 2:1–35.
Livingstone, David W. 1995. "Searching for Missing Links: Neo-Marxist Theories of Education," *British Journal of Sociology of Education* 16:53–73.
Merton, Robert K., and Alan Wolfe. 1995. "The Cultural and Social Incorporation of Sociological Knowledge," *The American Sociologist* 26:15–39.
Platt, Jennifer. 1995. "The United States Reception of Durkheim's 'The Rules of Sociological Method'" *Sociological Perspectives* 38:77–105.
Quah, Stella R. 1995. "Beyond the Known Terrain: Sociology in Singapore," *The American Sociologist* 26:88–106.
Sica, Alan. 1995. "A Sociology Archive and the Discipline's Future," *The American Sociologist* 26:70–77.
1995. "Gabel's 'Micro/Macro' Bridge: The Schizophrenic Process Writ Large," *Sociological Theory* 13:69–99.
Siemens, Robert Peter. 1995. "Henry George: An Unrecognized Contributor to American Social Theory," *The American Journal of Economics and Sociology* 54:107–127.
Smith, R. S. 1995. "Giving Credit Where Credit Is Due: Dorothy Swaine Thomas and the 'Thomas Theorem,'" *The American Sociologist* 26:9–28.
Alexander, Jeffrey C., and Sciortino, Giuseppe. 1996. "On Choosing One's Intellectual Predecessors: The Reductionism of Camic's Treatment of Parsons and the Institutionalists," *Sociological Theory* 14:154–171.
Chapoulie, Jean-Michel. 1996. "Everett Hughes and the Chicago Tradition," *Sociological Theory* 14:3–29.
Emirbayer, Mustafa. 1996. "Useful Durkheim," *Sociological Theory* 14:109–130.
Gerhardt, Uta. 1996. "Scholarship, Not Scandal," *Sociological Forum* 11:623–630.
Fararo, Thomas J. 1997. "Reflections on Mathematical Sociology," *Sociological Forum* 12:73–101.
Weinstein, Jay. 1997. "Applied Sociology Is the Answer, but What Was the Question?" *Michigan Sociological Review* 11:18–40.
Camic, Charles, and Neil Gross. 1998. "Contemporary Developments in Sociological Theory: Current Projects and Conditions of Possibility," *Annual Review of Sociology* 24:453–476.
Helmes-Hayes, Richard C. 1998. "Everett Hughes: Theorist of the Second Chicago School," *International Journal of Politics, Culture, and Society* 11:621–673.
Johnston, Barry V. 1998. "The Contemporary Crisis and the Social Relations Department at Harvard: A Case Study in Hegemony and Disintegration," *The American Sociologist* 29:26–42.
Martin, John Levi. 1998. "Authoritative Knowledge and Heteronomy in Classical Sociological Theory," *Sociological Theory* 16:99–130.

Rynbrandt, Linda J. 1998. "Caroline Bartlett Crane and the History of Sociology: Salvation, Sanitation, and the Social Gospel," *The American Sociologist* 29:71–82.
Finlay, Barbara. 1999. "Lester Frank Ward as a Sociologist of Gender: A New Look at His Sociological Work," *Gender and Society* 2:251–265.

Panel iii: 2000–2012

Allardt, Erik. 2000. "Edward Westermarck: A Sociologist Relating Nature and Culture," *Acta Sociologica* 43:299–306.
Buxton, William J. 2000. "Talcott Parsons and Japan in the 1970s," *The American Sociologist* 31:32–42.
Ekerwald, Hedvig. 2000. "Alva Myrdal: Making the Private Public," *Acta Sociologica* 43:343–352.
Hall, Elaine J. 2000. "Packaging Poverty as an Intersection of Class, Race, and Gender in Introductory Textbooks, 1982 to 1994," *Teaching Sociology*.
Tiryakian, Edward A. 2000," Parsons' Emergent Durkheims." *Sociological Theory* 18:60–83.
Mineva, Emilia, and Regina Raycheva. 2001. "On the Reception of Marxism in Bulgaria," *Studies in East European Thought* 53:61–74.
Samman, Khaldoun. 2001. "The Limits of the Classical Comparative Method," *Review (Fernand Braudel Center)*.
Shain, Farzana, and Jenny Ozga. 2001. "Identity Crisis? Problems and Issues in the Sociology of Education," *British Journal of Sociology of Education* 22:109–120.
Swedberg, Richard. 2001. "Sociology and Game Theory: Contemporary and Historical Perspectives," *Theory and Society*.
Wargon, Sylvia T. 2001. "Connections: Demography and Sociology in Twentieth Century Canada," *Canadian Journal of Sociology*.
Gerhardt, Uta. 2002. "Worlds Come Apart: Systems Theory versus Critical Theory. Drama in the History of Sociology in the Twentieth Century," *The American Sociologist* 33:5–39.
Grant, Linda, Marybeth C. Stalp, and Kathryn B Ward. 2002. "Women's Sociological Research and Writing in the 'AJS' in the Pre-World War II Era," *The American Sociologist* 33:69–91.
Helmes-Hayes, Rick. 2002. "John Porter: Canada's Most Famous Sociologist (and His Links to American Sociology)," *The American Sociologist* 33:79–104.
Lengermann, Patricia Madoo, and Jill Niebrugge-Brantley. 2002. "Back to the Future: Settlement Sociology, 1885–1930," *The American Sociologist* 33:5–20.
Richardson, Barbara. 2002. "Ellen Swallow Richards: 'Humanistic Oekologist,' 'Applied Sociologist,' and the Founding of Sociology," *The American Sociologist* 33:21–57.
Rynbrandt, Linda J., and Mary Jo Deegan. 2002. "The Ecofeminist Pragmatism of Caroline Bartlett Crane, 1896–1935," *The American Sociologist* 33:58–68.
Steinmetz, George, and Ou-Byung Chae. 2002. "Sociology in an Era of Fragmentation: From the Sociology of Knowledge to the Philosophy of Science, and Back Again," *The Sociological Quarterly* 43:111–137.
Deegan, Mary Jo. 2003. "Textbooks, the History of Sociology, and the Sociological Stock of Knowledge," *Sociological Theory* 21:298–305.

Pols, Hans. 2003. "Anomie in the Metropolis: The City in American Sociology and Psychiatry," *Osiris* 18:194–211.

Keith, Bruce, and Morten G. Ender. 2004. "The Sociological Core: Conceptual Patterns and Idiosyncrasies in the Structure and Content of Introductory Sociology Textbooks, 1940–2000," *Teaching Sociology* 32:19–36.

Lyon, E. Stina. 2004. "Researching Race Relations: Myrdal's American Dilemma from a Methodological Perspective," *Acta Sociologica* 47:203–217.

Nock, David. 2004. "The Myth about 'Myths of the Chicago School': Evidence from Floyd Nelson House," *The American Sociologist* 35:63–79.

Zerilli, Filippo M. 2004. "'Du déménagement comme coupure épistémologique.' Durkheim and Ethnographical Sources," *Revue européenne des sciences sociales* 42:349–361.

Coghlan, Catherine L. 2005. "Please Don't Think of Me as a Sociologist: Sophonisba Preston Breckinridge and the Early Chicago School," *The American Sociologist* 36:3–22.

McLaughlin, Neil, Lisa Kowalchuk, and Kerry Turcotte. 2005. "Why Sociology Does Not Need to Be Saved: Analytic Reflections on Public Sociologies," *The American Sociologist* 36:27–45.

Richard Swedberg. 2005. "Can There Be a Sociological Concept of Interest?" *Theory and Society* 34:359–390.

Steinmetz, George. 2005. "The Genealogy of a Positivist Haunting: Comparing Prewar and Postwar U.S. Sociology," *boundary 2* 32:109–135.

Williams, Joyce E., and Vicky M. MacLean. 2005. "Studying Ourselves: Sociology Discipline-Building in the United States," *The American Sociologist* 36:111–133.

Borch, Christian. 2006. "Crowds and Pathos: Theodor Geiger on Revolutionary Action," *Acta Sociologica* 49:5–18.

Scannel, Paddy. 2006. "Personal Influence and the End of the Masses," *Annals of the American Academy of Political and Social Science* 608:115–129.

Scheuch, Erwin K. 2006 (Reprinted from 1980). "Quantitative Analysis of Historical Material as the Basis for a New Cooperation Between History and Sociology (1980)," *Historical Social Research* 18:63–82.

Turner, Jonathan H. 2006. "American Sociology in Chaos: Differentiation without Integration," *The American Sociologist* 37:15–29.

Jacobs, Jerry A. 2007. "Further Reflections on ASR's Greatest Hits," *The American Sociologist* 38:99–131.

Sallaz, Jeffrey J., and Jane Zavisca. 2007. "Bourdieu in American Sociology, 1980–2004," *Annual Review of Sociology* 3:21–41.

Wark, Colin, and John F. Galliher. 2007. "Emory Bogardus and the Origins of the Social Distance Scale," *The American Sociologist* 38:383–395.

Oromaner, Mark. 2008. "Intellectual Integration and Articles in Core Sociology Journals, 1960–2000," *The American Sociologist* 39:279–289.

Misztal, Barbara A. 2009. "A Nobel Trinity: Jane Addams, Emily Greene Balch and Alva Myrdal," *The American Sociologist* 40:332–352.

5

History of Psychology since 1945

A North American Review

James H. Capshew

To underline the major claim of his 1929 *A History of Experimental Psychology*, Edwin Boring repeated Hermann Ebbinghaus's remark, made in 1908, that "psychology has a long past, but only a short history" (Boring 1929, p. vii). Such a comment could warrant appropriation of any of the relevant Western intellectual traditions for the new scientific approach. All of the fields that became new social science disciplines in the late nineteenth century could claim similar intellectual genealogies extending back to Aristotle, which provided not only a useful legacy but also a convenient contrast with their declarations of scientific aspirations. Although their specific histories emphasized different thinkers and ideas, the nascent disciplines needed histories to provide markers of identity and to bolster claims to legitimacy and relevance.

A usable past was constructed by and for psychologists in the midst of their professionalizing project. Emphasizing the breadth and the depth of philosophical thinking about mind since the Greeks and the rise of experimental science, particularly physiology, in the nineteenth century, a narrative of scientific progress was created (e.g., Brett 1912–21). By the late 1920s, competing histories revealed disciplinary fault lines about aims and approaches as the field contended with growth and diversification. "History, with its developmental logic, offered a way to integrate an epistemologically unruly field and an alternate means of defining a disciplinary identity" (Capshew 1999, p. 24). In the United States, where the discipline took root most vigorously, the Great Depression ushered in a decade of academic retrenchment and competition for resources. On the eve of World War II, one psychologist noted that the discipline was facing its "impending dismemberment" along ideological, organizational, and generational lines (Klüver 1949).

In the postwar period, American psychology experienced sustained exponential growth and its incorporation into nearly every facet of modern life (see Herman 1995; Capshew 1999). The history of psychology became a scholarly specialty in the 1960s, when American psychology became an influential if not the dominant idiom for professional discourse and practice in much of the world. This is the reason why this chapter, though it does draw in European work where necessary, concentrates on North American developments, focusing on scholarly contributions, with some attention paid to pedagogy and university textbooks. Although it is still little noticed by most professional psychologists, historical analysis and narrative offer perspectives and reflections on the complex and often surprising past. Ideas, theories and concepts, social and political engagements, institutional developments, and cultural influences are but a few of the main categories that the history of psychology encompasses.

The history of psychoanalysis complicates this picture. Considered as a major tributary of psychological knowledge, its history has been bound up with the peculiar features of its institutionalization, professionalization, and popularization. Psychoanalysis, as a body of theory and of practice, is closely identified with the work of Sigmund Freud and his associates. It emerged within the psychiatric specialty of the medical profession in the United States, mostly practiced by medical doctors with a few lay analysts. For much of the twentieth century, psychoanalysis carved its own channel, commingling upon occasion with the experimental psychology mainstream and its shadow, applied psychology, and psychologists were also exposed to psychoanalytic ideas from the general culture. More recently, as historians of psychoanalysis replace their assumptions of exceptionalism with a commitment to symmetrical analysis, there are encouraging signs of a rapprochement with history of psychology.

In addition to designating a field of study, history of psychology since 1945 can refer to historical writing on psychological subjects after World War II. As a chronologically bounded subset of the scholarly field, it has exhibited significant trends and emphases that will be discussed in the concluding section.

The development of the specialty can be divided roughly into three major periods. During the first, from 1945 to the late 1960s, the field coalesced around a shared interest in history on the part of scientific and professional psychologists. These individuals, assisted by a few professional historians, created scholarly societies, publication outlets, and archival resources. American psychology was growing rapidly, aided by effective organization during World War II, and there was a low threshold to achieve specialty status. The next period, lasting until the early 1990s, saw increasing diversity in recruitment to the field, a self-conscious turn to critical historiography, and a measure of academic establishment. During the past twenty-odd years, the academic fortunes of self-identified practitioners have been bound to the institutional fluctuations of higher education even as intellectual standards have been elevated and scholarly work of great historical depth and nuance has been produced. It remains a small part of the psychology discipline but it has also attained respectable status within the history of science field. Whether this arrangement will prove sustainable is an open question.[1]

Old Wine in New Bottles

World War II buoyed the fortunes of American psychology, causing an exponential growth in the protean discipline. Incorporating clinical psychology into the American Psychological Association in 1945 set the stage for the eventual dominance of professional psychologists over the experimentalists twenty-five years later, although both groups looked to scientific psychology as their common ancestor. Higher education and university-based research were also burgeoning in the United States, fueled by funds from the federal government, during the quarter-century following the Second World War. Psychologists had a collective sense that the recent war put "psychology on the map" of scientific respectability and professional salience. In the closing year of the war, the National Research Council authorized a Committee on the History of Psychology and the War, to document the discipline's

[1] On the importance of specifying emplacement for historians, see Danziger (1997a). My historiographical point of view has been shaped by my educational career and training, professional employment, and choices of research topics and approaches. In the late 1970s, I was an undergraduate majoring in psychology with a minor in philosophy at a Midwest public research university. Through the first half of the 1980s I studied for my doctorate at an elite private university in the urban East, in a department that prided itself on even-handed analysis of both the content and context of post-Enlightenment science, technology, and medicine. In 1990 I joined the faculty of Indiana University, in the Department of History and Philosophy of Science, where I remain as the sole historian concentrating on the human sciences, in America, during the twentieth century. Much of my research and publication dealt with the impact of World War II on psychology in the United States. I began attending professional meetings (regularly the Cheiron Society and the History of Science Society, occasionally the American Psychological Association and the American Historical Association, sporadically others) starting in 1980, and have been a participant in organizational affairs, serving as Editor of the journal *History of Psychology* from 2006 to 2009, as well as an interested observer for more than three decades.

achievements and review lessons learned. Elaborate plans were made for research and publication, but the principals found themselves pulled in other directions. It seems that psychologists were too busy creating a glorious future for the discipline to spend time on recounting past accomplishments, and the committee died quietly.

In the main, the history of psychology that emerged in the five years following the war had its origins in the interwar period. The Columbia functionalist Robert Woodworth's *Contemporary Schools of Psychology*, first published in 1931, came out in a lightly revised edition in 1948. Taken from his lecture notes, the book went through functional and structural psychology, associationism, behaviorism, gestalt, psychoanalysis, and hormic and holistic psychologies. The last chapter, "The Middle of the Road," contained his renewed plea for accepting the plural nature of the field (Woodworth 1948). In 1949, Gardner Murphy, a social psychologist at Columbia, published a revised version of his popular textbook, *An Historical Introduction to Modern Psychology* (1929). Attempting to place psychology in its social and cultural context, Murphy provided a readable narrative of the antecedents of modern psychology and the history of experimental psychology, coupled with a review of prominent systems of psychology (behaviorism, associationism, gestalt, field theory, Freudianism) and some representative research areas. Murphy (1949) recognized the existence of three major movements or approaches to psychology – as a natural science, a cultural science, and an arena for application.[2]

In 1950, the Harvard psychologist Edwin Boring published the second edition of his masterwork, *A History of Experimental Psychology* (1929). Major changes included a new chapter, "Dynamic Psychology," which he defined as the psychology of motivation that included Pierre Janet, Freud, psychoanalysis, and purposive psychology, among other topics. More important was his revised historical framework. Boring had moved away from his earlier reliance on the great-man theory of history by juxtaposing it to the influence of the Zeitgeist.

In 1939, less than a month after the Second World War started, Sigmund Freud died. For decades, he had promoted an authorized version of the origins and development of psychoanalysis, jealously protecting his priority claims and policing the borders of his movement. After his death, his daughter, Anna Freud, a psychoanalyst in her own right, became the chief

[2] Interestingly, he made reference to what is now known as reflexivity. He predicted that the "relativity approach," in which "the observer himself is an aspect of the whole field observed," will become more common in the next few years (Murphy 1949, p. 433).

promoter and enforcer of orthodoxy as she gathered loyal associates around her. Among those reliable associates were the neurologist and psychoanalyst Ernest Jones, who produced the official biography, *Sigmund Freud: Life and Work* (3 volumes; 1953–7), and translator James Strachey, who oversaw publication of the *Standard Edition of the Complete Psychological Works of Sigmund Freud* (24 volumes; 1956–74). These served as key texts, to supporters and detractors alike (Jones 1953–7; Freud 1953–74).

Republication and revision of existing texts from the interwar period underlined the minor role that the history of psychology played during the immediate postwar period. In the late 1920s and early 1930s, as psychology was struggling for scientific legitimacy and professional relevance, differing views of history competed for dominance. At stake were psychology's self-identification, relations to other sciences, and acculturation of recruits. The postwar repurposing of texts of Woodworth, Murphy, and Boring underlined the extent to which history seemed irrelevant to the regnant discipline. Struggles for psychology's scientific legitimacy and academic status were seemingly rendered superfluous by the war, replaced by a fervent wish for professional advancement and social relevance in the postwar period.

An Organization Man

One of the main proponents of the history of psychology specialty was Robert I. Watson, a 1938 Columbia psychology Ph.D. graduate and self-trained clinical psychologist. His first foray into historical writing was a long article in the *Psychological Bulletin* in 1953, entitled "A Brief History of Clinical Psychology." Completely on the basis of published sources, he surveyed the "men and ideas" that shaped clinical psychology; its style was akin to an extended background section of a scientific paper. Watson reported in his autobiography that this article, in contrast to his other publications, struck "a responsive chord" among psychologists, and by 1959 he decided to focus his research activities on the history of psychology (Brožek and Evans 1977, p. 13). Whatever his reputation as a scholar, Watson was an organizer.

He discovered an essential ally in John Burnham, who had completed his 1958 dissertation, "Psychoanalysis in American Civilization before 1918," in the Stanford University History Department (see Burnham 1967). Trained in the new interdisciplinarity of American studies, Burnham took a fresh approach to the emerging specialty with his deeply historicist stance as well as connections to the history of medicine. He had a three-year postdoctoral fellowship from Foundations' Fund for Research in Psychiatry that allowed study and research into the history of mental health. He took his fellowship at the Austen Riggs Center, a private clinical treatment and research facility in Massachusetts that was a noted center of psychoanalytic ego psychology. Watson and Burnham started exchanging letters and visits in 1959 and soon drew the psychologists David Bakan and Dale Dick, both at the University of Missouri, into the planning circle.[3]

Burnham was also in touch with the psychiatric historian Eric T. Carlson, of the Department of Psychiatry of the New York Hospital (Payne Whitney Psychiatric Clinic) – Cornell University Medical College. In 1958, Carlson launched the History of Psychiatry Section (later known as the Institute for the History of Psychiatry) to serve both scholars and medical students. The following year he started publishing the *History of the Behavioral Sciences Newsletter.* The introduction to the first issue of the *Newsletter* announced its broad audience: "all those interested in the history of any of the behavioral sciences" whether for historical research, bibliographic activities, or general study, including anthropologists, psychiatrists, psychologists, sociologists, biologists, neurologists, historians, and any others working in this area. The *Newsletter*'s mission was equally capacious: to identify and foster communication among people working in this field and to explore relevant bibliographical resources (Carlson and Watson 1965, p. 3).

Burnham, Watson, Bakan, and Dick compiled a list of American Psychological Association (APA) members who were interested in the history of psychology, and plans were made to gather interested parties together at the 1959 APA convention. (Burnham shared the APA list with Carlson for his *Newsletter.*) With the convention less than a month off, however, plans changed when Bakan and Burnham could not attend. The group decided to postpone the general meeting to the 1960 APA convention, scheduled for Chicago, giving them additional time to publicize their plans.[4]

In October 1959, Burnham published a short comment, "Preserving Historical Materials," in the *American Psychologist*, lamenting the general lack of manuscript resources for the history of psychology. Appealing to the pride of U.S. psychologists upon attaining world leadership in the discipline by World War II, he cautioned that "now records of this heroic age of American psychology are fast disappearing, and the future worker in history who attempts to chronicle and assess the course of the science and its role in civilization will have little with which to work except for surviving published writings. Personal papers, the chief sources of a rich history,

[3] Bakan had published the book *Sigmund Freud and the Jewish Mystical Tradition* in 1958.

[4] Burnham to Carlson, June 5, 1959; Burnham to Carlson, July 16, 1959; Burnham to Watson, July 21, 1959; and Burnham to Bakan, Dick, and Watson, August 9, 1959. Courtesy of John C. Burnham.

are scarce and neglected" (Burnham 1959, p. 655). In April 1960, Watson published an article, "The History of Psychology: A Neglected Area," in the *American Psychologist*. He defined history of psychology as

> a study of long-time cultural trends over time. Psychological contributions are embedded in the social context from which they emerge. Psychology has always responded in part to its social environment, but it also has been guided by an internal logic of its own. We cannot emphasize one of these trends at the expense of the other. Psychology neither reflects culture with passive compliance nor does it exist in a social vacuum. External and internal circumstances are present, and there is a constant interplay between them. (Watson 1960, p. 254)

the *American Psychologist* publications in six months had the potential to advertise the existence of historical concerns to a wide swath of professional psychologists.

Watson, Burnham, and twenty-four others attended the history of psychology interest group meeting at the 1960 APA convention. After self-introductions, discussion identified three areas of concern: lack of publication outlets for historical papers, an absence of university training programs for history of psychology, and neglect of records and historical documents at the American Psychological Association. Burnham and Watson prepared a summary of the first meeting of what came to be known as the History of Psychology Group, making plans to meet the next year and to investigate possible sponsorship by a division of the APA. The mailing list grew to more than ninety individuals, including any APA members who listed history as an interest in the membership directory. Subsequent meetings of the History of Psychology Group were held yearly at the APA convention and a periodic newsletter facilitated communication among the group. The group catalyzed the APA Board of Directors to appoint an Ad Hoc Committee on Psychological Archives and was successful in having their concerns aired to the APA Council of Editors. In 1962, the group sponsored a symposium on the teaching of the history of psychology at the APA meeting. Included among its participants was Edwin Boring, who stopped by the business meeting of the history group (Mayer 1997, pp. 129–32).

In 1964 the History of Psychology Group met for the fifth time and decided to pursue APA divisional status, in spite of the fact that each of their meetings had attracted only twenty to thirty persons. The American Psychological Association, concerned about organizational fragmentation as authorized divisions proliferated to more than twenty, had recently placed additional requirements for prospective divisions. One of the most daunting hurdles was the submission of a petition that had the signatures of no less than 1 percent of the entire APA membership, which stood at more than eighteen thousand. Watson suggested the mailing lists for the History of Psychology Group and the *History of the Behavioral Sciences Newsletter* be canvassed for possible signers, which totaled around eight hundred names. The University of Oregon psychologist Richard Littman drafted a statement:

> The purpose of this organization shall be (a) to encourage and facilitate original scholarship in the history of psychology; and (b) to extend the awareness and appreciation of the history of psychology as an aid to the understanding of (1) contemporary psychology in its aims as a science, profession and means of promoting human welfare, (2) its relation to other scientific and scholarly fields, and (3) its role in society. (Mayer 1997, p. 136)

A total of 222 signatures were collected, and the APA Council voted to approve the new division, christened Division 26, at their 1965 annual meeting.[5] The first formal meeting was held the year following, and Watson was elected as president, Gardner Murphy president-elect, and John Popplestone, secretary-treasurer. Behind-the-scenes maneuvering instigated the selection of Edwin Boring as honorary president of the new division (Hilgard 1982).

A Journal Established

In January 1961, a few months after Watson sent out the first mailing of what would become the newsletter of the History of Psychology Group, he became Consulting Editor in Psychology to the *History of the Behavioral Sciences Newsletter*. Apparently, both Carlson and Watson harbored unspoken hopes to establish a historical journal. As a founder and shareholder of Psychology Press, a private publishing company, Watson broached the idea with them and received support. In the fall of 1962, he informed Carlson of the proposal and asked him to serve as coeditor. After some consideration, Carlson begged off, citing his heavy research commitments. The following year, Psychology Press agreed to provide financial backing to the proposed *Journal of the History of the Behavioral Sciences* (Carlson and Watson 1965). By that time, Watson had given up responsibility for the newsletter of the History of Psychology Group.

[5] Mayer (1997, p. 135) states: "In retrospect, the manner in which the division was formed reflected the changing times. There was no great groundswell demanding a history division. Less than a dozen persons seemed particularly motivated. It appears that a few activists managed to marshal support from a wide array of friends and colleagues. Most of the signatories were either sympathetic colleagues or dedicated scholars whose major commitments were to other more traditional fields of psychology."

At the 1964 APA meeting, when the History of Psychology Group decided to pursue divisional status, Watson displayed little enthusiasm initially. Writing autobiographically later, he explained:

> Quite deliberately, the group was without officers, due, or even an official name. Many of us found this state of affairs congenial. When the possibility of a formal division within the APA was first broached, I demurred. The argument that convinced me that such a step was necessary was the comment of one young psychologist to the effect that the division of the history of psychology would give the stamp of authenticity to work in this area – that it would help bring recognition that the history of psychology is a form of specialization. (Watson 1972, p. 288)

Watson was already busy assembling an editorial board for the *Journal of the History of the Behavioral Sciences*, drawing heavily upon the readers of the *History of the Behavioral Sciences Newsletter* as well as of the newsletter of the much smaller History of Psychology Group. The *Journal of the History of the Behavioral Sciences* (*JHBS*) began publishing at the beginning of 1965. An editorial, "The Birth of a Journal," preceded the first article in the inaugural issue. Carlson is credited with writing the statement, "amplified" by Watson (Carlson and Watson 1965).

In 1967, Watson's efforts at organizing the specialty culminated in his relocation to the University of New Hampshire, where he was a principal in the new history track in their graduate psychology program. That program was a source of trained psychologists-historians for many decades.

American Psychology Archives

The year 1965 turned out to be a signal year for the new specialty. In addition to the founding of Division 26 of the American Psychology Association and the establishment of the *Journal of the History of the Behavioral Sciences*, a major effort was made to address the preservation and access to historical source materials. Two clinical psychologists at the University of Akron, John A. Popplestone and Marian White McPherson, responded to conversations and concerns about preserving the letters and records of American psychologists in order to preserve the documentary basis of historical writing. Garnering sufficient administrative support from the University of Akron, McPherson and Popplestone established the Archives of the History of American Psychology in October 1965, to collect, preserve, and make accessible manuscript materials to support scholarship in the history of psychology. The mission was to collect records, mainly from individual psychologists, to document the history of the field. Although the archives grew slowly, it eventually became an important center for research. Within its first ten years, about fifty scholars and twenty-five graduate students did research there; their disciplinary location was evenly split between psychology and history (Popplestone and McPherson 1976).[6]

A Scathing Critique

In the midst of ongoing efforts to establish the specialty, Robert M. Young, a recent Ph.D. of the History and Philosophy of Science Department at Cambridge University, offered a scathing critique of the field's methods. In 1966, working as a University Assistant Lecturer in Cambridge, he published a fifty-page essay in *History of Science*. Reviewing recent work as well as older publications, Young took historians of behavioral science (the bulk of them in history of psychology) to task for lax standards of scholarship, confusion about historiography, and "an extraordinarily naïve positivism" (Young 1966, p. 17).

Young, born and reared in Dallas, Texas, received his undergraduate education at Yale University and started medical school at the University of Rochester, but decamped to Cambridge in 1960. Working with the psychologist Oliver Zangwill and faculty in Cambridge's excellent History and Philosophy of Science Department, in 1964 he obtained perhaps the first doctorate in the history of psychology.[7] He became a Fellow and Graduate Tutor of King's College, and later the Director of the Wellcome Unit for the History of Medicine, before leaving academic life in 1976 for a career as a public intellectual.[8]

Many years later he admitted that he behaved arrogantly as a "Young Turk" in the lengthy review – his first substantial scholarly publication – with the egocentric mission of promoting the "One True Highest Standard."[9] Young's later apologies notwithstanding, the review provides a convenient

[6] Hurley (2005) gives the following account of AHAP's origins: "Forced to teach a course in the history of psychology, Dr. Popplestone casually said to his wife [McPherson] one evening that the field would never amount to anything without a central archive. He recalled her saying, 'That's the best idea you've had in quite a while.'" In 2010, the AHAP gave rise to the Center for the History of Psychology, including a Museum of Psychology, which provides scholarly support and educational programming. See also Faye and Baker, 2011.

[7] His dissertation was published in 1970 by Oxford University Press, under the title *Mind, Brain, and Adaptation in the Nineteenth Century: Cerebral Localization and Its Biological Context from Gall to Ferrier.*

[8] See Gary Werskey, "The Marxist Critique of Capitalist Science: A History in Three Movements?" published online at http://human-nature.com/science-as-culture/werskey.html (accessed July 11, 2012) for a fascinating account of Young's intellectual trajectory.

[9] Young, [later introduction to 1966], http://human-nature.com/rmyoung/papers/paper57.html (accessed 18, May 2012)

marker of an influential perspective and an entry into some of the perennial issues that have shaped the historiography of psychology.

Young singled out "perseveration" (or the tendency for persistent repetition) as a major problem, making the argument that "a scholarly tradition which is primarily based on textbooks has severe inherent limitations" (Young 1966, p. 16). This expository approach left out critical debate and controversy in favor of storytelling for didactic purposes and acculturation into the profession. Mainstream historians of science, he argued, were abandoning Whig history in favor of articulating a historicist view, displaying science's historical integrity in its own time.[10]

Young (1996, p. 16) mentioned Edwin Boring's book *A History of Experimental Psychology* (1929/1950) as an example. "If one began one's research in the history of psychology from Boring's footnotes," he suggested, "one would find a very exciting catalogue of unanswered questions. But the tendency has been to learn from the text and not from the footnotes." Expository history has its place, but only after a sufficient volume and quality of monographic and journal literature, he stated. Young welcomed the creation of the first specialized periodical in the field in 1965, the *Journal of the History of the Behavioral Sciences* (*JHBS*), as a promising sign of professional development. But he was dismayed by the content and symbolism of the first article in the inaugural issue: "On the Subjectivity of Important Historical Dates: Leipzig 1879" by Boring. This reference to the putative founding of experimental psychology by Wilhelm Wundt was a perfect example of the perseveration found in uncritical expository history.

Young's critique, harsh in tone as it was, nevertheless had a salutary effect on the field, initiating dialogues between psychologists and historians about historiography and scholarly standards. There was an essential tension besetting the history of psychology: The field of psychology gave the subject matter whereas the field of history provided methodology. Some psychologist-historians were committed to historical analysis as a route to improve psychology, and some historically trained historians of psychology were interested in aims that fell outside this agenda. Practitioners and students of the history of psychology were not very numerous and the paths they took were idiosyncratic and defied generalization.

[10] He cited Kuhn's 1962 book, *The Structure of Scientific Revolutions*, with approval, quoting, on page 19: "Rather than seeking the permanent contributions of an older science to our present vantage, they [historians] attempt to display the historical integrity of that science in its own time." Kuhn 1962, p. 3.

Cheiron Society Formation

In 1968, Watson and Josef Brožek, a psychologist at Lehigh University, joined forces and directed a Summer Institute for the History of Psychology for college teachers. Sponsored by the National Science Foundation (NSF), it was held at the University of New Hampshire in Durham. Thirty participants, including six predoctoral students, attended the six-week summer institute.[11] The scholars selected for the teaching staff reflected a broad vision of what the history of the behavioral sciences could include, with academics from psychology, medicine, and history of science as instructors. A rousing time was had, with seminars during the day and social events in the evening – sort of a "summer camp" for academics. Elizabeth Scarborough, who was among the graduate students attending, remembered "a warm camaraderie developed" among the group (Scarborough 2004, p. 208). The wish that Boring might pay a visit to the summer institute was dashed by his death in Massachusetts during the middle of the program.

Julian Jaynes, a Princeton psychologist, was so inspired by the intellectual excitement that he magnanimously offered to host a meeting in a year's time to share the results of research that participants were planning. The idea morphed into creating a new scholarly organization, one that would be international in scope and interdisciplinary in nature, so as not to compete directly with the new APA history group, Division 26. The new group was christened the International Society for the History of the Behavioral and Social Sciences and held their first meeting at Princeton University in the summer of 1969. By the following summer's meeting, held at the University of Akron, the awkward acronym, ISHOBSS, was replaced by the "wise and knowledgeable centaur of Greek mythology," Cheiron (Scarborough 2004, p. 209).

In 1971, another NSF summer institute was held, this time at Lehigh University, under the direction of Josef Brožek. Among the recurring themes were:

> 1) The importance of a broad knowledge of history, encompassing the socioeconomic and philosophical climate of the time and the development of related sciences; 2) The continuity of the past and the present in regard to the study of the process of scientific discovery, and the need to view the history of science within the broader framework of the science of science; 3) Alternative approaches to the

[11] Among the predoctoral students attending were Elizabeth Scarborough (Goodman) (University of New Hampshire), Michael Sokal (Case Western Reserve University), William Woodward (Princeton University master's student, who then went to Yale for his doctorate), and Barbara Ross (University of New Hampshire). Brožek et al. 1969, 1970.

history of science, their advantages and limitations; 4) The importance of firsthand contact with the work of individuals contributing to the development of psychology; and 5) Awareness of the nature and location of the sources of information for teaching and historical research. (Brožek and Schneider 1973, p. 91)

Panels were formed to examine some nineteenth-century psychological research as well as to ponder Thomas Kuhn's 1970 update of *The Structure of Scientific Revolutions* (originally published in 1962), and Imre Lakatos and Alan Musgrave's (1970) collection, *Criticism and the Growth of Knowledge.* Vigorous discussions about teaching – texts, approaches, and motivation of students – were held. In the published report on the summer institute, Brožek emphasized that the history of psychology is "not fully comprehensible without an understanding of the changing philosophical climate and the implications for psychology of developments in biology, medicine (including psychiatry), the social sciences, and the humanities" (Brožek and Schneider 1973, pp. 99–100). The organizers had planned on exploring these and other themes in the third summer institute, but a federal executive order caused the cancellation of the NSF program (Brožek 1999).

Thus by the early 1970s, a quarter-century after the Second World War, scholars and scientists had coalesced around shared interests in the history of psychology. A journal (*JHBS*), two societies (APA Division 26 and Cheiron), an archive (AHAP), and a graduate program (UNH) were institutional indicators. Ironically, this robust professional growth was not matched by a correspondingly deep scholarly vigor. The field was still dominated by positivist assumptions and concerns over the demarcation problem, symbolized by the continuing respect accorded Boring's nearly forty-year-old classic, *A History of Experimental Psychology.* Watson (1971) put forth a "prescriptive theory" of history, whereby psychologists of the past could be measured against a set of polarities, such as monism versus dualism or mentalism versus physicalism. He thought he could balance contrary impulses toward presentism and historicism: "This would be my way of 'telling it like it was' and yet showing the relation of the past to contemporary interest" (Watson 1971, p. 317). This form of positivism would make history subservient to psychology, with the result that "the modern development of psychological specialisms is seen against the background of historically permanent categorical parameters," leading to an ahistorical essentialism (Danziger 1997b, p. 11).

Although motivations of other practitioners from psychology were varied, among them was to recapture dreams of system and unity in the face of continuing fragmentation of psychological theory and practice. "It is a function of the systematic psychologist and of the historian of psychology to try to correct this situation by bringing the fragments together into a context," said the psychologists Mary Henle and John Sullivan (1974, p. 46). History of psychology occupied a marginal status within the parent discipline of psychology and was barely recognized within history of science, its alternate home. Although Robert Young's criticism was still fresh, there were hopeful signs of change.

New contributors, mostly students of U.S. history, introduced a focus on understanding the development of psychology as part of the American experience, including how psychology acquired and maintained professional status. In 1968, the historian of education Geraldine Jonçich published a massive biography of Edward L. Thorndike, an influential educational psychologist located at Columbia University's Teachers College (Jonçich 1968). In the same year, the Princeton graduate student Daniel J. Kevles published "Testing the Army's Intelligence: Psychologists and the Military in World War I" in the prestigious *Journal of American History*, reexamining the episode through the lens of science and politics (Kevles 1968). Another student, Thomas M. Camfield, wrote his 1969 dissertation at the University of Texas with a similar focus on the First World War but with the theme of how psychology achieved scientific legitimacy and professional respect. In 1973, he published "The Professionalization of American Psychology, 1870–1917" in the *Journal of the History of the Behavioral Sciences* (Camfield 1973). That work articulated with a growing interest within the history of science community in studies on the social history of disciplines and of the scientific community. In an exemplary biography published in 1972, the intellectual historian Dorothy Ross placed the psychologist G. Stanley Hall into the rich context of the late nineteenth-century emergence of the American university (Ross 1972).

Within the history of psychoanalysis, a wave of revision attempted to place "Freud's endeavor back into its social and intellectual context" (Marinelli and Mayer 2006, p. 8). Using letters and other unpublished sources, this historiography tried to decenter the authority of Freud and confront the myths created by him and his followers. One high point in this approach was the 1970 publication of *The Discovery of the Unconscious*, by the Canadian-Swiss psychiatrist and medical historian Henri Ellenberger. He identified elements of the "Freud legend," calling into question Freud's status as an originator, in either theory or practice, and recontextualized history of psychoanalysis in late nineteenth-century neurology, psychiatry, and related areas (Ellenberger 1970).

Kuhn and the Study of Science

Intellectual developments within the history and philosophy of science, coupled with funding for research from the federal government and support for new university positions, led to the academic institutionalization of the two-headed field in the United States. Thomas Kuhn's 1962 book, *The Structure of Scientific Revolutions*, captured the public fascination with the importance of science as well as engendering great scholarly attention and debate over his intertwined philosophical framework and historical argumentation (Kuhn 1962). Some of his terms, such as "paradigm" and "incommensurability," influenced discourse in many fields. Although Kuhn barely mentioned psychology in his predominant focus on the exact sciences, commentators debated whether psychology had attained paradigmatic status or still was preparadigmatic. One useful but unintended consequence was a renewed attention paid to the nature and functioning of the scientific community.

In 1971, David Palermo, a developmental psychologist with interests in language and cognition at Penn State, wrote "Is a Scientific Revolution Taking Place in Psychology?" in the second issue of the new journal *Science Studies* (Palermo 1971).[12] He argued, on the basis of Boring and other secondary sources, that psychology already had one revolution, when American behaviorism replaced German structuralism, and that a new revolution was brewing in the psychology of language, spearheaded by Chomsky's critique of Skinner's *Verbal Behavior* (1957). His article garnered some critical responses and induced Palermo to collaborate with his Penn State colleague Walter B. Weimer to produce "Paradigms and Normal Science in Psychology," published two years later (Weimer and Palermo 1973). They argued that Kuhn's model of science was not a template but a generative framework and went on to defend its applicability to psychology. Exploring philosophical frameworks provided by Kuhn, Popper, and Lakatos, Weimer published a two-part article, "The History of Psychology and Its Retrieval from Historiography: I. The Problematic Nature of History" and "II. Some Lessons for the Methodology of Scientific Research," which dealt with a framework for testing these models (Weimer 1974a, 1974b). Although Weimer's and Palermo's sojourn in the history of psychology came to an end, their collaboration continued, in the area of cognition and symbolic processes.

[12] *Science Studies* changed its name to *Social Studies of Science* in 1975.

Looking toward history rather than philosophy, a more productive methodological vein was explored by the social psychologist Franz Samelson, located at Kansas State University, in his 1974 article "History, Origin Myth and Ideology: 'Discovery' of Social Psychology." Writing during a time of questioning the identity of the specialty, he took issue with Gordon Allport's rendering of Auguste Comte as the founder of social psychology that appeared in the standard reference *Handbook of Social Psychology*, first published in 1954 and revised in 1968 (Allport 1954, 1968). Samelson criticized not only Allport's selective quotations but also misrepresentation of the purpose of Comte's work, and the lack of citation to scholarship in the history of science. He extended the critique to other recent texts in the history of psychology and found "their bibliographies show no awareness of the field of history of science, except for a few which refer to outdated works, with an occasional passing reference to Kuhn's (1962) 'revolutions' and 'paradigms' thrown in for up-to-dateness" (Samelson 1974, p. 223).[13] After a thorough review of the vices of "presentism" (or "whiggish" history), Samelson summarized the ideological thrust of Allport's account and suggested that history of psychology's goal should be "a critical examination of the past leading to a better understanding of the present" (p. 229).

Wundt Reappraisal

The growing number of critiques of standard views or conventional interpretations within the history of psychology demonstrated the growing practice of revisionism, the essence of historical analysis. With interests in psycholinguistics, a lively topic in the 1960s, Arthur L. Blumenthal read many of the classic German works in their original language as he prepared his first book, *Language and Psychology: Historical Aspects of Psycholinguistics* (1970). He was surprised to discover a very different picture of the German scholar and scientist Wilhelm Wundt than the standard textbook sources offered. In 1975 he published "A Reappraisal of Wilhelm Wundt" in the *American Psychologist*, outlining the major tenets of Wundt's theoretical system and empirical methodology. He offered six aspects of Wundt's psychology that had current relevance and made a generous assessment of the simplistic textbooks that were written during a time "when early behaviorist

[13] Samelson continued, "Typically, their presentation of history, conceived as a mix of doxographic and biographic chronicle, starts without any discussion of what the problems of history and history-writing are" (p. 223).

and positivist movements were eager to encourage a break with the past, hence giving understandably little effort to careful description of the enormous body of writings they were discarding" (Blumenthal 1975, p. 1087). A year later, in an article that was substantially the same, Blumenthal pointed explicitly to Boring's example and the practice of "citing only isolated passages (and peculiar translations) that would support the popular negative views of [Wundt's] work." (Blumenthal 1976, p. 21).

Taking the distorted picture of Wundt's system that Boring expounded as its starting point, the York University psychologist-historian Kurt Danziger (1979) analyzed "The Positivist Repudiation of Wundt" in an article published in the *Journal of the History of the Behavioral Sciences*. He argued that Wundt's two-part psychological system bridged the *Naturwissenschaften* and the *Geisteswissenshaften*, with the key concept of psychic causality. Younger psychologists, most notably Wundt's student Kulpe, following the precepts of the positivist philosophers Mach and Avenarius, rejected psychic causality in favor of explanations involving the corporeal individual in their efforts to establish psychology as a natural science. After detailing the intellectual consequences of this approach, Danziger explained how positivism paved the way for the dominance of behaviorism.

Generations of textbooks, Boring's included, emphasized the significance of Wundt's establishment of a psychological laboratory in 1879 at the University of Leipzig as marking the founding of psychology. John O'Donnell (1979), a University of Pennsylvania doctoral student, reinterpreted Boring's mobilization of history as a strategy to bolster the fortunes of experimentalism in the 1920s, both at Harvard and in the discipline generally. As the 1970s wore on, perhaps most psychologists were aware of the approaching centennial, and many works in the history of psychology appeared. Not all of them were products of the self-identified practitioners of the new specialty, however. One such was *The First Century of Experimental Psychology*, edited by the animal behaviorist Eliot Hearst (1979) at Indiana University. Hearst, trained at Columbia University in the mid-1950s (when he took Woodworth's famous course on schools of psychology), had a lively interest in history and taught the Indiana history-and-systems course regularly. He recruited contributors to the volume, seeking experienced research psychologists to author chapters about their own specialties, which ranged across the entire field of psychology. Most of the contributors had obtained their doctorates in the 1940s or 1950s. Nearly all wrote what amounted to a historically inflected literature review, perhaps more useful to working psychologists than historians. Richard Littman, a University of Oregon developmental psychologist, did more as he surveyed the intellectual, social, and institutional factors that defined the new psychology, ranging widely in his sources and speculations.

A different approach was taken by the psychologist Sigmund Koch, a Boston University generalist who edited a massive six-volume survey probing scientific psychology's epistemology and empirical findings in the late 1950s and the early 1960s before turning to more humanist concerns (Koch 1959–63). He teamed up with the historian of psychology David Leary, a University of Chicago doctorate and a faculty member in the University of New Hampshire's graduate history of psychology program, to edit a nearly thousand-page volume assessing *A Century of Psychology as Science* (1985). Not surprisingly, the many contributors took varied approaches to the assignment, and Koch introduced the volume with his trademark skepticism and a sharp analytic scalpel. In his foreword ("Wundt's Creature at Age Zero – and as Centenarian: Some Aspects of the Institutionalization of the 'New Psychology'"), he argued that Wundt's "founding" is properly understood as a semantic and rhetorical achievement to stabilize the meaning of the word "psychology" and its domination by the adjectives "scientific" and "experimental" (Koch 1985, p. 8). The volume was reprinted a few years later by APA Books, as part of the 1992 centennial observance of the American Psychological Association.

The ferment coinciding with the Wundt centennial was also the occasion for new publications in university textbooks designed for history of psychology courses. Among the most notable was Raymond Fancher's *Pioneers of Psychology* (1979). Fancher, a psychology faculty member at York University, was part of an emerging history of psychology group there. He took a biographical approach to major figures of psychological thought and narrated their contributions in their historical context. It was a far cry from the "great men" approach exemplified in Robert Watson's textbook, *The Great Psychologists: From Aristotle to Freud* (1963).

Rise of "Critical History"

Another response to the centennial celebration of the founding of Wundt's lab in 1879 was the coalescence of a scholarly movement around the idea of "critical history." Although critical history meant many things to different people, among the shared attitudes were a rejection of positivist historiography and an embrace of historical contingency and an emphasis on social factors and causation. The French philosopher Michel Foucault became an exemplar and touchstone with his analytic marriage of power and knowledge, dissecting how knowledge production is part and parcel of the inherently political nature of human activity. A shift in the historian's stance from the omniscient narrator to a more nuanced appreciation of her status as an interested party was a welcome consequence. More self-consciousness about the reflexive issues of historical scholarship can be traced to this period as well.

A critical history approach was exemplified in the work of Ben Harris, a 1975 Ph.D. in social psychology from Vanderbilt University who was working at Vassar College. In February 1979, he published a historical study, "Whatever Happened to Little Albert?" in the *American Psychologist*. Similar in conception to Samelson's 1974 article on the creation of a historical myth, Harris (1979) delineated John Watson's experimental conditioning of fear in an infant boy and how later psychologists distorted the story to serve various purposes. A follow-up note in the *American Psychologist* argued against "celebratory" history in favor of "critical" history.

"Critical history" was aired at the annual meetings of the Cheiron Society during the 1980s (see also Woodward 1980). The topic first appeared in 1979 with a "Workshop on Historiographic Methods," chaired by Jill Morawski, followed by an evening discussion at the 1980 meeting. During the next three years, programming was added to extend the length of the conference with either a half-day or a full-day "Critical History Workshop" prior to the start of the regular sessions. In 1984, the workshop name was changed to "Issues and Methods in History of Psychology." The next year, Franz Samelson organized a post-Cheiron workshop to discuss "Where Have We Been and Where Do We Go from Here?" This rump session continued through 1987. By drawing together both psychologists and historians interested in questions about methodology and aims, it succeeded in changing the discourse in Cheiron as well as the field more generally.

Mitchell Ash (1983), who earned his Ph.D. in history at Harvard in 1982, made a valuable contribution to understanding what was at stake in his 1983 paper "The Self-Presentation of a Discipline: History of Psychology in the United States between Pedagogy and Scholarship." He explored the tension of historical studies that served to socialize and acculturate students into the prevailing worldview of scientific psychology versus historicist perspectives that bracket the truth claims of psychology in their attempts to contextualize the field along a variety of social and intellectual dimensions.

In the early 1980s, at York University in Toronto, Bakan, Fancher, and Danziger formed the backbone of a History and Theory option within the Psychology Department's graduate program (Fancher 2003). At the same time, increasing numbers of students trained in history or history of science departments entered the field, coinciding with the interest in "critical" history in Cheiron and other places. Their professional ideology easily accommodated this attitude and approach. In 1981, Donald Napoli, an American historian trained at University of California – Davis, published his lightly revised dissertation, *Architects of Adjustment: The History of the Psychological Profession in the United States* (1981), in which he analyzed the rise of psychology through the entrepreneurial efforts of its practitioners rather than by some inherent scientific logic. With an exquisite balance between intellectual and institutional factors, the University of Pennsylvania–trained historian John M. O'Donnell wrote an exemplary study of the emergence of American psychology and its dominant discourse in *The Origins of Behaviorism* (1985). In 1982, there was sufficient interest to form Cheiron-Europe, an offshoot of the largely North American membership of the parent organization. The inaugural meeting was held in Amsterdam, Netherlands.

Twenty years after the first Cheiron Society meeting, another scholarly organization took root, providing another avenue for the work of historians of psychology. During the 1988 Cheiron meeting, coincidentally also at Princeton, a gathering of younger scholars, dissatisfied with the standing of their field within the history of science profession, established an additional scholarly group:

> The Forum for History of Human Science (FHHS) is a new organization that has been formed to promote scholarship in the history of the social and behavioral sciences. "Human science" is broadly defined, and encompasses anthropology, economics, geography, history, linguistics, political science, psychiatry, psychology, sociology, statistics, as well as aspects of the biological and physical sciences, medicine, education, law, and philosophy. The primary aim of the organization is to foster research and education in the history of human science and to encourage communication among scholars, scientists, and others working in the area.[14]

After a couple of years, the Forum for History of Human Science successfully petitioned the History of Science Society for formal recognition as a special-interest group. From the beginning, FHHS has sponsored sessions and panels at the annual meeting of the History of Science Society and has maintained a periodic newsletter (see www.fhhs.org).

At that same 1988 Cheiron meeting at Princeton, some generational strains became visible. John Carson, a graduate student in the history of science program at Princeton, read a paper, "Is the Mental Test a Foucaultian

[14] *Forum for History of Human Science Newsletter 1*, Summer 1989. The first steering committee included James Capshew (chair), Laurel Furumoto (corresponding secretary), John I. Brooks III (recording secretary), Ben Harris (treasurer), and three at-large representatives, Timothy Alborn, Elazar Barkan, and Jack Pressman.

Panopticon?" Foucault had written about Jeremy Bentham's 1791 idea of a prison with a radial structure that allowed for constant surveillance of the inmates. Carson used the panopticon as a literary trope, a metaphor to suggest that the modern regime of mental tests, begun in childhood and continuing through adulthood, has served as a powerful way to enforce social norms. In the discussion following the paper, John Popplestone, head of the Archives of the History of American Psychology, rose and denounced Foucault, saying in effect, "does anybody really believe this nonsense?" It soon became clear, with nobody in the audience following Popplestone's lead, that he expressed a minority point of view.[15]

The Freud Industry

Although psychoanalysis ramified greatly in the postwar era, and was the subject of much cultural commentary as well as internal development, historians were slow to probe its post-1945 past.[16] But by the mid-1970s, the term "Freud Industry," with biographical studies at its center, emerged to characterize a burgeoning field as historians contributed to a growing literature. In 1973, the York University historian of psychology Raymond Fancher published *Psychoanalytic Psychology: The Development of Freud's Thought* (1973). The Harvard University historian of science Frank Sulloway published *Freud, Biologist of the Mind* (1979) in an attempt to assimilate Freud's ideas to Darwinian evolution. The subtitle, *Beyond the Psychoanalytic Legend*, gestured to the growing critical response to the orthodox view of the history of psychoanalysis promulgated by Freud and his disciples. The Freud Industry meant that the debate over Freud and psychoanalysis would be fierce and long-lasting and would escalate into the so-called Freud Wars.

Literary critics, philosophers and historians, and other cultural commentators were involved, and debates often produced more heat than light. For instance, in 1985, the British-Czech philosopher and social anthropologist Ernest Gellner wrote *The Psychoanalytic Movement*, with the polemical subtitle *The Cunning of Unreason*. Quoting W. H. Auden's poem about Freud (1950) – "To us he is no more a person / Now but a whole climate of opinion / Under whom we conduct our differing lives." – Gellner (1996, p. 5) defined psychoanalysis broadly, as "a theory, a technique, an organization, a

[15] Popplestone continued to be exercised by this episode, spoke about it at a 2000 symposium in his honor, and then published an account in Popplestone 2005.

[16] Notably, the sociologist Philip Rieff (1959, 1966) critically examined Freud and the rise of the therapeutic society.

language, an ethos, an ethic, a climate." He wanted to examine how and why Freudian psychoanalysis came to be "the dominant idiom for the discussion of the human personality and of human relations." Despite untestable epistemological claims and questionable therapeutic efficacy, as the philosophers Karl Popper and Adolf Grünbaum had pointed out earlier, psychoanalysis was successfully institutionalized, the book concluded, because it filled the overriding social need for human warmth and solace.

Biography continued to flourish within Freud studies. In 1988, the historian Peter Gay published *Freud: A Life for Our Time* (1988), which became a best seller (see also Young-Bruehl 1992). The explosive growth of the secondary literature was fertilized by a huge increase in access to primary source materials.

A Measure of Maturation

In 1987, the historians of psychology Elizabeth Scarborough and Laurel Furumoto (1987) published their path-breaking study *Untold Lives: The First Generation of American Women Psychologists*, which analyzed and narrated patterns of collective change in this important group. Although the discipline had always attracted a substantial number of women, patriarchal attitudes and sex discrimination had diminished their chances of conventional professional success. Through a series of moving biographical sketches, the volume traced the career trajectories of female psychologists, identifying the multiple obstacles they faced as well as their differing career strategies. This work was a fruit of the feminist wave in psychology. As early as 1974, the feminist psychologists Maxine Bernstein and Nancy Russo (1974) published a call to action, "The History of Psychology Revisited: Or, Up with Our Foremothers," in the *American Psychologist*. Following up, in 1980 Russo and Agnes O'Connell (1980) published a collection of autobiographies of eminent women psychologists. Not only did it provide raw material for historical analysis; it also began to redress the male dominance of psychologist autobiographies.[17]

In 1987, the psychologist Ernest Hilgard, at Stanford University, published a thousand-page synthesis, *Psychology in America: A Historical Survey* (1987), aimed toward the college textbook market. A veteran textbook writer, the author was a participant-observer for more than fifty years

[17] The great portion of contributors to the series *A History of Psychology in Autobiography*, begun in 1930 and still published today, have been men, as is also true of the more recent series, *The Psychologists*, published in three volumes in 1972–8. See Murchison (1930) and Krawiec (1972–8).

and among the most accomplished generalists of psychology.[18] Hilgard's quest for comprehensiveness, combined with his tolerant pluralistic stance, led him to range beyond the boundaries of the United States in considering the sources and ramifications of American developments. In explaining the rise of modern psychology he relied mainly on accounts of theories and experiments, although he did not neglect the role of personalities, institutional settings, and social factors. Because the text championed diversity and mirrored psychology's complex character, it challenged the teacher to construct her or his own pedagogical framework, while its encyclopedic quality might have made it difficult for students to discern connections across topics and to identify larger historical forces. In my review, I approvingly noted the inclusion of personal anecdotes scattered throughout the book, giving some insight into Hilgard's long career, and suggested, "Like Boring's book, Hilgard's history is destined to become a classic text for psychologists and an important source for historians of science" (Capshew 1988, p. 112).

Ludy T. Benjamin Jr., an active historian of psychology working in the Psychology Department at Texas A&M University, was especially interested in introducing psychology students to the issues and techniques of historical research. In 1981, he authored *Teaching History of Psychology: A Handbook* (1981), and, in 1988, *A History of Psychology: Original Sources and Contemporary Research* (1988). Cognizant of the rich tradition in history (or history and systems) of psychology courses in American colleges and universities, Benjamin's 1988 book took a new approach in a textbook genre that had been suffering from the ills of excessive standardization and perseveration. Organized as a reader with a combination of subject-matter primary sources and interpretive secondary sources, it attempted to provide a window into the process of constructing historical explanations. The first chapter, "Research in the History of Psychology," introduced various working methods and framing issues and reiterated Benjamin's key themes:

> (1) a keen awareness of the necessity to understand psychology's past for its own sake (historicism) and (2) a recognition that psychology has not evolved in a vacuum, that it is the product of a complex forces within psychology as well as the cultural, political, economic, and geographic forces external to psychology (a view of historical writing usually called *external history*). (Benjamin 1988, p. 4)

[18] Hilgard published one of the first postwar textbooks in general psychology, *Introduction to Psychology* (1953). Hugely popular, it went through edition after edition and later added coauthors Richard and Rita Atkinson. The 15th edition, published in 2009, is called *Atkinson and Hilgard's Introduction to Psychology*. Hilgard served as APA president in 1949, and he was the editor of the sourcebook *American Psychology in Historical Perspective: Addresses of the Presidents of the American Psychological Association, 1892–1977* (1978), which appeared on the eve of Wundt's laboratory centennial.

The rest of the book exhibited a typical topical organization, proceeding chronologically from Descartes to Gestalt psychology, with both primary and secondary sources within each chapter.

In 1988, the historian of psychology Laurel Furumoto (1989), who taught at Wellesley College, summarized the ongoing shift in perspectives and methods in an APA lecture, "The New History of Psychology." Addressing teachers of psychology, she emphasized the move away from great men, great events, and great ideas toward a more nuanced, contextual viewpoint that placed external factors in a dynamic relationship to disciplinary developments. Historians of psychology, she argued, were becoming more critical of sources and interpretations in an effort to avoid historical errors such as presentism. She also noted an increase in the use of archival materials. Furumoto's lecture, after publication, became a touchstone as historians of psychology contemplated their professional progress.

In a 1987 article titled "Of What Is History of Psychology a History?" the British historian of psychology Graham Richards wrestled with difficult epistemological questions raised by the many connotations of "psychology." He suggested the use of an uppercase "P" to designate the discipline and the lowercase "p" to refer to the subject matter of psychology. "The status of past Psychological work has a character quite different form the status of past work in other disciplines, for it can always be reconstrued as subject matter data." Richards (1987, pp. 210–11) argued this reflexive feature gives rise to "numerous ambiguities and paradoxes," which historians of psychology needed to explore.

Following similar themes, the historian of science Roger Smith, at Lancaster University in Great Britain, argued against a transhistorical subject matter for psychology in "Does the History of Psychology Have a Subject?" In the first volume of a new British journal, *History of the Human Sciences*, in 1988, Smith (1988, p. 153) criticized Boring and the textbook tradition in positing "a conception of psychology as a discipline with a continuous and profound tradition of describing what it really is to be human." In a nuanced discussion of presentism, he writes:

> we can suggest that historians construct the historical subject out of the tension between present purposes and what, it must be assumed, may have been quite another subject. What they cannot do is presuppose that the subject pre-exists the historian's activity and purposes. (p. 164)[19]

[19] For a comparison of *History of the Human Sciences* with the *Journal of the History of the Behavioral Sciences*, see Cravens (1990).

Once psychology became an occupation after 1850, historians were on firmer ground to take the social identity of psychology as a starting point.

The history of psychology was not immune to the turn toward philosophical relativism and rise of social constructionism in science studies. Jill Morawski, a historian of psychology at Wesleyan University, edited *The Rise of Experimentation in American Psychology* (1988), in which authors used historical case studies to subvert the standard narrative of inexorable progress toward scientific rationality. A sympathetic reviewer, Kenneth Gergen (1989, p. 410), author of the 1973 article "Social Psychology as History," applauded the authors' intent: "they are formulating interpretations of why certain events occurred in history – the advent of quantification, the form of the experimental report, the terms of description and explanation, and the like – and generating evidence to show how such events were dictated not by a foundationalist logic but by social processes within the culture of science and the culture more broadly."

In the late 1980s, Mitchell Ash, in the History Department at the University of Iowa, and William Woodward, in the history of psychology program at the University of New Hampshire, convinced Cambridge University Press to launch a new series, the Cambridge Studies in the History of Psychology, under their editorship. Their place as part of the rising generation in the specialty, aided by the imprimatur of the venerable publisher, made their assertive solicitation of sophisticated manuscripts possible. The Cambridge Studies kicked off with an instant classic, Danziger's *Constructing the Subject: Historical Origins of Psychological Research*, published in 1990. The book teased apart methodological traditions and their origins in different national contexts, and the development of the discipline's ability to construct wholly artificial categories of subjects that have no analog in the natural world. For the next dozen years, the Cambridge Studies series published, on average, one monograph per year, greatly enriching the historiography of psychology.[20]

Among the outstanding works that appeared in the Cambridge series was Nikolas Rose's *Inventing Our Selves: Psychology, Power, and Personhood* (1996), a set of essays that extended earlier work. Rose, professionally identified with the discipline of sociology, wrote a Foucaultian critique of the rise of the "psy" disciplines, relating how they provided new ways of conceptualizing and controlling human behavior in modern society. He developed a theory of "governmentality" to explain the paradox of the modern

[20] The Cambridge University Press Web site lists eleven titles published in the Cambridge Studies in the History of Psychology.

autonomous self coexisting with the increasing regulation of individual and collective behavior through institutions such as schools, psychotherapy, and corporations (see also Rose 1990).

In 1991, another marker of professional salience was achieved by the appearance of an article on the history of psychology in the *Annual Review of Psychology*, a disciplinary series in existence since 1950. The well-connected Ernest Hilgard, active in the affairs of the *Annual Review* publishing company, pushed for such an article in 1988, soon after his *Psychology in America* was published. He found two coauthors: the historian of psychology David Leary, a faculty member at the University of New Hampshire, and Gregory McGuire, a graduate student at York University, who supplied an extensive bibliography. The review dealt with the history of the field, historiographical issues, and the teaching of the history of psychology (Hilgard et al. 1991).[21] Skillfully, the field was presented as a natural outgrowth of the parent discipline of psychology while dependent upon the exercise of humanistic methods not originating from science. In their conclusion to the historiography discussion, the authors felt compelled to reiterate:

> Historians do not simply read texts and write history. Decisions about topical or thematic focus, the nature of relevant data, the means of gathering this information, the appropriate mode of analysis and interpretation, and the construction of narrative or other genres of presentation are all at issue, each and every time an historical project is undertaken. (p. 94)

Sage advice, whether given to acolytes or seasoned veterans.

In the mid-1990s, Kurt Danziger noted that the breakdown of the "stark opposition between scientific and historical sensibilities" occasioned by greater awareness of polycentric and agonistic voices in psychology could give hope for historians. He suggested: "Where the insider's engagement with the discipline's concepts and practices is combined with the moral distance maintained by the outsider, one has reason to look for the emergence of a historiography that is both critical and effective" (Danziger 1994, p. 479). Adrian Brock, a student of Danziger who trained in both psychology and history of science, contrasted the differing commitments required to do historical work from within psychology and from without. In a 1995 article, "Why I Am Not a Historian of Science," he drew on his own educational career, in which he started with psychology for his B.A., switched to history of science for his M.A., and back to psychology for his Ph.D. Noting the agonistic structure of the discipline, characteristic of the human

[21] Before the article reached print, Leary had moved to the University of Richmond and McGuire had acquired a position at St. Francis Xavier College.

sciences, Brock (1995), like his mentor, wanted to be in conversation with psychology and working psychologists, not just other historians of science. Brock, who obtained a position in psychology at University College Dublin, was active in both Cheiron and Cheiron-Europe. Inspired by the example of the Forum for History of the Human Science and the journal *History of the Human Sciences*, he suggested at the 1992 Cheiron meeting that it consider a name change that would incorporate the phrase "human sciences." Older members of the organization strenuously opposed the suggestion. A few years later, in 1996, he suggested something similar at a Cheiron-Europe meeting, where it was favorably received. The organization henceforth was the European Society for the History of the Human Sciences (ESHHS).[22]

The Big Picture, Redux

In his 1966 critique, Robert Young suggested that scholars should spend their time producing high-quality journal articles and monographs based on primary sources rather than grand narratives, derived from other secondary sources, of how psychology developed. As history of psychology emerged as a specialty, certain intellectual trends, such as critical revisionism, and various institutional factors, such as new publication outlets, reinforced that message. As a consequence, there was a remarkable flowering of superior scholarship produced in the ensuing three decades, much of it in the realm of analytical microhistory. Critical history even flowed to textbook history, as the British psychologist Graham Richard's wrote *Putting Psychology in Its Place: An Introduction from a Critical Historical Perspective* (1996).[23] There were exceptions to this dynamic picture, however, as most history and systems textbooks evinced little change, repeating the standard narrative through edition after edition.[24]

In the last few years before the turn of the millennium, two historians of psychology returned to big-picture concerns. In *Naming the Mind: How Psychology Found Its Language* (1997b), Danziger explored the history of discursive formations (i.e., language) in psychology, looking at key concepts such as intelligence, behavior, and attitudes. Rejecting the deep-rooted

[22] Adrian Brock, personal communication, October 28, 2012.

[23] The book was revised in 2002 and 2010.

[24] For example, in 1969, Duane Schultz published *A History of Modern Psychology*. Over the next forty years, it was revised and republished every five years, on average. The 10th edition, with Ellen Schultz as a coauthor, came out in 2011. Although there have been many changes over the years, the overall structure remains about the same, with little attention to post–World War II developments and few signs of engagement with primary source materials. Schultz (1969) and Schultz and Schultz (2011).

ahistoricism of the discipline, he argued that psychological categories are "historically constructed objects" (p. 12). Moreover, discursive formations constitute semantic networks: "a coherent framework for representing a kind of knowledge that it regarded as true and a kind of practice regarded as legitimate" (p. 13). They are not the creation of individuals, but formed collectively. Starting with the ancients and the "great transformation" of the eighteenth century, Danziger historicized key categories of psychological discourse in the nineteenth and twentieth centuries. In the conclusion, he reminded his audience that language was the first and most powerful tool for investigation, although its role, being constitutive of the phenomena under investigation, has been often overlooked (p. 187).

The history of psychology was at the center of the multistranded narrative by Roger Smith, published in 1997 as *The Fontana History of the Human Sciences* in England and as *The Norton History of the Human Sciences* in the United States. Trained under Robert Young, he obtained his doctorate at Cambridge's History and Philosophy of Science Department. Smith used the term "human sciences" for convenience, but he reminded the reader, "it also implies that questions are on the agenda about what *is* a science of being human. There is no agreement, … either in the past or in the twentieth century, about what a human science should be like" (Smith 1997, p. 4).[25] The book took a grand tour of thought and practice in a variety of fields that grappled with such questions since the Renaissance. Coverage got thicker in the nineteenth century and thickest in the twentieth, with the rise of natural and social science, and the discipline of psychology was at the center of the analysis. This book, with nine hundred pages of text and one hundred pages of source notes, set a new standard for the history of psychology and its operation within the broader context of the human sciences.[26]

Another Journal

In the early 1990s, activists in Division 26 of the American Psychological Association began to advocate the creation of a new journal focused exclusively on the history of psychology. Although the two existing journals, the *Journal of the History of the Behavioral Sciences* and the *History of the*

[25] The term "human sciences" came into widespread use by the 1980s. The journal, *History of the Human Sciences*, was founded in 1988, and the History of Science Society's interest group, Forum for History of Human Science, was organized in the late 1980s.

[26] It is fittingly ironic that a student of Young published this superb exposition thirty-one years after Young's diatribe against expository history.

Human Sciences, had published many articles in the history of psychology, their overlapping catchments were broader. It was felt that the history of psychology, perhaps the most robust specialty in the history of the behavioral sciences/human sciences, deserved its own publication venue and that APA had the resources to make it work. The 1996–97 division president, Raymond Fancher, of York University, chaired the committee that selected Michael Sokal, of Worcester Polytechnic Institute's Department of Humanities and Arts, as founding editor of *History of Psychology.* Sokal, trained in the history of science and technology at Case Western Reserve University, was widely known in history of science circles, serving as executive secretary of the History of Science Society from 1988 to 1992 and a noted contributor to the history of psychology literature.

The first issue of *History of Psychology* appeared in February 1998. Editor Sokal (1998) wrote a five-page editorial for the inaugural issue to explain the aims and rationale for the new journal. He invoked the market provided by the nearly one thousand members of Division 26 as well as citing seven other similar membership organizations. Noting the pedagogical demand for history and system courses in U.S. colleges and universities, he averred that *History of Psychology* would accelerate the trend of the latest scholarship's finding its way into the textbook literature. The journal would be open to psychohistory and historical psychology as well as history of psychology.

"New Freud Studies"

Within the history of psychoanalysis, the 1990s saw a historiographical shift that was dubbed "New Freud Studies" and was characterized by increased concern with the consumption, not production, of psychoanalysis (Burnham 2006). This movement allowed the image of Freud to take on new meanings, not as an originator but as a figure that was buffeted by cultural currents and synthesized an influential version of late modernism. The New Freud Studies gained impetus from British historians of science such as John Forrester and Sonu Shamdasani, among others. In 1997, Forrester (1997) analyzed the Freud Wars and called for a wide-ranging investigation of the varieties of psychoanalysis and the local conditions that had shaped it. Shamdasani, a specialist in the life and work of Carl Jung, has fashioned a career out of responding to Jung's critics on the basis of a thorough reconstruction of primary sources with the larger goal of understanding the formation of modern psychological disciplines and therapeutics. "The figure of 'Jung' stands at the interfaces of academic psychology, psychiatry, psychotherapy, popular psychology, and New Age psychologies," he has suggested. "The rise of these disciplines and movements is one of the decisive developments in twentieth-century Western society" (Shamdasani 2003, p. 3).

The historian of medicine and science John Burnham, at the Ohio State University, who not only witnessed a half-century of psychoanalytic historiography but also was a signal contributor to the subject, edited *After Freud Left: A Century of Psychoanalysis in America* (2012). Maintaining that scholars had formed a loose consensus around the fate of Freud's ideas in America during the twentieth century, he stated:

> In 1909, hardly any Americans had heard of Freud's writings [but] by the mid-twentieth century, Freud's ideas had become a conspicuous – indeed, unavoidable – part of the American cultural landscape. Another half century later, Freud's name was still familiar, but American cultural leaders had many new ways of looking at the world, and only infrequently did they make detailed, direct references to any of Freud's ideas. (Burnham 2012, p. 3)

Burnham has been perhaps the most consistent historicist voice calling for wide-ranging analysis of psychological science and therapeutics across institutional and professional boundaries (see Burnham 1988).

In 2006, the historians of psychoanalysis Lydia Marinelli and Andreas Mayer (2006) coedited a special issue of *Science in Context* in which the contributors go beyond the polarizing debate of the Freud Wars to explore aspects of specific theoretical developments and clinical interventions against a richly textured historical context. The figure of Freud has proved remarkably resilient to epistemological critiques and has survived waves of historical revisionism. Taking issue with the "exceptionalism of psychoanalysis, removed from context, history, and verification," a recent book, long in the making, by Mikkel Borch-Jacobsen and Sonu Shamdasani (2012) attempted to make the case that "psychoanalysis is vulnerable to its history," its very identity held together by the Freudian legend.

A Textbook in Context

As we have seen, a continuing challenge to the history of psychology is how to bridge the gap between cutting-edge scholarship and college-level teaching, specifically, how to simplify scholarly research findings without too much distortion, as well as making them palatable to students. A recent textbook, *A History of Modern Psychology in Context* (2010), by Wade Pickren and Alexandra Rutherford, goes a long way toward that goal. Pickren obtained his Ph.D. from the University of Florida, working with psychologists and historians of science; Rutherford acquired her doctorate (2001) from the history and theory of psychology program at York University, where she was hired subsequently as a faculty member. "Context" in the title is a hopeful sign. A description by the publisher explains the book's aims:

> The authors resist the traditional storylines of great achievements by eminent people, or schools of thought that rise and fall in the wake of scientific progress. Instead, psychology is portrayed as a network of scientific and professional practices embedded in specific temporal, social, political, and cultural contexts. The narrative is informed by three key concepts – indigenization, reflexivity, and social constructionism – and by the fascinating interplay between disciplinary Psychology and everyday psychology.... The text also moves beyond an exclusive focus on the development of North American and European psychologies to explore the development of psychologies in other indigenous contexts, especially from the mid-20th-century onward. (Pickren and Rutherford 2010)

A critical attitude is assumed, and the conceptual framework endeavors not to take the dominance of the American style for granted. This book gives fresh hope to the alliance of researchers and teachers of the history of psychology that sophisticated explanation and understanding of psychology's past can be made available to students and the lay public.

Does Our Present Past Have a Future?

"Since 1945" is an open code for the past two-thirds of a century following World War II, the cataclysm that left an indelible imprint on the world's institutions, politics, societies, and cultures. Although historians of psychology often concentrate on earlier periods, particularly the rise and institutionalization of modern psychology in Europe and America, there is an increasing emphasis on the postwar period as it recedes from living memory. Of course, since the development of the specialty occurred in this period, it provides an unmarked background and an implicit comparison to all work of the period. Just as the history of science resisted studying the Second World War and the development of atomic weapons, preferring to reify the scientific revolution of the seventeenth century, at least until the 1970s, the history of psychology swallowed the positivistic assumptions of psychology's effort to be considered a natural science, for the same period. Since that time, some historians of science (including psychology) have struggled for independence from the totalizing ideology of science to do their work (see Forman 1991; cf. Brock 1995).

Even as late as 1980, history and systems of psychology textbooks, at least in the United States, did not cover World War II and postwar developments, but ended with the various flavors of 1930s neobehaviorism and a brief sop to Freudian ideas. Some innovative textbooks, such as Benjamin (1988), have ventured into the postwar territory, however. Beginning in the 1990s, historians started producing monographs that dealt specifically with wartime contexts and their aftermath. In *The Romance of American Psychology: Political Culture in the Age of Experts* (1995), the American historian Ellen Herman begins her story with the war, when psychologists sold themselves as experts, and traces the expansion of psychology into the public sphere and private life until the 1960s, to mixed results. My own contribution, *Psychologists on the March: Science, Practice, and Professional Identity in America, 1929–1969* (1999), explored the impact that the war had on the community of psychologists as they forged a postwar self-concept that balanced their scientific aspirations with their urge to practical expertise. Exploring the practice of applied psychology, Ludy Benjamin and David Baker, head of the Archives of the History of American Psychology, published *From Séance to Science: A History of the Profession of Psychology in America* (2004). Since the psychologist Robert Guthrie's indictment contained in *Even the Rat Was White* (1976), historians of psychology have produced detailed accounts of the nature and varieties of scientific racism, within psychology and beyond, including wide-ranging studies contained in the British historian of psychology Graham Richard's *"Race," Racism, and Psychology: Towards a Reflexive History* (1997/2011), the psychologist-historian Andrew Winston's collection *Defining Difference: Race and Racism in the History of Psychology* (2003), and the work of the historians John Jackson and Nadine Weidman, in *Race, Racism, and Science* (2005), aimed toward college teaching.

Both Danziger (1997) and Smith (1997), mentioned earlier as exemplars of the big-picture approach, deal with postwar developments extensively. In his article on psychology for the Cambridge History of Science's volume on the modern social sciences, Mitchell Ash (2003) dealt mostly with the prewar period, while his contribution to *The History of the Social Sciences since 1945* (2010) covered cognitive neuroscience, social psychology, and reflexivity. And on the pedagogical side, Richards (1996 et seq.) and Pickren and Rutherford (2010) are among the authors treating the postwar period in some detail.

Among the themes that look most promising from the present vantage point are polycentrism, indigenization, and reflexivity. In the early 1990s, Danziger (1991) pointed out the replacement of the center-and-periphery metaphor with a polycentric understanding of disciplinary developments as affected by local conditions. That, coupled with an emphasis on intellectual and social contextualization, has led to a new foundation for relevant and significant historical investigation (see also Danziger 1994, 1996; Baker 2012). Critiques of American psychology's imperial ambitions have given way to a positive interest in forms of indigenous psychology, the process of globalization, and the relation between subjectivity and culture in international contexts (Brock et al. 2004; Brock 2006; Danziger 2006). Reflexivity, whether considered as an inherent characteristic of the human sciences or in its theoretical and practical dimensions, has been an intriguing challenge to historians of psychology (Cohen-Cole 2005; Morawski 2005; Smith 2005).

A recent issue of *Theory & Psychology* contained a minisymposium on historiographical issues, displaying the contrasting views of Daniel Robinson, Kurt Danziger, and Thomas Teo. Robinson (2013), a distinguished intellectual historian of psychology, defended the perspective of historically transcendent foundational issues in psychology, thus warranting the investigation of "Aristotle's psychology" because of its conceptual resonance with contemporary issues in the discipline. Danziger (2013), another eminent specialist, sharply opposed this view, arguing that the modern discipline projected the idea of psychology back to ancient times and that the proper starting point should be researching the historical emergence of the current multiplicity of psychological objects. Teo (2013), a self-described critical historian and philosopher of psychology, suggested that Robinson's approach confused the relationship between history and philosophy of psychology and offered a dialectic perspective on the two subdisciplines.[27] This exchange reprised a longstanding debate in the history of psychology about proper approaches to the past, pitting presentists against historicists once again. It is also a sign of a healthy professional community concerned about foundational issues. No doubt historians of psychology will pursue these and other themes in the future as they endeavor to make sense of the psychological enterprise in its human complexity. Whether psychologists will listen to them is another matter entirely.

Acknowledgments

An earlier version of this paper was presented at the joint meeting of the Cheiron Society and the European Society for the History of the Human Sciences at Dawson College in Montreal in 2012. I am grateful for comments and references from colleagues, including Adrian Brock, John

[27] Adcock (this volume) delineates a move by the historian of political science Brian Schmidt (1998) to draw "a sharp dichotomy between an analytic tradition (a parade of past figures constructed by scholars in the present on the basis of what appears retrospectively and selectively as similar concerns) and a historical tradition (a historical lineage of actual intellectual inheritance)."

Burnham, Raymond Fancher, David Leary, Annette Mülburger, Elizabeth Scarborough, Michael Sokal, two anonymous reviewers, and the editors of this volume, Philippe Fontaine and Roger Backhouse.

References

Allport, Gordon W. 1954. "The Historical Background of Modern Social Psychology." In *Handbook of Social Psychology*, ed. G. Lindzey. Reading, MA: Addison-Wesley, 3–56.

Allport, Gordon W. 1968. "The Historical Background of Modern Social Psychology." In *The Handbook of Social Psychology*, 2nd ed., ed. G. Lindzey and E. Aronson. Reading, MA: Addison-Wesley, 1–80.

Ash, Mitchell G. 1983. "The Self-Presentation of a Discipline: History of Psychology in the United States between Pedagogy and Scholarship." In *Functions and Uses of Disciplinary Histories*, ed. L. Graham, W. Lepenies, and P. Weingart. Dordrecht and Boston: Reidel, 143–89.

2003. "Psychology." In *The Cambridge History of Science*, Vol. 7: *The Modern Social Sciences*, ed. T. M. Porter and D. Ross. Cambridge: Cambridge University Press, 251–74.

2010. "Psychology." In *The History of the Social Sciences since 1945*, ed. R. E. Backhouse and P. Fontaine. New York: Cambridge University Press, 16–37.

Backhouse, Roger E., and Philippe Fontaine, eds. 2010. *The History of the Social Sciences since 1945*. New York: Cambridge University Press.

Bakan, David. 1958. *Sigmund Freud and the Jewish Mystical Tradition*. Princeton, NJ: Van Nostrand.

Baker, David B., ed. 2003. *Thick Description and Fine Texture: Studies in the History of Psychology*. Akron, OH: University of Akron Press.

2012. *The Oxford Handbook of the History of Psychology: Global Perspectives*. New York: Oxford University Press.

Benjamin, Ludy T., Jr. 1981. *Teaching History of Psychology: A Handbook*. New York: Academic Press.

1988. *A History of Psychology: Original Sources and Contemporary Research*. New York: McGraw-Hill.

Benjamin, Ludy T. Jr., and David B. Baker. 2004. *From Séance to Science: A History of the Profession of Psychology in America*. Belmont, CA: Wadsworth/Thomson Learning.

Bernstein, Maxine D., and Nancy F. Russo. 1974. "The History of Psychology Revisited: Or, Up with Our Foremothers," *American Psychologist* 29:130–4.

Blumenthal, Arthur L. 1975. "A Reappraisal of Wilhelm Wundt," *American Psychologist* 30:1081–8.

1976. "Wundt – Revisions and Reappraisals," *Annals of the New York Academy of Sciences* 270:21–30.

Borch-Jacobsen, Mikkel, and Sonu Shamdasani. (2012). *The Freud Files: An Inquiry into the History of Psychoanalysis*. Cambridge: Cambridge University Press.

Boring, Edwin G. 1929. *A History of Experimental Psychology*. New York: Appleton-Century-Crofts. 2nd ed., 1950.

Brett, George S. 1912–21. *A History of Psychology*, 3 Vols. London: George Allen and Unwin.

Brock, Adrian C. 1995. "Why I Am Not a Historian of Science," *History and Philosophy of Psychology Bulletin* 7:27–31.

Brock, Adrian C., ed. 2006. *Internationalizing the History of Psychology*. New York: New York University Press.

Brock, Adrian C., Johann Louw, and Willem van Hoorn, eds. 2004. *Rediscovering the History of Psychology: Essays Inspired by the Work of Kurt Danziger*. New York: Kluwer.

Brožek, Josef. 1999. "History of a Historian of Psychology in the United States," *History of Psychology* 2:83–101.

Brožek, Josef, and Leslie S. Schneider. 1973. "Second Summer Institute on the History of Psychology," *Journal of the History of the Behavioral Sciences* 9:91–101.

Brožek, Josef, Robert I. Watson, and Barbara Ross. 1969. "A Summer Institute on the History of Psychology: Part I," *Journal of the History of the Behavioral Sciences* 5:307–19.

1970. "A Summer Institute on the History of Psychology: Part II," *Journal of the History of the Behavioral Sciences* 6:25–35.

Brožek, Josef, and Rand B. Evans, eds. 1977. *R. I. Watson's Selected Papers on the History of Psychology*. Hanover, NH: University Press of New England.

Burnham, John C. 1959. "Preserving Historical Materials," *American Psychologist* 14:655–6.

1967. *Psychoanalysis and American Medicine, 1894–1918: Medicine, Science, and Culture*. New York: International Universities Press.

1988. *Paths into American Culture: Psychology, Medicine, and Morals*. Philadelphia: Temple University Press.

2006. "The 'New Freud Studies': A Historiographical Shift," *Journal of the Historical Society* 6(2):213–33.

Burnham, John C., ed. 2012. *After Freud Left: A Century of Psychoanalysis in America*. Chicago: University of Chicago Press.

Camfield, Thomas M. 1973 "The Professionalization of American Psychology, 1870–1917," *Journal of the History of the Behavioral Sciences* 9:66–75

Capshew, James H. 1988. Review of *Psychology in America: A Historical Survey* and *A History of Psychology: Main Currents in Psychological Thought*. *Isis* 79:111–12.

1999. *Psychologists on the March: Science, Practice, and Professional Identity in America, 1929–1969*. New York: Cambridge University Press.

Carlson, Eric T., and Robert I. Watson. 1965. "Editorial: The Birth of a Journal," *Journal of the History of the Behavioral Sciences* 1:3–4.

Cohen-Cole, Jamie. 2005. "The Reflexivity of Cognitive Science: The Scientist as Model of Human Nature," *History of the Human Sciences* 18:107–39.

Cravens, Hamilton. 1985. "History of the Social Sciences," *Osiris* 1:183–207.

1990. Review of the *Journal of the History of the Behavioral Sciences* and *History of the Human Sciences*, *Isis* 81:306–8.

Danziger, Kurt. 1979. "The Positivist Repudiation of Wundt," *Journal of the History of the Behavioral Sciences* 15:205–30.

1990. *Constructing the Subject: Historical Origins of Psychological Research*. Cambridge: Cambridge University Press.

1991. "Introduction," *History of the Human Sciences* 4:327–33.

1994. "Does the History of Psychology Have a Future?" *Theory & Psychology* 4:467–84.

1996. "Towards a Polycentric History of Psychology." Unpublished paper, 26th International Congress of Psychology, Montreal. Revised and expanded version. Downloaded from www.kurtdanziger.com.

1997a. "The Moral Basis of Historiography," *History and Philosophy of Psychology Bulletin* 9(1):6–15.

1997b. *Naming the Mind: How Psychology Found Its Language*. London: Sage.

2006. "Comment," *International Journal of Psychology* 41:269–75.

2013. "Psychology and Its History," *Theory & Psychology* 23:829–39.

Ellenberger, Henri F. 1970. *The Discovery of the Unconscious: The History and Evolution of Dynamic Psychiatry*. New York: Basic Books.

Fancher, Raymond E. 1973. *Psychoanalytic Psychology: The Development of Freud's Thought*. New York: Norton.

1979. *Pioneers of Psychology*. New York: Norton.

2003. "A Tale of Two Institutions: York University's History of Psychology Program and the Archives of the History of American Psychology." In *Thick Description and Fine Texture*, ed. D. B. Baker. Akron: University of Akron Press.

Fancher, Raymond E., and Alexandra Rutherford. 2012. *Pioneers of Psychology: A History*, 4th ed. New York: Norton.

Faye, Cathy, and David B. Baker. 2011. "Sources: The Center for the History of Psychology at the University of Akron," *History of Psychology* 14:204–9.

Forman, Paul. 1991. "Independence, Not Transcendence, for the Historian of Science," *Isis* 82:71–86.

Freud, Sigmund. 1953–74. *The Standard Edition of the Complete Psychological Works of Sigmund Freud*, 24 Vols., trans. James Strachey London: Hogarth Press & Institute of Psychoanalysis.

Furumoto, Laurel. 1989. "The New History of Psychology." In *The G. Stanley Hall Lecture Series*, Vol. 9, ed. Ira S. Cohe. Washington, DC: American Psychological Association, 9–34

Gellner, Ernest. 1996. *The Psychoanalytic Movement: The Cunning of Unreason*. Evanston, IL: Northwestern University Press.

Gergen, Kenneth J. 1973. "Social Psychology as History," *Journal of Personality and Social Psychology* 26:309–20.

1989. Review of *The Rise of Experimentation in American Psychology*, *Contemporary Sociology* 18:409–10.

Goodman, Elizabeth S. 1974. "Follow-Up Study: Uncle Sam's Dollars at Work." Unpublished paper, Cheiron Society annual meeting.

Guthrie, Robert V. 1976. *Even the Rat Was White: A Historical View of Psychology*. New York: Harper & Row, 2nd ed., 1998. Boston: Allyn & Bacon.

Hale, Nathan G., Jr. 1995. *The Rise and Crisis of Psychoanalysis in the United States: Freud and the Americans, 1917–1985*. New York: Oxford.

Harris, Benjamin. 1979. "Whatever Happened to Little Albert?" *American Psychologist* 34:151–60.

Hearst, Eliot, ed. 1979. *The First Century of Experimental Psychology*. Hillsdale, NJ: Lawrence Erlbaum Associates.

Henle, Mary, and John Sullivan. 1974. "Seven Psychologies Revisited," *Journal of the History of the Behavioral Sciences* 10:40–6.

Herman, Ellen. 1995. *The Romance of American Psychology: Political Culture in the Age of Experts.* Berkeley: University of California Press.

Hilgard, Ernest R. 1982. "Robert I. Watson and the Founding of Division 26 of the American Psychological Association," *Journal of the History of the Behavioral Sciences* 18:308–11.

1987. *Psychology in America: A Historical Survey.* San Diego: Harcourt Brace Jovanovich.

Hilgard, Ernest R., David E. Leary, and Gregory R. McGuire. 1991. "The History of Psychology: A Survey and Critical Assessment," *Annual Review of Psychology* 42:79–107.

Hurley, Dan. 2005. "Bizarre and Infamous Join Scholarship in an Archive of Psychology," *New York Times,* 27 September.

Jackson, John P., Jr., and Nadine M. Weidman. 2005. *Race, Racism, and Science: Social Impact and Interaction.* New Brunswick, NJ: Rutgers University Press.

Jonçich, Geraldine. 1968. *The Sane Positivist: A Biography of Edward L. Thorndike.* Middletown, CT: Wesleyan University Press.

Jones, Ernest. 1953–57. *Sigmund Freud: Life and Work*, 3 Vols. London: Hogarth.

Kevles, Daniel J. 1968. "Testing the Army's Intelligence: Psychologists and the Military in World War I," *Journal of American History* 55:565–81.

Klüver, Heinrich. 1949. "Psychology at the Beginning of World War II: Meditations on the Impending Dismemberment of Psychology Written in 1942," *Journal of Psychology* 28:383–410.

Koch, Sigmund, ed. 1959–63. *Psychology: A Study of a Science.* New York: McGraw-Hill.

Koch, Sigmund. 1985. "Wundt's Creature at Age Zero – and as Centenarian: Some Aspects of the Institutionalization of the 'New Psychology.'" In *A Century of Psychology as Science*, ed. S. Koch and D. E. Leary. Washington, DC: American Psychological Association, 7–35.

Koch, Sigmund, and David E. Leary, eds. 1985/1992. *A Century of Psychology as Science.* Washington, DC: American Psychological Association.

Krawiec, T. S., ed. 1972–78. *The Psychologists.* New York: Oxford University Press.

Kuhn, Thomas S. 1962. *The Structure of Scientific Revolutions.* Chicago: University of Chicago Press. 2nd ed., 1970.

Lakatos, Imre, and Alan Musgrave, eds. 1970. *Criticism and the Growth of Knowledge.* New York: Cambridge University Press.

Marinelli, Lydia, and Andreas Mayer. 2006. 'Editors' Introduction: Forgetting Freud? For a New Historiography of Psychoanalysis," *Science in Context* 19:1–13.

Mayer, Ronald W. 1997. "A History of Division 26 (History of Psychology)." In *Unification Through Division: Histories of the Divisions of the American Psychological Association*, Vol. II, ed. D. W. Dewsbury. Washington, DC: American Psychological Association, 127–51.

Morawski, Jill G., ed. 1988. *The Rise of Experimentation in American Psychology.* New Haven, CT: Yale University Press.

Morawski, Jill G. 2005. "Reflexivity and the Psychologist," *History of the Human Sciences* 18:77–105.

Murchison, Carl, ed. 1930. *A History of Psychology in Autobiography*. Worcester, MA: Clark University Press.
Murphy, Gardner. 1929/1930/1949. *An Historical Introduction to Modern Psychology*. New York: Harcourt, Brace & World.
Napoli, Donald S. 1981. *Architects of Adjustment: The History of the Psychological Profession in the United States*. Port Washington, NY: Kennikat Press.
O'Connell, Agnes N., and Nancy Felipe Russo, eds. 1980. *Models of Achievement: Reflections of Eminent Women in Psychology*. New York: Columbia University Press.
O'Donnell, John M. 1979. "The Crisis of Experimentalism in the 1920s: E. G. Boring and His Uses of History," *American Psychologist* 34:289–95.
1985. *The Origins of Behaviorism: American Psychology, 1870–1920*. New York: New York University Press.
Palermo, David S. 1971. "Is a Scientific Revolution Taking Place in Psychology?" *Science Studies* 1:135–55
Pickren, Wade E., and Alexandra Rutherford. 2010. *A History of Modern Psychology in Context*. Hoboken, NJ: John Wiley & Sons.
Popplestone, John A. 2005. "Reinventing the Past through Reinterpretation: Reflections on the History of Psychology – 35 Years in the Trenches." In *The Life Cycle of Psychological Ideas: Understanding Prominence and the Dynamic of Intellectual Change*, ed. T. C. Dalton and R. B. Evans. New York: Kluwer, 59–81.
Richards, Graham. 1987. "Of What Is History of Psychology a History?" *British Journal for the History of Science* 20:201–11.
1996/2002/2010. *Putting Psychology in Its Place*. New York: Routledge.
1997/2011. *"Race," Racism, and Psychology: Towards a Reflexive History*. London: Routledge.
Rieff, Philip. 1959. *Freud: The Mind of the Moralist*. New York: Viking Press.
1966. *The Triumph of the Therapeutic: The Uses of Faith after Freud*. New York: Harper & Row.
Robinson, Daniel N. 2013. "Historiography in Psychology: A Note on Ignorance," *Theory & Psychology* 23:819–28, 852–4.
Rose, Nikolas. 1990. *Governing the Soul: The Shaping of the Private Self*. London: Routledge.
1996. *Inventing Our Selves: Psychology, Power and Personhood*. Cambridge: Cambridge University Press.
Ross, Dorothy. 1972. *G. Stanley Hall: The Psychologist as Prophet*. Chicago: University of Chicago Press.
Samelson, Franz. 1974. "History, Origin Myth and Ideology: 'Discovery' of Social Psychology," *Journal for the Theory of Social Behaviour* 4:217–34.
Scarborough, Elizabeth. 2004. "Cheiron's Origins: Personal Recollections and a Photograph," *Journal of the History of the Behavioral Sciences* 40:207–11.
Scarborough, Elizabeth, and Laurel Furumoto. 1987. *Untold Lives: The First Generation of American Women Psychologists*. New York: Columbia University Press.
Schultz, Duane P. 1969. *A History of Modern Psychology*. New York: Academic Press.
Schultz, Duane P., and Sydney Ellen Schultz. 2011. *A History of Modern Psychology*, 10th ed. Belmont, CA: Wadsworth.
Shamdasani, Sonu. 1998. *Cult Fictions: C. G. Jung and the Founding of Analytical Psychology*. London: Routledge.

2003. *Jung and the Making of Modern Psychology: The Dream of a Science*. Cambridge: Cambridge University Press.

Smith, Roger. 1988. "Does the History of Psychology Have a Subject?" *History of the Human Sciences* 1:147–77.

1997. *The Norton History of the Human Sciences*. New York: Norton.

2005. "Does Reflexivity Separate the Human Sciences from the Natural Sciences?" *History of the Human Sciences* 18:1–25.

Sokal, Michael M. 1998. "On *History of Psychology*'s Launch," *History of Psychology* 1:3–7.

Teo, Thomas. 2013. "Agnotology in the Dialectics of the History and Philosophy of Psychology," *Theory & Psychology* 23:840–51.

Watson, Robert I. 1953. "A Brief History of Clinical Psychology," *Psychological Bulletin* 50:321–46.

1960. "The History of Psychology: A Neglected Area," *American Psychologist* 15:251–5.

1963. *The Great Psychologists: Aristotle to Freud*. Philadelphia: Lippincott.

1972. "Working Paper." In *The Psychologists*, ed. T. S. Krawiec . New York: Oxford University Press, 275–98.

Watson, Robert I., and Donald T. Campbell, eds. 1963. *History, Psychology, and Science: Selected Papers by Edwin G. Boring*. New York: Wiley.

Weimer, Walter B. 1974a. "The History of Psychology and Its Retrieval from Historiography, I: The Problematic Nature of History," *Science Studies* 4:235–58.

1974b. "The History of Psychology and Its Retrieval from Historiography, II: Some Lessons for the Methodology of Scientific Research," *Science Studies* 4:367–96.

Weimer, Walter B., and David S. Palermo. 1973. "Paradigms and Normal Science in Psychology," *Science Studies* 3:211–44.

Winston, Andrew S., ed. 2003. *Defining Difference: Race and Racism in the History of Psychology*. Washington, DC: APA Books.

Woodward, William T. 1980. "Towards a Critical History of Psychology." In *Historiography of Modern Psychology*, ed. J. Brožek and L. Pongratz.

Woodworth, Robert S. 1931/1948/1964. *Contemporary Schools of Psychology*. New York: Ronald Press.

Young, Robert M. 1966. "Scholarship and the History of the Behavioural Sciences," *History of Science* 5:1–51.

Young-Bruehl, Elisabeth. 1992. "A History of Freud Biographies," *Studies in Psychoanalytic Theory* 1:3–21.

6

Contested Identities

The History of Economics since 1945

Roger E. Backhouse and Philippe Fontaine

In 2007, when the Australian Bureau of Statistics (ABS) proposed a new classification in which "history of economic thought" was moved from "economics" to "history, archeology, religion and philosophy," some in the field were up in arms, protesting that this amounted to its destruction (see Kates and Millmow 2008a, b). As most Australian historians of economics are affiliated to economics departments, this change threatened to render their research worthless within their institutions. However, their reaction also reflected a belief that what they were doing fell under the jurisdiction of economics and that it could not therefore be considered a form of the history and philosophy of science.

This episode and others like it point to an identity problem: Most historians of economics are trained as economists and think of themselves as such, but the remainder of the economics profession cannot see the significance of the history of economics for what they are doing. Some historians of economics, such as those who challenged the ABS reclassification, are committed to trying to change this situation while others contend that what they do is a form of history and accordingly feel less concerned about economists' lack of interest.

Attempts have been made to mitigate this identity problem by terminological clarification. To take but one example among many, Waterman (2008) identifies two kinds of "history of economics": the history of economic analysis, the purpose of which is "to enlarge our understanding of present-day economic theory by a careful consideration of its intellectual pedigree" (p. 107), and the "intellectual history of economic thought," which places textual developments into a broad context including disciplines other than economics and "is of little or no value to working economists" (p. 106). The former concerns the logical structure of economic ideas and their evolution; it may require technical abilities of the kind used by working economists.[1]

The problem of identity cannot so readily be resolved. Language has its own history and cultural resonance, making it hard to change usages overnight, however rational the proposed clarifications. More important, there is no completely sharp distinction between intellectual history of economic thought and history of economic analysis.[2] There is also little connection between such a classification, made on intellectual grounds, and the institutional situation in which the field finds itself. Even if they do not consider it to be part of economics, economists can be more interested in the intellectual history of their own field than they are in what Waterman calls history of economic analysis.[3]

The uncertainties affecting historians of economics (we use this as a generic term, interchangeable with historians of economic thought) result from the pressures created by the gradual distancing of the economics profession as a whole from the history of economics, as witnessed by its almost complete disappearance from the pages of the leading general journals.[4] Losing ground in economics, historians of economics have found themselves challenged by cultural and intellectual historians, sociologists and historians of science, scholars from various branches of science studies, and even journalists, who have no training in economics but who write on the history of economics arguing that the subject can, and perhaps should, be studied outside economics.

Even if historians of economics see themselves as historians, they do not escape issues of identity. In what sense can it be said that they are historians? Do they endorse research methods common to historical scholarship and, if so, what kind of historical scholarship? There have been calls to see the history of economics as history of science (Schabas 1992) or as history

1 Two other distinctions have been used to analyze the field: one between absolutism and relativism, which is used in the first edition of Mark Blaug's *Economic Theory in Retrospect* (1962); the other, between historical and rational reconstructions, which appears in later editions (Blaug 1996; see also Blaug 1990 and 2001).

2 Waterman (2002) himself implicitly recognizes this point when he argues that the work of the "Sussex school" in intellectual history is potentially of interest to those engaging in history of economic analysis, and that intellectual historians need to understand economic analysis.

3 There is also the issue of heterodox economics, discussed later.

4 As an indication of the early recognition of that development, note that in the "avant-propos" to the newly created *History of Political Economy*, Craufurd Goodwin et al. (1969, 1) wrote: "In 1967 the thirty-five articles and communications published in the [*American Economic*] *Review* include only one article dealing with the history of economic thought."

of social science (Backhouse and Fontaine 2010). And yet, departments of the history of science have not been especially welcoming to historians of economics. Moreover, the notion that economics can be seen as a science standing alongside the natural sciences has met with the resistance of those who see such a position as linked to a view of science as cumulative and therefore in no need of its past (Kurz 2006, p. 466). Likewise, the notion that the history of economics is tied to the histories of the other social sciences challenges the view that it moved away from them after the Second World War, as suggested by Solow (1997, p. 54). Aligning history of economics with intellectual history (Winch 1978, 2000), where it would therefore be seen "as a part of history, part of the attempt to understand past human experience" (Collini 1985, p. 46), is another option. However, intellectual historians have paid more attention to political science and sociology, perhaps because these bear a more easily understood relationship to broader cultural developments, perhaps because they consider they lack the technical skills needed to discuss economics, though this has changed as economics has become an increasingly dominant element in public discourse (Rodgers 2011; Burgin 2012).[5]

Perhaps one reason that other historians keep their distance is the implicit belief of some historians of economics that published texts offer an immediate access to the past that renders its recreation a trivial task. Clearly, some historians of economics see their main task as unveiling the authorial intentions contained in published texts so as to reveal to the wider community their hidden meanings.[6] This tendency of historians of economics to consider texts independently of their relation to the external world stems from what other contributors to this volume term a "presentist" perspective. Texts are read in the light of modern theory or are seen as a source of forgotten ideas that might be worth recovering, leading to neglect of the questions of the historical reconstruction of the past and its limits. Because of the frequent association of the historical past with the chronological past, there is thus much more discussion of when the history of economics begins – whether with Adam Smith or in the ancient world (e.g., Lowry 1991) – than of when it ends. There are discussions of how to

[5] Waterman (2002) provides an interesting discussion of the limited engagement of intellectual historians with economics.

[6] The focus on published texts by many historians of economics may explain why intellectual historians, who also see their main task as the elucidation of texts, have had much difficulty with traditional history of economics. Here we leave aside the philosophical problems relating to the meaning of a text. Peter Burke (2005, p. 103) thinks that historians would be ill advised to take sides on this question.

write the history of twentieth-century economics (e.g., Weintraub 1999) and of the history of recent economics as a model for writing the history of economics in general (Davis 1998), but it is harder to find discussions of how to draw the line between engaging in contemporary economics, which has numerous surveys, many of which are arranged chronologically, and writing its history.

This takes us back to questions of identity: To be recognized as an economist it is necessary to participate in the process of creating and propagating economic knowledge, whereas to be recognized as a historian it is necessary to make historical claims that go beyond what might be found in a survey in an economics journal. As we get close to the present, these two roles enter into conflict.[7]

In this chapter we show that the changing identity problem of the history of economics cannot be understood without taking account of the changes affecting economics from 1945, especially as the claim that the history of economics is economics has, for many of its practitioners, been central to the legitimation of the field up to the present.[8] Until the 1950s or so, economists had usually attached importance to history, including both economic history and the history of economic theories, but as the discipline became more technical and acquired a more scientific self-image, this view found fewer and fewer supporters within the profession.[9] As a result, whereas the history of economics, in the 1940s, had an established, if limited, place in the curriculum, sometimes taught by leading economic theorists, the subject is today widely seen as peripheral, as symbolized by its frequent association with "heterodox" economics – for most economists a label for out-of-date and nonrigorous economics.[10]

[7] Coats (1969b, p. 11) already saw the role of the history of economic thought in teaching, commonly used to defend the field, as diminishing. That development may illustrate the tendency, from this period, for economists to define their identity in terms of practices rather than beliefs. On the distinction between beliefs and practices in relation to that of subject matter and discipline, see Chandler (2009).

[8] For a characterization of the history of economics before 1945, see Goodwin (2008).

[9] Outsiders regularly confuse economic history and the history of economics (history of economic thought, history of economic doctrines, history of economic analysis, etc.). Economic history relates to the study of historical economic phenomena (e.g. the Great Depression) and economic institutions (e.g. slavery, the World Bank). Our concern is not with economic history except as it impinges on the history of economics.

[10] Some publishers even include history of economic thought alongside heterodox economics in their catalogs, and some historians of economic thought, who use history to advance heterodox causes, concur. Kurz (2006, p. 468), for instance, writes: "it should come as

Times of Doubt

The late 1940s is often seen as the period when American institutionalism, a movement with historicist roots, began to be displaced by a more formal, abstract, and ahistorical neoclassical economics (see, for instance, Yonay 1998; Morgan and Rutherford 1998; Rutherford 2011). One of the main features of institutionalist work was its highly empirical and inductive character so that the ascendancy of neoclassical economists came to be associated with mathematical modeling and a higher level of abstraction.[11] In view of this development, it is hardly surprising that in his report on graduate education in economics, Howard R. Bowen (1953) contrasted the technical-theoretical and the historical-philosophical-institutional approaches, arguing that in recent years the balance had been tipped in favor of the former. Bowen even explained the growth of interest in economic history as a result of the overemphasis of economic theory following the Great Depression (p. 112).

In contrast, though he noted its presence among the traditional core courses at many institutions, Bowen suggested that the history of economic thought had "declined in popularity" (p. 115). As his report made clear, the field was second only to economic theory among the fields required or usually elected by students at reporting institutions, but the trend, Bowen surmised, was in favor of more technical fields. In this respect, it is of some interest that Bowen concluded the "History of Economic Thought" section in the report by citing the view of Jacob Viner – who had left Chicago for Princeton in the mid-1940s – that "the demands of technical professionalism should not be permitted to crowd out interest in scholarship" (p. 116), which Viner described as "the pursuit of broad and exact knowledge of the history of the working of the human mind as revealed in written records" (Viner quoted by Bowen 1953, p. 115). As economics became more technical in the years following the report, there was an increasing sense that

no surprise that people interested in the history of economic thought often happen to be heterodox economists of various leanings." This remark follows a reference to Whig history à la Samuelson, which suggests that the latter, because of its presentist motivation, does not count as "history of economic thought." Weintraub (2007, p. 277), on the other hand, argues that the association of history of economics with heterodox economics undermines it: "in economics it is heterodox economics [as opposed to economic science studies] that is considered de-legitimizing in the sense that in numerous ways it challenges the epistemic authority of 'neoclassical' or 'mainstream' economics."

11 Mary Morgan and Malcolm Rutherford's (1998) distinction between interwar pluralism and postwar neoclassicism allows a more balanced approach to the transformation of American economics, but it does not seem to be at variance with our broad outline description.

mainstream practices and the writing of the history of economic thought were separate activities: that although economists might have an interest in the history of economics, it was a separate activity informed by economic theory rather than vice versa.

The situation had been different only a few years earlier. Even leading economic theorists and opponents of institutionalism, who might be expected to be the least sympathetic to history, such as Lionel Robbins at the London School of Economics (LSE), Joseph Schumpeter at Harvard, and Frank Knight and Jacob Viner at Chicago, considered that the history of the subject should be an integral part of the economics curriculum. At Chicago, the educationist Robert M. Hutchins, as president from 1929 to 1945 and the university's chancellor until 1951, contributed vigorously to the debate over general education and instituted his "great books" program. This was of concern even to economists who attached importance to history, such as Knight and Viner, for its effect was to allow departmental faculty to free themselves from the responsibility of general education and to focus on educating specialists (Emmett 1998, p. 139). By the 1940s, though the economics department had endorsed a more constraining range of course offerings, focusing on economic theory and statistics, the history of economic thought was still "part of the economic theory core that all doctoral students had to take and was taught by Knight" (p. 144).[12] However, the fact that the luminaries of economics departments at leading research universities – Knight and Viner at Chicago, and Schumpeter at Harvard – considered history of economic thought a central part of an economics education did not augur a bright future. Once convinced that it would be better to forget about past mistakes rather than try to learn from them, economists had few scruples about withdrawing the history of economic thought from their curricula. Bowen, who connected the decline of the field with the ascendancy of technicality and abstraction, overlooked that dependence on economic theory also carried some risks for the history of the economics discipline.

The link between the perceived decline of the history of economic thought (and interdisciplinary work) and the increased technicality of economics was also pointed out at Harvard on the occasion of the writing of the Ford Foundation commissioned self-study of the behavioral sciences. *The Behavioral Sciences at Harvard* (Harvard University, Faculty Committee

[12] As noted by Henderson (1976 [1993], p. 354), "For the several decades both preceding and following the turn of the century, the history of economic thought was a much more active area of research than it was after mathematics began to assert itself."

on the Behavioral Sciences, 1954) emphasized the significance of the main traditions of economic theory as against the "assaults of institutionalists and other critics of abstract theory"; it likewise pointed out that some of the "younger men" at Harvard believed research was lagging in the field of mathematical economics compared with Chicago and Stanford (p. 128). More importantly, though it separated the discussion of economic theory from that of other fields, the report stressed the superficiality of that separation since specializations were not only regarded as applications and extensions of the methods of economic theory but were also valued according to their degree of theoretical development.[13] That placed the history of economic thought in a difficult position: As a part of economic theory, it could hardly appear as one of its applications so that its value to economics resided mainly in the perception of its usefulness to economic theorizing. If that were challenged, then the history's place in the curriculum would be in jeopardy.[14]

Schumpeter, who had taught the history of economic thought at Harvard from 1939 to 1948, might have considered it essential for economists to develop some familiarity with the field, but it is doubtful his younger colleagues at the economics department concurred.[15] By the time his monumental *History of Economic Analysis* came out posthumously in 1954, his university's report to the Ford Foundation could only deplore "a notable absence of younger men in the field – a situation in sharp contrast with the lively activity in intellectual history and the history of political thought." Not only the increased technicality of economics but also "its divorcement [*sic*] in America from the European traditions of broad, diffuse scholarship were suggested as possible explanations" (1954, p. 145).

13 Nearly a decade after the publication of *General Education in a Free Society* (1945), the tensions between general education and specialism, which permeated every chapter of the book, had lessened. By then, it was clear that general education, which might have appeared as inadequate to cope with the postwar challenges, had survived the "age of specialism," as the "red book" described it. To some extent, the Department of Social Relations could be seen as a vehicle of general education. It should be remembered that the members of the Harvard Committee "recommend[ed] that a course in the field of 'human relations' be carefully considered by the standing committee and ... be offered as one of those in general education" (p. 220).

14 Another, no less significant, element is that after 1945 history of economics, unlike economic theory, could hardly benefit from the strong emphasis on basic science. A couple of decades later, when the emphasis shifted toward the applied, the position of the history of economics was no better.

15 Schumpeter, the historian of economic thought, did not comment on Schumpeter, the economic theorist, in a book of almost thirteen hundred pages (McCraw 2007, p. 444). In his lectures, too, he did not emphasize his own work.

One of the reviewers of *History of Economic Analysis*, Friedrich von Hayek, another Austrian, who had spent some twenty years at London School of Economics before relocating to Chicago, was well placed to appreciate the incongruity of the book in relation to recent developments in American economics: "Nobody should profit more from [the book] than the economists of the younger generation … no work is better suited to show what they ought to know if they are to be not merely economists but cultivated persons competent to use their technical knowledge in a complex world" (Hayek quoted in McCraw 2007, pp. 464–5).[16] For Hayek, as for his colleague Robbins, the dominant influence on economics at LSE, it was as important to learn from the work of previous generations as from economists in other countries.[17]

At the more insular University of Cambridge, United Kingdom, feelings toward the history of economic thought were more ambivalent. The professor of political economy, Arthur Cecil Pigou, was not quite so dismissive of the field as has been claimed but he was not sympathetic towards it and it played no role in his work.[18] In contrast, being fascinated by biography (see Backhouse 2007), his colleague John Maynard Keynes was much more interested in the history of economic thought, and undertook some serious historical study, including the recovery of lost texts, but this remained essentially separate from his economics.[19] This position was shared by most of their younger colleagues at Cambridge, some of whom became very influential, few of whom took an interest in the history of their field. Piero Sraffa did, producing a major edition of the works of Malthus's contemporary David Ricardo, but from 1927 to 1959 he published nothing of significance in economics.

[16] In arguing over monetary policy in the 1930s, Hayek had taken the view that had his leading opponent, John Maynard Keynes, been thoroughly trained in the nineteenth-century classics, he would never have been able to make some of the claims he did.

[17] After the war, Robbins shared the teaching of the subject with Terence Hutchison, a Cambridge-trained specialist in the philosophy of economics whose *A Review of Economic Doctrines, 1870–1929* (1953) was eclipsed by Schumpeter's *History*.

[18] Blaug (2001, p. 154), echoing the view he had expressed in his widely cited textbook (1962, 1996) claimed that Pigou dismissed the field as "the wrong opinions of dead men." Pigou (1902, p. 374) admitted a prejudice against the field when he wrote "These antiquarian researches have no great attractions for one who finds it difficult enough to read what is now thought upon economic problems, without spending time in studying confessedly inadequate solutions that were offered centuries ago," but though he was "little disposed to be sympathetic" he found the book on early economic thought that he was reviewing "full of interest."

[19] This is not to deny that there may have been occasions when reading past texts may have helped him formulate his theoretical ideas.

The ambivalence toward the history of economic thought among economists persisted long into the early 1960s, which probably stands as a pivotal moment in higher education in Britain. It reflected the existence of more general divisions between those who emphasized the broad functions of education and those who insisted on its more specialized objectives. Perhaps the most telling illustration of these divisions manifested itself in the well-known "two cultures controversy," which, beyond the opposition between arts and sciences, evidenced the existence of different worldviews as to the role of higher education. It is no accident that C. P. Snow was asked to serve on the Robbins committee on higher education (even though he eventually declined) and that the "two cultures" problem surfaced on a number of occasions during the committee's deliberations (see Ortolano 2009, pp. 107–9). The controversy had momentous significance in the transition of British higher education to the modern era. The report produced by the Robbins Committee, which became one of the central documents underwriting the expansion of higher education, continued to recognize the necessity for universities to produce "cultivated" men and women, despite its acknowledgment of the increasing role of science and technology in British society. The history of economics could have served this purpose, as it has continued to do in American liberal arts colleges (Bateman 2002), but this did not happen. In the following years Robbins witnessed the gradual eviction of historical scholarship from economics as the demands of technical professionalism increased, a development that his friend Viner had pointed out as an unfortunate possibility on the other side of the Atlantic.

In Continental Europe, the situation was very different. German economics, the center of the historical approach, had become a shadow of what it once was as a result of the mass migration resulting from National Socialist policies and the Second World War. In France, economics remained strong though it had little influence on the United States, which now dominated the field. When linguistic and other barriers fell, there was increased harmonization with trends in the United States – a process variously perceived as "internationalization" or "Americanization" (see Coats 1996, 2000). In France, the internationalization of economics can be dated from the late 1960s (see Fourcade 2009, pp. 212–15). In the twenty years preceding that development, the field continued to exhibit a variety of orientations, approaches, and influences that could hardly encourage the disappearance of a form of pluralism (see Arena 2000). In that context, and following the tradition inherited from Charles Gide and Charles Rist's *Histoire des doctrines économiques* (1909) and perpetuated by Daniel

Villey and Colette Neme's *Petite Histoire des grandes doctrines économiques* (1944), scholarly interest in the history of economic thought tended to emphasize doctrinal issues, in which value judgments were prominent, even if from the 1950s authors like Émile James (1950) may have wished to provide their readers with a better grasp of theoretical problems by putting more emphasis on economic theories. A number of factors combined to maintain the place of the history of economic thought in higher education curricula. The role of the faculties of law in the teaching of economics long encouraged the emphasis on general knowledge; likewise, with few exceptions, the tardy internationalization of French economists slowed down the endorsement of more technical-theoretical approaches; and finally, promotion at the full professor level required candidates to take an examination, the *agrégation*, which, until the late 1990s, included presenting a separate lecture in either the history of economic thought or economic history.[20]

France may have been an exception, though not the only one, for after 1945, in part propelled by the expansion of the economics profession and the influx into academia of a generation far better trained in mathematics and statistics than their elders, economics became progressively more technical. Some of the leading figures (notably Paul Samuelson, George Stigler, and William Baumol), trained in the 1930s and 1940s, retained strong interests in the history of economic thought, but they were a small minority. Economics was seen as a science in which what mattered was logical and empirical rigor, and an understanding of history was a luxury. This move was arguably impelled by the "Keynesian revolution" and the emergence of macroeconomics, in which Keynes's *General Theory of Employment, Interest and Money* (1936) was believed to involve so profound a break with the past as to render earlier work superfluous, a break that may have likewise precipitated the neglect of the history of more recent economics.[21]

[20] Italy may well stand as another significant exception, as illustrated by Marcuzzo and Rosselli (2002, p. 98), who "look at the peculiar Italian way of doing HET, which germinated in the late 1960s, blossomed in the mid-1970s, and withered away in the early 1980s, involving people who considered themselves and were generally perceived as economists rather than historians of economic thought."

[21] Milton Friedman (1956) might challenge this, arguing for the "traditional" quantity theory of money going back to Hume, but his focus was as much on the importance of Chicago as an appeal to history for which a caricature would suffice. Friedman's claims were, however, later to stimulate the serious historical scholarship needed to undermine them (Patinkin 1969; Johnson 1971; Laidler 1993).

Institutional Reactions to Perceived Decline

In the United States and to a lesser extent the United Kingdom, the research university experienced significant changes in the sixties due to increasing recognition of knowledge as a factor of economic growth and instrument of national purpose (Kerr 1963). That development encouraged greater involvement in national policy making on the side of economists who succeeded in constructing an image of professional rigor and objectivity for their discipline on the basis of increased technicality. Though the origins of technical economics can be traced to the 1930s, it was not until the 1960s and 1970s that it became the generally accepted way to do economics. By then, a level of mathematics (including differential and integral calculus, matrix algebra, probability theory, statistics, and, somewhat later, set theory and topology) significantly more advanced than that expected in 1945, was acknowledged as a prerequisite for serious graduate studies, with the result that less room was left in the curriculum for courses with a historical dimension. If economic theories consisted of mathematical theorems that were demonstrably correct and testing was done through formal statistical methods, then knowing about their history was a luxury.[22] It was still possible to obtain supervision for a thesis in the field, but it became hard to have material published in the leading journals or to be recruited at the leading research universities. Unless, as was very common, they acquired credentials in some other field of economics, perhaps turning to its history after obtaining tenure, historians of economics were much more likely to find employment in liberal arts colleges. There thus arose a significant literature discussing, sometimes in the top journals, the role of the history of economic thought in economics (Samuelson 1962; Gordon 1965).[23]

Increasingly aware that other economists did not necessarily share their interests, historians of economics, especially in the United States

[22] Note the influential "What Price the History of Economic Thought," in which Winch (1964) noted the loss of relevance of the teaching of the history of economic thought to the training of economic theorists and deplored the divorce of the field from other branches of intellectual history. In that article, which followed Samuelson's (1962) presidential address on "Economists and the History of Ideas" at the 1961 meeting of the American Economic Association, Winch also pointed to the widening rift between the history of ideas and intellectual history.

[23] Discussing contributions to a symposium on the history of economics in the *American Economic Review*, William R. Allen (1965, p. 143) noted: "Some of my best friends take me as a friend only in spite of my interest in dead economists. It is better in the eyes of these colleagues to be even a traditionalist in labor or public finance than to have an active interest in the evolution of economic theory."

and Britain, where the field was losing ground, began to organize. In the United States, after a symposium on the history of economic thought held in Durham on December 6–7, 1968, a specialist journal, *History of Political Economy* (*HOPE*), was established in 1969, and shortly afterward the History of Economics Society was formed. It held its first meeting in 1973, opening with a session on methods of intellectual history and closing with a roundtable on the teaching of the history of economics. At the conference, Warren J. Samuels (1974) pointed to higher quality of work and brighter future for the field as possible benefits of considering the history of economic thought as a branch of intellectual history. Inspired by the history-of-ideas tradition, it is doubtful his endeavor connected with that of Donald Winch on the other side of the Atlantic. A few years earlier, at a time when intellectual history was picking up at the University of Sussex, Winch organized the first of what would become an annual UK History of Economic Thought Conference. Significantly, Robbins and John Hicks, two of Britain's leading economic theorists, attended the event. After the second conference, an archivist was commissioned to produce a survey of archives and other manuscript collections of economists' papers (Sturges 1975).[24]

Despite great concern about its institutional future in the United Kingdom and the United States in the mid-1970s, there was significant research activity in the history of economic thought. Some outsiders even talked of a revival of interest, though they pointed to the risk of a split between economists and historians because of possible differences in training and professional identification and the subsequent unawareness of mutual interests (e.g., Horowitz 1974, p. 454). Aside from a number of individuals at the very top of the economics profession who did significant historical work, there was a cohort of younger economists for whom history of economic thought was a major concern. The focus of their work remained, as it had long been, the eighteenth and nineteenth centuries, that is, the classics of the subject. This involved not simply textual exegesis, but serious historical scholarship, and resulted in the publication of scholarly editions of the works and, crucially, correspondence, of many of the past figures (including Adam Smith, James Mill, Jeremy Bentham, Ricardo, McCulloch, Stanley Jevons, and Léon Walras), as well as interpretations based on extensive

[24] An indication of the prevailing pessimism in the field at the time is Bernard A. Corry's (1975, 258) encouragement to his readers to be realistic and to accept that the history of economics was actually not important to economists and accordingly to consider its potential capacity to fill gaps in the standard teaching of economics.

research in the archives. Involving leading economic theorists as well as those approaching him from other angles, scholarship on Karl Marx was also very active because of the discovery of the "Young Marx." Significantly, the period's most notable textbook, Blaug's *Economic Theory in Retrospect* (1962), which was to go through five editions and become widely cited, did not reflect the historical sensibility of its author's earlier book, *Ricardian Economics* (1958); instead, it analyzed past economists' ideas using modern economic theory.[25]

The other development, the significance of which was perhaps not apparent for a decade or more, was the emergence of self-consciously heterodox groupings of economics (see Lee 2010). There had always been groups that stood for unorthodox approaches, and Marxist economics, because of its historical antecedents as a critique of political economy and its connections with active political movements, was clearly always a special case. The increasing emphasis on mathematical rigor, however, provoked a reaction from those who found their work excluded as not being sufficiently rigorous. They began to organize conferences, journals, and societies, in which they could assert separate identities.[26] The reason why this was significant for the history of economic thought was that several of these groups formed identities centered on historical figures – post-Keynesians on Keynes, neo-Ricardians (Sraffians) on Ricardo and Sraffa, and "Austrians" on the late nineteenth-century economist Carl Menger and his followers including Hayek – many of whom were linked with distinctive political as well as economic positions. For such heterodox economists as for Marxists, the boundaries between economic analysis and history of economic thought barely existed. As long as the latter retained a significant presence outside such circles, there was no danger that it would be identified with heterodox economics. However, as the field came under increasing pressure toward the end of the century, pushed out of mainstream economics departments, heterodox economists versed in the history of economic thought became numerically more prominent, giving mainstream economists (the large majority) even more reason to reject it.

25 Characteristically for the period, Blaug was not given tenure at Yale – they had no need of a tenured professor in the field – and he ultimately made a career in Britain in the economics of education.

26 Among new heterodox journals, one should note *Cahiers d'économie politique*, created in 1974; the *Cambridge Journal of Economics*, founded in 1977; and the *Journal of Post Keynesian Economics*, established in 1978.

New Horizons

During the 1980s, the ideas of Thomas Kuhn and Imre Lakatos were widely used to frame discussions of the history of economic thought. As is well known, Kuhn's *Structure of Scientific Revolutions* (1962 [1970]) had a profound effect on the history and philosophy of science and on several social sciences. In contrast, economics was, aside from the use of Kuhn by marginalized, heterodox economists, entirely unaffected. His work, however, attracted the attention of historians of economic thought and economic theorists writing on the subject (Gordon 1965; Coats 1969a). One of the reasons was that his view of scientific development as involving periods of normal science interspersed with scientific revolutions fitted well with the long-held belief that there were revolutions in the history of economics. There might be controversy over details, but it was widely agreed that significant changes took place with Adam Smith, the "marginalists" of the 1870s, and Keynes. Even Schumpeter, in his magnum opus, had written in terms of "classical periods" analogous to Kuhnian normal science. At the same time, Kuhn's conclusion that theories belonging to different paradigms are literally incommensurable could easily antagonize those who saw the history of economics as one of progress, thereby reducing the impact of *The Structure of Scientific Revolutions* in the field.[27]

However, the stimulus to structure histories of economics around a methodological framework originated not so much with Kuhn but with Lakatos, who proposed a way to use history of science to test his "methodology of scientific research programmes" (MSRP), a more formal theory inspired by his LSE colleague Karl Popper. One of the reasons why this had an influence not matched by earlier discussions of Kuhn was a symposium, planned by Lakatos himself, though he did not live to attend it, spanning physics and economics. The volume on economics, *Method and Appraisal in Economics* (1976), edited by Spiro Latsis, one of Lakatos's students, was significant because it drew together eminent historians of economics (Blaug, Coats, and Terence Hutchison) as well as leading economists (Hicks and Axel Leijonhufvud) who explored whether the history of economics could be understood in terms of either Kuhnian or Lakatosian philosophy. This question structured much work on the history of economics during the 1980s.[28] For example, Roy Weintraub's *General Equilibrium Analysis* (1985)

[27] See Backhouse (1996) for a comparison of Schumpeter's approach with Kuhn's.

[28] This is not to say that there were no other influential questions shaping the field. Donald (now Deirdre) McCloskey's (1983, 1985) analysis of rhetoric (drawing in turn on Wayne Booth and Richard Rorty) put forward another one. It argued that even economics, with

sought to tell the story of general equilibrium theory through the lens of a "neo-Walrasian research program."

By the end of the decade, interest in this approach was waning, as Neil De Marchi and Mark Blaug (1991) found when, in 1989, they organized a major conference on the applicability of MSRP to economics. Many of the participants were more interested in drawing on the sociology of scientific knowledge (SSK), influenced by writers such as Karen Knorr-Cetina and Harry Collins, than in discussing MSRP.[29] Weintraub's *Stabilizing Dynamics* (1991), published shortly afterward, was a manifesto for the view that economic knowledge was not found but constructed in communities.

By the early 1990s, very few historians of economics would have described themselves as historians of science. There was, however, significant activity at the intersection of these fields. An influential example was the publication of the English translation of *La Mano Invisibile* of 1987, by the economist Bruna Ingrao and the mathematician Giorgio Israel (1990), bearing the subtitle *Economic Equilibrium in the History of Science*. Shortly afterward, Philip Mirowski's *More Heat than Light* (1989 [1991]) sought to present the so-called marginal revolution as a mistranslation of energy physics into economics. Both books were widely discussed, with Mirowski's being particularly controversial (see, for example, Walker 1991 and the wide range of views presented in De Marchi 1993). They testified to the necessity for historians of economics investigating what was increasingly described as the mathematization of economics to adopt a cross-disciplinary and transnational approach (Weintraub 1992, p. 4).

In writing "Breaking Away: History of Economics as History of Science" for the leading journal in the field, Margaret Schabas (1992) was consciously seeking to open up the field to the history of science, but her intention was also to point out the scant attention paid to the history of economic thought by historians of science. In addition to her detailed analysis of the reasons

its strong mathematical orientations, employed rhetorical means of persuasion, which in turn suggested that literary methods could shed light on its history. More generally, McCloskey's approach reflected a move toward thinking in terms of discourse, a term that had been introduced into discussions of the history of economics in Tribe (1978), following Michel Foucault's *Les mots et les choses* (1966) and *L'Archéologie du savoir* (1969). In these books, the idea of discourse opened the way to an analysis of texts in which the reference to objective reality was less important than the reference to a collective construction organized in a system of rules.

29 This move toward SSK can be read as an indirect consequence of the immersion of historians of economic thought in Kuhn's work. Indeed, as suggested by Gordon (2012, p. 143), "The great emphasis Kuhn placed on the social consensus of the research collective in his portrait of normal science helped pave the way for the full-blown sociology of scientific knowledge."

why these two strands of intellectual history had remained so detached, she argued that if economics no longer welcomed its historians, they should consider moving to history of science departments.[30] The responses collected in a *HOPE* minisymposium adduced many reasons, both intellectual and practical, against this. They showed that in the early 1990s most historians of economics were still strongly attached to their self-image as economists and found it hard therefore to accept Schabas's main point that greater historical sensibility could make their work stronger.

New horizons were also opened up by the availability of new source materials. For example, scholarship on Adam Smith was stimulated by the Glasgow edition of his works and correspondence, produced to mark the bicentenary of his *Wealth of Nations* (Smith 1976). One reason for the volume of work on Smith was that his writings were of great interest not only to historians of economic thought but to intellectual historians concerned with the culture of which it formed an important part. Part of the inspiration here was from the work of Quentin Skinner and John Pocock on the history of political ideas. As two Cambridge intellectual historians, Istvan Hont and Michael Ignatieff (1983, p. 1), argued, it was impossible to define the identity of political economy in eighteenth-century Scotland without understanding the central questions Smith was trying to answer when writing *Wealth of Nations*. When Winch (1978), whose training had been in economics, turned to study Smith, he found it useful to go beyond the history of economics to show that Smith's work could be read in diverse contexts depending on the language in which his texts were located; he emphasized that Smith's economic reasoning needed to be understood in the context of his politics, not as something standing on its own. He later collaborated with his Sussex colleagues John Burrow and Stefan Collini on *That Noble Science of Politics* (Burrow, Collini, and Winch 1983), a study of nineteenth-century political economy based on the premise that the disciplinary boundaries that became established in the twentieth century were not then meaningful.[31]

Engagement between the history of economics and the history of political ideas, drawing on newly available source materials, was not confined to those concerned with the eighteenth and nineteenth centuries.[32]

[30] Trained as a historian of economics in an economics department, Schabas was then affiliated to the Philosophy Department at York University.

[31] Winch (2009) has produced his own account of his break with the history of economic thought and collaboration with Burrow and Collini.

[32] We could also cite the literature on John Stuart Mill, admittedly less extensive than that on Smith, and the Toronto edition of Mill's work.

Publication by the Royal Economic Society of a thirty volume edition of *The Collected Economic Writings of John Maynard Keynes*, which began to appear in 1971, was followed by immense research, including two major biographies, one by an established historian of economics (Moggridge 1992), another by a historian whose previous work had been focused on political thought (Skidelsky 1983–2000). As with scholarship on Smith, Malthus, and Marx, work on Keynes was being undertaken by scholars from different disciplines.[33]

These new approaches, however, were not uncontested, quite apart from intense discussion over the merits of particular cases. One of the most forceful defenses of a more traditional position appeared in a keynote address to the History of Economics Society delivered by Samuelson (1987), one of the leading mathematical economic theorists of the post Second World War era, in which he outlined "A Program for the Whig History of Economic Science." This defended the approach to history that lay beneath his widely discussed article "The Classical Canonical Model" (1978), in which he had offered a consistent mathematical model of the "classical" theory of growth. Debates focused both on the details of his interpretation (notably whether it was consistent with what Smith had said) and on whether this was the right way to write history.

Into the Twenty-First Century

The traditional canon was dominated by the publications of European economists working between the late eighteenth century and the early decades of the twentieth, culminating with Keynes. However, in the 1990s historians of economics turned their attention increasingly to American economics and to the late twentieth century. (That this was not uncontroversial is shown by the reaction when, at the 1994 meeting of the History of Economics Society, Mary Morgan and Malcolm Rutherford proposed to set up a network of scholars interested in the history of American economics, only to encounter the response, from many distinguished figures, that it did not contain ideas of significant value.) Bob (A. W.) Coats, a British economic historian, whose interest in the history of ideas had been fostered by attending Lovejoy's seminar at Johns Hopkins, had been a pioneer in the study of American economics and adopted a sociological approach. Two collaborative projects documented the increasing dominance of the economics profession after the Second World War by American economics (Coats

[33] See Backhouse and Bateman (2008) for a survey of recent work on Keynes.

1996, 2000).[34] Where Coats focused on the international transmission of ideas, Morgan and Rutherford (1998) focused on the transformation, between 1920 and 1960, of economics within the United States itself.

One of the most important factors in increased attention to the history of recent economics was the greater availability of archives of modern economists' papers.[35] Though it was far from the only such source, given the natural tendency of economists to deposit their papers at the university to which they were affiliated, a particularly important source was the Economists' Papers Project, established at Duke University, which collected together the papers of more than fifty twentieth-century economists, mostly deceased but a significant number still alive.[36] The size of this collection at a university that was active in the history of economics increased the visibility of the materials and helped open up the study of late twentieth-century economics. Weintraub et al. (1998, p. 1498), in an article advertising the project in the *Journal of Economic Literature*, adopted a missionary tone, albeit aimed at persuading economists to donate their papers as much as urging historians to use them, pointing out that "each collection is a potentially rich mine of information, allowing the researcher with sufficient patience to reconstruct opinions and ideas which were unpublished due to lack of time, apparent lack of popular interest, or confidentiality."

History of economics has also been studied in several other disciplines – in history, in sociology, and in political science (in the guise of political economy). Economic historians had always been interested in policy. For example, Martin Daunton's (2002, 2007) work on taxation required him to think about the economic ideas that lay behind changing policies in relation to taxation. Economic historians concerned with policy in the interwar period were similarly forced to engage with competing economic ideas in order to understand the ways in which the unemployment problem was tackled (e.g., Barber 1985,1996; Middleton 1983) and some ventured beyond policy into the history of the profession that generated those ideas (Middleton 1998; Bernstein 2001). Economists' arguments about trade policy and empire also interested intellectual historians, for whom it was part of a much broader political culture (e.g., Howe 1998; Cain 2002; Hont 2005; Trentmann 2008).

[34] They followed previous projects on economists in government and in international organizations (Coats 1982, 1987).

[35] Of course, there remained many historians of economics who focused simply on published texts, ignoring pleas such as that of Coats (1969b, pp. 17–18).

[36] On May 2, 2012, the archive contained papers of fifty-six economists. However, for a very small number of these, the main holdings are elsewhere, and one is a nineteenth-century economist.

There has also been increased interest among intellectual historians in the history of post–Second World War economics, driven in part by the increased pervasiveness of economics in public discourse. Given that historians of economics have increasingly been examining this period in ways that relate to the methods of intellectual historians, there have been increasing cross-disciplinary engagements, even if the latter have fallen short of integration into a single community. Daniel Rodgers (2011) made developments in economics central to his account of how, between the 1950s and 1980s, the notion of the "social" became fractured with people in many spheres thinking in terms of individualism. Though his thesis was that this fracturing of the social transcended any left-right political divide, it has been associated above all with the rise to prominence in political discourse of what has been termed "neoliberalism," a topic that because of its political resonance has attracted much attention from economists, historians, political scientists and journalists (Klein 2007; Foucault 2008; Mirowski and Plehwe 2009; Burgin 2012).

An excuse for writing the history of economics in isolation from other disciplines is that cross-disciplinary engagements have been few. However, during the Second World War and its aftermath, that was not the case. Economists clearly engaged with mathematicians and scientists, the towering figure of John von Neumann attracting attention (Mirowski 1992, 2002, chap. 3; Leonard 1995, 2010) along with John Nash (Leonard 1994).[37] Likewise, as has increasingly become evident, though economists often saw themselves as standing apart from other social scientists, there was nonetheless significant intellectual interaction (Backhouse and Fontaine 2010a). A widely discussed location for such interaction was RAND, the U.S. Air Force think tank that employed scientists, economists, and social scientists (Jardini 1996; Amadae 2003; Abella 2008). Another significant location was the field of Soviet studies, which grew rapidly during the Cold War (Dawidoff 2003; Engerman 2009). Clearly, the various issues historians of science have discussed under the heading "Cold War science" encompassed the natural sciences but also the social sciences (see, for instance, Heyck and David Kaiser 2010; Solovey and Cravens 2012), including economics, if only because, in the Cold War era, social scientists played an important role in the changes affecting Western societies as well as in the efforts to understand them (see Backhouse and Fontaine 2010b). Ironically, the increasing sensitivity of historians of economics to the role of the natural sciences in

[37] See also Weintraub (2002b) and Düppe and Weintraub (2014) on interactions between economics and mathematics.

postwar economics and the growing interest of historians of science in the postwar social sciences have occasioned a rapprochement between the two fields, eventually prompting historians of economics to consider the role of the other social sciences in postwar economics.

However, though the field was thriving intellectually, its institutional position, and hence its identity, was precarious. Alarmed by what was seen as the field's imminent demise within economics, Weintraub opened a symposium on the *Future of the History of Economic Thought* (2002a) with an essay entitled "Will Economics Ever Have a Past Again?" It was possible to find grounds for optimism in the range of disciplines – history, sociology, science studies – within which scholars were turning their attention to the history of economics, but, equally, the lack of any secure disciplinary home for the field as economics departments excluded it from their curricula gave grounds for pessimism. The problem was that the long-standing decline in the place of the history of economics in the U.S. graduate curriculum had by then proceeded to the point where, except in a tiny minority of places, those graduating with a Ph.D. in economics no longer had any opportunity to study the history of their discipline as part of their formal training. Given that they constituted the supply of future teachers, this would surely lead to the extinction of the field. In undergraduate education, in particular in liberal arts colleges, the situation was different in that there was a demand for courses in a subject that was attractive to students. However, though the best liberal arts colleges might encourage research, they did not produce the new Ph.D.s who would keep the subject going. In the UK economics departments the picture resembled that in U.S. graduate schools, an additional factor being the Research Assessment Framework (now the Research Excellence Framework), which involved a national system of assessment that linked funding to the evaluations of research made by a national committee of economists.[38]

It was only in parts of Continental Europe and Japan, with different institutional structures in higher education, and to some extent Australia, that a different picture obtained. For example, in France and Italy, there remained a large number of historians of economics, protected from the pressures exerted on their British and North American colleagues by the strong presence of the public sector in higher education. The number

[38] Research is judged by an expert panel of assessors expected to read work submitted; however, it is widely believed that their decisions conform closely to what a system based on journal rankings would produce. Members of the economics panel do not usually include any historians of economics, though history panels have included historians who have published in the subject.

of European historians of economics was sufficiently high to support not merely national societies and journals, but also the *European Journal of the History of Economic Thought* (established 1993) and the European Society for the History of Economic Thought (established in 1995). However, in the twenty-first century, partly because of the Bologna process aimed at harmonizing European higher education systems and partly because of increasing competitiveness in higher education, there have been further pressures making the situation of historians of economics in those countries more similar to that of their counterparts in the United States and the United Kingdom.[39]

Conclusions: Identity Again

Ten years after reflecting on the relationships between history of science and history of economics, Schabas (2002, p. 210) noted that in her own experience it was no longer the case that historians of science regarded the writing of the history of economics as a "deviant pursuit." Schabas went so far as to argue that by "the mid-1990s, history of economics had become part of mainstream history of science" (p. 210). Judging from the contents of *Isis*, the premier journal in the field, that seems a rather optimistic assessment, though it is true that history of science journals have become more hospitable to work in the history of economics and that a minority of historians of economics have increasingly considered these journals as natural outlets for some of their work.

Despite the opening up of the history of economics to the history, philosophy, and sociology of science and to a lesser extent to history, most work in the field continues to follow more traditional paths. Some, and perhaps the majority of, historians of economics see the function of their work as pointing out errors or restoring forgotten ideas to life so as to enrich or reconstruct economic theory. They focus on work that they consider relevant to the traditions that they believe should become more influential, or on critiques of what increasingly came to be called "mainstream" economics. Such work, linking history of economics to critiques, and sometimes denunciations, of contemporary economics, did not endear them to economists.[40] Referring to debates over the role of history of economic thought

[39] Though it was perceived as a threat to the history of economic thought, the ABS reclassification was not motivated by any desire to change what academics did, merely to improve the classification system.

[40] For example, the History of Economics Society Presidential Address by Jerry Evensky (2012), bears the title "What's Wrong with Economics?"

in economics, Weintraub (2007, p. 279) has concluded: "The argument, the war, is over except that the losers still say 'you need to deal with us, why won't you pay attention to us?' The economic science war is over and, institutionally speaking, historians of economics have lost. Tarred with the heterodox brush, it could not have been otherwise for them."

In view of these conflicting views, it is hardly a surprise that a growing number of historians of economics have commented about the directions the field should take at the same time as they have endorsed a let-a-thousand-flowers-bloom approach to the field.[41] While some would like to see the lack of a clear identity for the field as a sign of its liveliness, richness, and even strength, it may equally be taken as the expression of its very uncomfortable position within academe.

References

Abella, Alex. 2008. *Soldiers of Reason: The Rand Corporation and the Rise of the American Empire.* Boston: Mariner Books.

Allen, William R. 1965. "Discussion," *American Economic Review* 55.1/2:143–9.

Amadae, Sonja. 2003. *Rationalizing Capitalist Democracy: The Cold War Origins of Rational Choice Liberalism.* Chicago: Chicago University Press.

Arena, Richard. 2000. "Les économistes français en 1950," *Revue économique* 51.5:969–1007.

Backhouse, Roger E. 1996. "Vision and Progress in Economic Thought: Schumpeter after Kuhn." In *Joseph A. Schumpeter: Historian of Economics*, ed. L. Moss. London: Routledge, 21–32.

2007. "Lives in Synopsis: The Production and Use of Short Biographies by Historians of Economics." In *Life Writing and the History of Economics*, ed. E. R. Weintraub and E. Forget. Annual Supplement to Volume 39 of *History of Political Economy.* Durham, NC: Duke University Press.

Backhouse, Roger E., and Bradley W. Bateman. 2008. "John Maynard Keynes: Recent Developments." In *The New Palgrave Dictionary of Economics*, ed. S. Durlauf and L. Blume. London: Palgrave Macmillan.

Backhouse, Roger E. and Philippe Fontaine, eds. 2010a. *The Unsocial Social Science? Economics and Neighboring Disciplines since 1945.* Annual Supplement to Volume 42 of *History of Political Economy*. Durham, NC: Duke University Press.

2010b. *The History of the Social Sciences since 1945.* Cambridge: Cambridge University Press.

[41] Characteristically, in their introduction to a minisymposium on the future of the history of economics, voicing the young scholars' perspective, Tubaro and Angner (2008, p. 82) write: "we encouraged contributors to explore not only what they think is happening and will happen, but also what they think should happen." Winch (2000, p. 480) also has a strong prescriptive flavor: "instead of working in a walled garden marked the History of Economic Thought, with a sign on the door warning all those not trained in economics to stay away, why don't we knock down one or two of the walls and swap a few plants with fellow historians working in the neighbouring gardens?"

Barber, William J. 1985. *New Era to New Deal: Herbert Hoover, the Economists and American Economic Policy, 1921–1933.* Cambridge: Cambridge University Press.

1996. *Designs within Disorder: Franklin D. Roosevelt, the Economists, and the Shaping of American Economic Policy, 1933–1945.* Cambridge: Cambridge University Press.

Bateman, Bradley W. 2002. "Sitting on a Log with Adam Smith: The Future of the History of Economic Thought at the Liberal Arts Colleges." In *The Future of the History of Economics*, ed. E. Roy Weintraub. Annual Supplement to Volume 34 of *History of Political Economy*. Durham, NC, and London: Duke University Press.

Bernstein, Michael A. 2001. *A Perilous Progress: Economists and Public Purpose in Twentieth-Century America.* Princeton, NJ, and Oxford: Princeton University Press.

Blaug, Mark. 1958. *Ricardian Economics.* New Haven, CT: Yale University Press.

1962. *Economic Theory in Retrospect*. Homewood, IL: R. D. Irwin.

1990. "On the Historiography of Economics," *Journal of the History of Economic Thought* 12.1:27–37.

1996. *Economic Theory in Retrospect*, 5th ed. Cambridge: Cambridge University Press.

2001. "No History of Ideas, Please, We're Economists," *Journal of Economic Perspectives* 15.1:145–64.

Bowen, Howard R. 1953. "Graduate Education in Economics," *American Economic Review* 43.4 (Part 2): ii–xv and 1–223.

Burgin, Angus. 2012. *The Great Persuasion: Reinventing Free Markets since the Depression.* Cambridge, MA: Harvard University Press.

Burrow, John, Stefan Collini, and Donald M. Winch. 1983. *That Noble Science of Politics.* Cambridge: Cambridge University Press.

Burke, Peter. 2005. *History and Social Theory*, 2nd ed. Ithaca, NY: Cornell University Press.

Cain, Peter. 2002. *Hobson and Imperialism: Radicalism, New Liberalism, and Finance 1887–1938.* Oxford: Oxford University Press.

Chandler, James. 2009. "Introduction: Doctrines, Disciplines, Discourses, Departments," *Critical Inquiry* 35.4:729–46.

Coats, A.W. 1969a. "Is There a 'Structure of Scientific Revolutions' in Economics?" *Kyklos* 22.2:289–296.

1969b. "Research Priorities in the History of Economics," *History of Political Economy* 1.1:9–18.

1982. *Economists in Government.* Durham, NC: Duke University Press

1987. *Economists in International Organizations.* New York: Praeger.

1996. *The Post-1945 Internationalization of Economics.* Annual Supplement to volume 28 of *History of Political Economy*. Durham, NC: Duke University Press.

2000. *The Development of Economics in Western Europe.* London: Routledge.

Collini, Stefan. 1985. "What Is Intellectual History?" *History Today* 35.10:46–8.

Conant, James Bryant et al. 1945. *General Education in a Free Society*. Cambridge, MA: Harvard University Press.

Corry, Bernard A. 1975. "Should Economists Abandon HOPE?" *History of Political Economy* 7.2:252–60.

Daunton, Martin. 2002. *Just Taxes: The Politics of Taxation in Britain, 1914–1979.* Cambridge: Cambridge University Press.

2007. *Wealth and Welfare: An Economic and Social History of Britain, 1851–1951.* Oxford: Oxford University Press.

Davis, John B. 1998. "Introduction." In *New Economics and Its History*, ed. John B. Davis. Durham, NC, and London: Duke University Press, 1–9.

Dawidoff, Nicholas. 2003. *The Fly Swatter: Portrait of an Exceptional Character.* New York: Vintage.

De Marchi, Neil, ed. 1993. *Non-Natural Social Science: Reflecting on the Enterprise of More Heat than Light.* Annual Supplement to Volume 25 of *History of Political Economy.* Durham, NC, and London: Duke University Press.

De Marchi, Neil, and Mark Blaug, eds. 1991. *Appraising Economic Theories: Studies in the Methodology of Scientific Research Programs.* Aldershot: Elgar.

Düppe, Till, and Weintraub, E. Roy. 2014. *Finding Equilibrium: Arrow, Debreu and McKenzie and the Problem of Scientific Credit.* Princeton, NJ: Princeton University Press.

Emmett, Ross B. 1998. "Entrenching Disciplinary Competence: The Role of General Education and Graduate Study in Chicago Economics." In *From Interwar Pluralism to Postwar Neoclassicism*, ed. M. S. Morgan and M. Rutherford. Annual Supplement to Volume 30 of *History of Political Economy.* Durham, NC, and London: Duke University Press.

Engerman, David C. 2009. *Know Your Enemy: The Rise and Fall of America's Soviet Experts.* Oxford: Oxford University Press.

Evensky, Jerry. 2012. "HES Presidential Address: What's Wrong with Economics?" *Journal of the History of Economic Thought* 34.1:1–20.

Foucault, Michel. 1966. *Les mots et les choses.* Paris: Gallimard.

1969. *L'Archéologie du savoir.* Paris: Gallimard.

2008. *The Birth of Biopolitics.* London Macmillan. Trans. Graham Burchell from *Naissance de la biopolitique: Cours au Collège de France. 1978–1979.* Paris: Seuil/Gallimard.

Fourcade, Marion. 2009. *Economists and Societies: Discipline and Profession in the United States, Britain, and France, 1890s to 1990s.* Princeton, NJ, and Oxford: Princeton University Press.

Friedman, Milton. 1956. "The Quantity Theory of Money: A Restatement." In *Studies in the Quantity Theory of Money*, ed. M. Friedman. Chicago: University of Chicago Press.

General Education in a Free Society. 1945. Cambridge, MA: Harvard University Press.

Gide, Charles, and Charles Rist. 1909. *Histoire des doctrines économiques depuis les Physiocrates jusqu'à nos jours.* Paris: Larose and Tenin.

Goodwin, Craufurd D., Joseph J. Spengler, and Robert S. Smith. 1969. "Avant-Propos," *History of Political Economy* 1.1:1–4.

2008. "History of Economic Thought." In *The New Palgrave Dictionary of Economics*, ed. Steven N. Durlauf and Lawrence E. Blume, 2nd ed., Vol. 4. London: Palgrave Macmillan, 48–57.

Gordon, Donald F. 1965. "The Role of the History of Economic Thought in the Understanding of Modern Economic Theory," *American Economic Review* 55.1/2:119–127.

Gordon, Peter E. 2012. "Agonies of the Real: Anti-Realism from Kuhn to Foucault," *Modern Intellectual History* 9.1:127–47.

Harvard University, Faculty Committee on the Behavioral Sciences. 1954. *The Behavioral Sciences at Harvard: Report by a Faculty Committee.* Cambridge, MA: Harvard University Press.

Henderson, John P. 1976 (1993). "The History of Thought in the Development of the Chicago Paradigm." In *The Chicago School of Political Economy*, ed. W. J. Samuels. New Brunswick and London: Transactions.

Heyck, Hunter and David Kaiser. 2010. "'Introduction' to Focus: New Perspectives on Science and the Cold War," *Isis* 101.2:362–6.

Hont, Istvan 2005. *Jealousy of Trade: International Competition and the Nation State in Historical Perspective.* Cambridge, MA: Harvard University Press.

Hont, Istvan, and Michael Ignatieff, eds. 1983. *Wealth and Virtue: The Shaping of Political Economy in the Scottish Enlightenment.* Cambridge: Cambridge University Press.

Horowitz, Daniel. 1974. "Historians and Economists: Perspectives on the Development of American Economic Thought," *History of Political Economy* 6.4:454–62.

Howe, Anthony. 1998. *Free Trade and Liberal England, 1846–1946.* Oxford: Clarendon Press.

Hutchison, Terence W. 1953. *A Review of Economic Doctrines, 1870–1929.* Oxford: Oxford University Press.

Ingrao, Bruna, and Giorgio Israel. 1987. *La Mano Invisibile: L'equilibrio economico nella storia della scienza.* Bari: Laterza.

1990. *The Invisible Hand: Economic Equilibrium in the History of Science*, trans. Ian McGilvray. Cambridge, MA: MIT Press.

James, Émile. 1950. *Histoire des théories économiques.* Paris: Flammarion.

Jardini, David R. 1996. *Out of the Blue Yonder: The RAND Corporation's Diversification into Social Welfare Research, 1946–1968.* PhD Dissertation, College of Humanities and Social Sciences, Carnegie-Mellon University.

Johnson, Harry G. 1971. The Keynesian Revolution and the Monetarist Counter-revolution," *American Economic Review* 61.2:1–14.

Kates, Steven, and Alex Millmow. 2008a. "The History Wars of Economics: The Classification Struggle in the History of Economic Thought," *History of Economics Review* 47 (Winter):110–24.

2008b. "A Canary in the Coalmine: The Near Death Experience of the History of Economics in Australia," *History of Economic Ideas* 16.3:79–94. (This article is followed by five comments and a reply.)

Kerr, Clark. 1963. *The Uses of the University.* Cambridge, MA: Harvard University Press.

Keynes, John Maynard. 1936. *The General Theory of Employment, Interest and Money.* London: Macmillan.

Klein, Naomi. 2007. *The Shock Doctrine.* London: Penguin Books.

Kuhn, Thomas S. 1962. *The Structure of Scientific Revolutions.* Chicago: University of Chicago Press.

Kurz, Heinz. 2006. "Whither the History of Economic Thought? Going Nowhere Rather Slowly?" *European Journal of the History of Economic Thought* 13.4:463–88.

Laidler, David E. 1993. "Hawtrey, Harvard, and the Origins of the Chicago Tradition," *Journal of Political Economy* 101.6:1068–1103.

Latsis, S. J., ed. 1976. *Method and Appraisal in Economics.* Cambridge: Cambridge University Press.

Lee, Frederic S. 2010. *A History of Heterodox Economics.* London: Routledge.

Leonard, Robert J. 1994. "Reading Cournot, Reading Nash: the Creation and Stabilisation of the Nash Equilibrium," *Economic Journal* 104.424:492–511.

1995. "From Parlor Games to Social Science: von Neumann, Morgenstern and the Creation of Game Theory, 1928–1944," *Journal of Economic Literature* 33.2:730–761.

2010. *Von Neumann, Morgenstern, and the Creation of Game Theory: From Chess to Social Science, 1900–1960.* Cambridge: Cambridge University Press.

Lowry, S. Todd. 1991. "Are There Limits to the Past in the History of Economic Thought," *Journal of the History of Economic Thought* 13.2:134–58.

Marcuzzo, Maria Cristina, and Annalisa Rosselli. 2002. "Economics as History of Economics: The Italian Case in Retrospect." In *The Future of the History of Economics*, ed. E. Roy Weintraub . Annual Supplement to Volume 34 of *History of Political Economy*. Durham, NC, and London: Duke University Press.

McCloskey, Donald N. 1983. "The Rhetoric of Economics," *Journal of Economic Literature* 31.2:482–504.

McCraw, Thomas K. 2007. *Prophet of Innovation: Joseph Schumpeter and Creative Destruction.* Cambridge, MA, and London: Belknap Press of Harvard University Press.

1985. *The Rhetoric of Economics*. Madison: University of Wisconsin Press.

Middleton, Roger. 1983. *Government versus the Market*. Aldershot: Edward Elgar.

1998. *Charlatans or Saviours? The British Economics Profession from Marshall to Meade.* Cheltenham: Elgar.

Mirowski, Philip. 1989 (1991). *More Heat than Light: Economics as Social Physics, Physics as Nature's Economics.* Cambridge: Cambridge University Press.

1992. What Were von Neumann and Morgenstern Trying to Accomplish?" In *Toward a History of Game Theory*, ed. E. Roy Weintraub. Annual Supplement to Volume 24 of *History of Political Economy.* Durham, NC, and London: Duke University Press.

2002. *Machine Dreams: Economics Becomes a Cyborg Science.* Cambridge: Cambridge University Press.

Mirowski, Philip, and Dieter Plehwe, eds. 2009. *The Road from Mont Pelerin: The Making of the Neoliberal Thought Collective.* Cambridge, MA: Harvard University Press.

Moggridge, Donald E. 1992. *Maynard Keynes: An Economist's Biography.* London: Routledge.

Morgan, Mary S., and Malcolm Rutherford, eds. 1998. *From Interwar Pluralism to Postwar Neoclassicism.* Annual Supplement to Volume 30 of *History of Political Economy.* Durham, NC: Duke University Press.

Ortolano, Guy. 2009. *The Two Cultures Controversy: Science, Literature and Cultural Politics in Postwar Britain.* Cambridge: Cambridge University Press.

Patinkin, Don. 1969. "The Chicago Tradition, the Quantity Theory, and Friedman," *Journal of Money, Credit and Banking* 1.1:46–70.

1976. *Keynes's Monetary Thought: A Study of Its Development.* Durham, NC: Duke University Press.

1982. *Anticipations of the General Theory?* Chicago: Chicago University Press.

Pigou, Arthur Cecil. 1902. Review of *Theories of Value before Adam Smith*, by A. R. Sewall. *Economic Journal* 12.47:374–375.

Rodgers, Daniel T. 2011. *Age of Fracture*. Cambridge, MA: Harvard University Press.

Rutherford, Malcolm. 2008. *The Institutionalist Movement in American Economics, 1918–1947*. Cambridge: Cambridge University Press.

Samuels, Warren J. 1974. "The History of Economic Thought as Intellectual History," *History of Political Economy* 6.3:305–323.

Samuelson, Paul A. 1962. "Economists and the History of Ideas," *American Economic Review* 52.1:1–18.

1978. "The Canonical Classical Model of Political Economy," *Journal of Economic Literature* 16.4:1415–34.

1987. "Out of the Closet: A Program for the Whig History of Economic Science," *History of Economics Society Bulletin* 9.1:51–60.

Schabas, Margaret, "Breaking Away: History of Economics as History of Science," *History of Political Economy* 24.1:187–203.

2002. "Coming Together: History of Economics as History of Science." In *The Future of the History of Economics.*, ed. E. Roy Weintraub. Annual Supplement to Volume 34 of *History of Political Economy.* Durham, NC, and London: Duke University Press.

Schumpeter, Jospeh A. 1954. *A History of Economic Analysis*. London: George Allen and Unwin.

Skidelsky, Robert. 1983. *John Maynard Keynes*, Vol. 1: *Hopes Betrayed, 1883–1920*. London: Macmillan.

1992. *John Maynard Keynes*, Vol. 2: *Economist as Saviours, 1920–1937*. London: Macmillan.

2000. *John Maynard Keynes*, Vol. 3: *Fighting for Britain*. London: Macmillan.

Smith, Adam 1976. *An Inquiry into the Nature and Causes of the Wealth of Nations*. Oxford: Oxford University Press.

Solovey, Mark, and Hamilton Cravens, eds. 2012. *Cold War Social Science: Knowledge Production, Liberal Democracy, and Human Nature*. London: Palgrave Macmillan.

Solow, Robert M. 1997. "How Did Economics Get that Way and What Way Did It Get?" *Dædalus* 126.1:39–58.

Sturges, P. 1975. *Economists' Papers, 1750–1950: A Guide to Archive and Other Manuscript Sources for the History of British and Irish Economic Thought*. London: Macmillan.

Trentmann, F. 2008. *Free Trade Nation: Commerce, Consumption and Civil Society in Modern Britain*. Oxford: Oxford University Press.

Tribe, Keith. 1978. *Land, Labour and Economic Discourse*. London: Routledge and Kegan Paul.

Villey, Daniel, and Colette Neme. 1944. *Petite Histoire des grandes doctrines économiques*, rev. ed. Paris: Génin, 1985.

Walker, Donald A. 1991. "Economics as Social Physics," *Economic Journal* 101.406:615–31.

Waterman, Anthony M. C. 2002. "The 'Sussex School' and the History of Economic Thought: British Intellectual History, 1750–1950," *European Journal of the History of Economic Thought* 9.3:452–63.

2008. "Two Kinds of 'History of Economics,'" *History of Economic Ideas* 16.3:106–11.

Weintraub, E. Roy. 1985. *General Equilibrium Analysis*. Cambridge: Cambridge University Press.

1991. *Stabilizing Dynamics*. Cambridge: Cambridge University Press.

1992. "Introduction." In *Toward a History of Game Theory*, ed. E. Roy Weintraub. Annual Supplement to Volume 24 of *History of Political Economy*. Durham, NC, and London: Duke University Press.

1999. "How Should we Write the History of Twentieth-century Economics?" *Oxford Review of Economic Policy* 15.4: 139–52.

2002a. *The Future of the History of Economic Thought*. (Annual Supplement to Volume 34 of *History of Political Economy*). Durham, NC: Duke University Press.

2002b. *How Economics Became a Mathematical Science*. Durham, NC: Duke University Press.

2007. "Economic Science Wars," *Journal of the History of Economic Thought* 29.3: 267–82.

Weintraub, E. Roy, Stephen J. Meardon, Ted Gayer and H. Spencer Banzhaf. 1998. "Archiving the History of Economics," *Journal of Economic Literature* 36.3: 1496–1501.

Winch, Donald N. 1964. "What Price the History of Economic Thought?" *Scottish Journal of Political Economy* 11.3:193–204.

1978. *Adam Smith's Politics*. Cambridge: Cambridge University Press.

2000. "Does Progress Matter?" *European Journal of the History of Economic Thought* 7.4:465–84.

2009. Intellectual History and the History of Economic Thought: A Personal View, Working paper, Sussex Center for Intellectual History.

Yonay, Yuval P. 1998. *The Struggle over the Soul of Economics: Institutionalist and Neoclassical Economists in America between the Wars*. Princeton, NJ: Princeton University Press.

7

A Disciplinary History of Disciplinary Histories

The Case of Political Science

Robert Adcock

Each generation redefines its own image of political science.
David Easton (1953, p. 148)

The phrase "political science" has been in use since the eighteenth century (Farr 1988b).[1] From its first uses in the Scottish and French Enlightenments into the late nineteenth century, it carried a wide and practical meaning. Political science in this older sense encompassed multiple areas of focused knowledge and skills – such as political economy, jurisprudence, and history – and involved applying one or more of these areas to inform practical judgments about what was possible and preferable in matters of present-day politics and policy. Political science in this sense was exemplified by Alexis de Tocqueville's 1835/1840 *Democracy in America* (2000, p. 7), and later expounded by him in his 1852 address as president of France's Académie des sciences morales et politiques (Tocqueville 2010). The wide practical science Tocqueville exemplified in France was just as prominent in Britain. When introducing their history of the 'science of politics' in nineteenth century Britain, Collini, Winch, and Burrow (1983, p. 3) observed wistfully, however, that the science they had surveyed "no longer appears on modern maps of knowledge, at least not as the extensive though vaguely delimited empire it once was."

Between the late nineteenth and mid-twentieth centuries, the older wide and practical sense of political science gave way to a new, narrower, and professionalized sense that maps "political science" onto just one of

[1] I thank Emily Hauptmann, Nicolas Guilhot, Mark Vail, Amy Hsieh, James Farr, the editors of this volume, and the anonymous referees for generous and insightful comments on earlier drafts of this chapter that have pushed me to refine both its details and my clarity about what I am trying to do in narrating those details.

the array of research-centered academic disciplines collectively labeled as the "social sciences." Where the wide sense had been born in Europe and exported to America (where it was also standard into the 1880s, and in some settings longer), the narrower sense that supplanted it was developed in early twentieth century America, was later exported to Europe, and is today globally dominant. If we inquire into the history and historiography of "political science," and, in doing so, use the phrase in its now dominant disciplinary sense, then we direct attention to studies largely focused upon developments in America's academy or their overseas offspring. Most such studies are disciplinary, not simply in the figures and agendas they focus upon, but in their authorship and audience: They are written *by* members of the discipline, and *for* members of the discipline. These disciplinary histories of political science are the subject of my chapter.

Disciplinary histories are, with varying levels of explicitness, informed by contemporary identities and agendas within political science, and concerned to inform the present and future of the discipline, or some section of it. Rather than approach this orientation as a problem, I treat it as giving direction and purpose to disciplinary history as a genre pursued by a subset of political scientists, first in America, and now globally. The evolution of this genre has been integrally interwoven with the twists and turns of what we might call the "disciplinary project" in political science. The genre was inaugurated in interwar America alongside the project of turning political science into a discipline – that is, a field centered on, and validating, professionalized academic research production. But, as this project advanced in subsequent decades, critics of it also took up and expanded the genre of disciplinary history to produce, from the 1950s on, critical histories of American political science. Finally, in the late twentieth century – after the disciplinary project initiated in America had gained critical mass in other countries, while it fragmented along the lines of subfields and more specialized research agendas in America – globalizing and specializing trends moved to the fore in disciplinary history.

In this chapter I survey these successive developments and relate them to changes in the institutions of political science and identities of political scientists. I offer, in sum, a disciplinary history of disciplinary histories of political science. More specifically, my history is, at once, a self-conscious offspring of the specializing and globalizing trends in recent disciplinary history and a somewhat skeptical reflection on the first of these trends. By sympathetically remembering earlier examples of the genre, contextualizing and unpacking the admonition to tell properly historical disciplinary histories that valorized specialization in the late 1980s and early 1990s, and stressing the continuing contributions of nonspecialists, I seek a critical distance from the specializing dynamics that have shaped my own previous scholarship in this area, as they, much more generally, shape research production all too much in today's globalizing political science.

From Association to Discipline: Political Science in Pre–World War II America and the Inauguration of Disciplinary History

The founding of the American Political Science Association (APSA) in 1903 to represent the "special interests" of "Political Science, as distinguished from History and Economics," was a watershed in the transatlantic history of political science (APSA 1904, p. 9).[2] Previous institutions created to promote political science in America primarily followed European models embodying a sense of political science as a wide practical domain that encompassed and employed focused fields like political economy, rather than itself being such a field. For example, founders of the School of Political Science at Columbia in 1880 took as a model the École Libre des Sciences Politiques founded in Paris in 1872 (Adcock 2014, chap. 4). By contrast, there was no European prototype for the founding of the APSA a generation later, or for the narrowing differentiation of "political science" from history and economics invoked to explicate and promote that founding.

Yet, as significant as the APSA founding was, we should be wary about interpreting it as establishing political science as an academic *discipline*.[3] If the founding appears in retrospect as a crucial step in that direction, it does so in large part because of subsequent steps, taken later in the twentieth century and not envisioned by the association's founding generation. The APSA was created in 1903 by men and for men – I say "men" deliberately in light of the gendered nature of the association (Silverberg 1998) – at the vibrant Progressive Era intersection between academic teaching about politics, administrative or political officeholding, and the progressive movement more broadly. While the APSA today is an association *of* professors *for* professors, this is what it became in the course of the twentieth century,

[2] I quote here from the circular letter sent to several hundred individuals in October 1903 inviting them to attend the meeting that formally founded the American Political Science Association that December.

[3] For an example of a disciplinary history that unreflexively approaches the APSA founding as if it were the founding of a discipline, see Adcock (2003). Thanks to conversations with Paul Forman I would now differentiate between "field" as a broader term and "discipline" as a narrower term denoting fields with specific disciplining institutional and identity traits. Such traits are unpacked in general terms in a sympathetic fashion by Forman (2012), and critically and with specific regard to political science by Luke (1999).

not what it was initially created to be at the dawn of the century. The fifteen-member committee that in 1903 canvassed support for and organized the creation of the APSA included, in addition to professors: the head of the Interstate Commerce Commission, two judges, a census official, a legislative librarian, and a religious minister nationally prominent in social service (APSA 1904, p. 7). The association's first president, Frank Goodnow, was a Columbia professor. But he stressed at the first annual APSA meeting that its conferences were to be a "common meeting ground" providing "an opportunity for those whose work savors somewhat of the closet, to meet those engaged in the active walks of political life" (1905, pp. 45–6). APSA turned for its second president to the progressive magazine editor Albert Shaw, for its third to the progressive lawyer F. N. Judson, and for its fourth to the then British ambassador James Bryce.

It is only during the second generation of APSA's existence that political science started acquiring more discernibly disciplinary institutional and identity traits. For its first two decades, APSA usually held its meetings in conjunction with the American Historical Association (AHA), and regularly gave its presidency to figures – Woodrow Wilson, A. B. Hart, William Dunning, and Charles Beard – who at other times served as AHA presidents. But, by the end of the 1920s, these kinds of overlap ended.[4] This shift paralleled changes in the internal structure of American colleges and universities. It was during the 1920s that freestanding departments housing political science apart from history, law, philosophy, economics, or sociology started to become more the norm than the exception. The remaking of "political scientist" as an intellectual identity distinct from that of "historian," "economist," and so on, was a differentiating process that, in its American first incarnation, was extended over decades, acquiring critical mass in the interwar era in the second generation of the APSA's existence.

At the same time as differentiation between political science and other fields solidified in the American academy, political science also moved toward a more professionalized conception of scholarship. This involved departure from the previous Progressive Era belief that journalists, political actors, and government officeholders not only were a desired audience, but could also themselves produce cutting edge works of political science. Among the first generation of APSA presidents, Woodrow Wilson (1889, pp. 154–5) had, for example, hailed James Bryce's experience as a British Member of Parliament as a major aid to the political analysis offered in Bryce's *The American Commonwealth* (1888). By contrast, in the writings of

[4] On the overlap with the AHA in the first generation of APSA's existence, see Farr (2007).

Charles Merriam in the early 1920s, we begin to find the "practical political wisdom or prudence" of political actors differentiated from "scientific" or "systematic" inquiry (1923, pp. 289–90) in a manner alien to the political science of earlier figures like Bryce and Wilson. Merriam still saw active involvement in politics as able to nourish a "political prudence" relevant for political science, but he set apart "scientific assembly and analysis of this material" as a task for "professional students of politics" (1921, p. 176).

The distinctions and arguments that Merriam advanced in a series of *American Political Science Review* articles – under such titles as "The Present State of the Study of Politics" (1921), "Recent Advances in Political Methods" (1923), and "Progress in Political Research" (1926) – announced the onset of a disciplinary project in political science. As chair of APSA's Committee on Political Research, and the University of Chicago's department of political science, as well as a lead figure in the 1923 creation of the Social Science Research Council, Merriam propounded a disciplinary vision of political science as becoming something produced by academics with ample research time, trained in the latest technical methods, and with funding to pursue extensive data gathering and organize collaborations of multiple scholars.[5] Finally, and most notably for my purposes, when Merriam charted a disciplinary vision for political science, he also advanced an account of its recent past that promoted his present efforts. In doing so he inaugurated a way of conceiving and telling the history of political science that was recognizably disciplinary.

In inaugurating the genre of disciplinary history in the early 1920s, Merriam forged basic contours of its application to American materials. Reading his own distinction between "political prudence" and "systematic" science into the past, Merriam's *American Political Ideas, 1865–1917* separated out from American political thought more broadly a specific current of "greatly increased attention to the scientific study of politics," which had become "very clearly marked" in the "last twenty-five years, particularly." The individuals – notably all academics – to whom Merriam gave the most attention as he attributed origins, and sketched a growth, of "Systematic Studies of Politics" (1920, chap. 13) – Francis Lieber, Theodore Woolsey, John W. Burgess, Woodrow Wilson, W. W. Willoughby, and Frank Goodnow – remain even today the pre-1920s figures most addressed in disciplinary histories of American political science. Merriam further refined

[5] On Merriam's discipline-promoting activities, the place of these interwar endeavors in relation to his earlier education and writings, and his wartime and political experiences in the latter half of the 1910s, see Karl (1974).

his disciplinary history in "Recent Advances in Political Methods" (1923) to incorporate certain general claims – for example, "historical and comparative method" dominated in the latter half of the nineteenth century; the earliest graduate training in political science at Hopkins and Columbia promoted research largely based on the German *Staatswissenschaften* – that likewise became, and largely remain, commonplaces of disciplinary histories of American political science.

Up into the period of Merriam's initiation of a new genre, the activity of telling a "history of political science" had drawn upon the earlier wider meaning of political science and involved telling a broad history of Western political thought. Where the British jurist Fredrick Pollock (1914) preferred to give the founding father position in such a history to Aristotle, his fellow Briton the Reverend Robert H. Murray (1926) gave it to Plato. In writing what they understood as histories of "political science," both pursued an activity decidedly different from the genre the American academic Merriam inaugurated. The newer academy-centered genre would first gain book length treatment with Anna Haddow's (1939) detailed survey of *Political Science in American Colleges and Universities, 1636–1900*, which culminated with a final part on "The Emergence of Political Science as a Separate Discipline, 1865–1900." Where Merriam employed the word "profession," with Haddow we find "discipline" being used to identify what "political science" had become (or was becoming) in America. Though first functioning as a synonym for "profession," a generation later "discipline" would come in America – and notably in the hands of lead figures (Key 1958; Almond et al. 1962; Truman 1965) of the behavioral revolution – to supplant "profession" as the prevailing way of referring to what "political science" was and/or should be.[6]

Situating the inauguration of disciplinary history relative to the developing character of political science in twentieth century America highlights two main points, both of which we will eventually see travel beyond America in the latter half of the century. First, the initial founding of a national association is not equivalent to the establishment of a full-fledged discipline. It creates the institutional basis for a field that can later become the focus of a disciplining project, but the advance of such a project entails institutional and identity changes that require decades to initiate and diffuse. Second, the inauguration of disciplinary history as a distinct genre of writing among

[6] For a non-American example of the different connotations that "discipline" and "profession" might convey, see the distinction as explicated by the Canadian political scientists Trent and Stein (1991, p. 85, fn 2).

political scientists is integrally interwoven with the disciplining project. Toward the end of this chapter, when I look briefly beyond America to stress the late twentieth century globalization of disciplinary histories, we will find the genre also arising in other national contexts in the second generation after the founding of a national political science association.

The Post–World War II Behavioral Revolution in America: From Critical Histories to Continuities

Interwar convergence in America toward the freestanding political science department as a standard institution – and the accompanying tying of the identity "political scientist" to location in such an institution – neither assumed nor entailed a consensus on the substance, methods, or aims of political science. There has, arguably, never been an era in which political scientists have agreed to any great extent on such matters (if certain departments, at certain times, enjoy/enforce more consensus, that is another matter). Conversation, conflict, and compromise on such charged matters involve judgments – with varying levels of explicitness – over what political science has been and is, and what it might and should become. While disciplinary history was inaugurated by Merriam in the interwar era alongside his promotion of technically (and financially) demanding modes of research, the genre broadened in the post–World War II era as disciplinary histories came to be written by critics as well as advocates of a more "scientific" political science. This broadening occurred as disciplinary history became one of the mediums – philosophy of science was another – that political scientists used to make sense of, and take positions relative to, what has come to be known, in retrospect and perhaps over-grandly, as the "behavioral revolution" in American political science (Farr 1995; Adcock 2007; Hauptmann 2012).

Behavioralism was first envisioned as transformative, not to characterize an accomplished intellectual shift, but to advocate major changes in political science. Its classic such formulation was in David Easton's *The Political System: An Inquiry into the State of Political Science* (1953). Easton's book holds a pivotal, but ambivalent position in the evolution of disciplinary histories. On the one hand, his advocacy of "systematic" theory took up one of Merriam's favorite adjectives and interwove it with a call to distinguish "pure" from "applied science" (1953, pp. 78–89) that might be seen as reworking Merriam's previous differentiation between "systematic" political science and political "prudence." But, for Easton, "systematic" and "scientific" had particular meanings (Gunnell 2013) far more demanding than Merriam's vague use of these terms, and thereby excluding a good part of the works Merriam had reverentially included under them. Where Merriam presented his discipline-promoting agenda as a next step to extend the "progress" in "systematic" studies made by some half a century of preceding scholars, Easton sharply criticized the half-century of political science before him as having led into a "malaise." He saw his precursors as led astray by a mistaken conception of science promoting "hyperfactualism" and "premature policy science" (1953, chaps. 2 and 3). When we remember Easton's 1953 classic for its prescription of "systematic theory" and "pure science," we should also remember that it promoted this prescription in conjunction with a sharply *critical* diagnosis of the condition of political science at midcentury and how it had gotten that way.

In advancing a critical narrative that portrayed political science in America as led astray by a mistaken conception of science, Easton favored a narrative form that was soon redeployed at greater length, but with almost entirely opposite substantive content, by the young British scholar Bernard Crick in *The American Science of Politics* (1959). Crick and Easton diverged in the specific beliefs about science that they took aim at, in when they saw American political science as having begun to go astray, and in the prescriptions accompanying their narratives. Where Easton had criticized early figures like Bryce and Wilson, and saw too much later political science as maintaining a problematic path started by such pioneering APSA presidents, Crick found in the same earlier figures a largely admirable practical political science. For him, trouble began more in the interwar era, with appeal to naturalistic conceptions of science infiltrating political science primarily from sociology and starting largely with Merriam. Crick took care to note, however, that such appeals still faced opposition, at the time of his writing in the late 1950s, from more historically and institutionally oriented political scientists in America. Hence, what Crick offered was a narrative of an incipient threat that might yet be averted, even in America – and its potential importing to his own British context resisted – where that threat was precisely natural-science-based conceptions of "science" such as Easton had recently prescribed as a cure for the "malaise" of midcentury American political science.

In the years after Crick's book appeared, the prescriptions Easton and other behavioralists made in the name of "science" advanced from rising agendas toward disciplinary preeminence. As behavioralism hit its high tide in the 1960s, it attracted the ire of an increasingly divergent set of opponents. Crick's criticisms of Merriam and his students soon came to seem relatively tame as compared to the conservative assault launched by Leo

Strauss and his students in *Essays on the Scientific Study of Politics* (Storing 1962). Later in the decade, as American campuses became centers of growing student protests, behavioralism was next targeted from the opposite end of the political spectrum, when it was charged with being inherently conservative by the edited volume *Apolitical Politics* (McCoy and Playford 1967; see esp. part II). Hence, even as discontent with behavioralism and its naturalistic conception of "science" became widely voiced, the discontents disagreed among themselves over whether a better, more practical, kind of science was found in the ancient political science of Aristotle, the liberal republicanism of a Tocqueville, or Marxian radicalism. Agreeing in their discontent with the present, but disagreeing over what alternative to revive, the diverse critics of behavioralism did not offer any one critical narrative of disciplinary history, but discrepant suggestions as to when, how, and why political science had gone awry.

Instead, the most significant development in disciplinary histories during the 1960s occurred as authors more amenable to behavioralism reframed its relationship to earlier political science. In Albert Somit and Joseph Tanenhaus's *The Development of Political Science: From Burgess to Behavioralism* (1967) the now powerful behavioralism appeared, no longer as a prescription for a discipline in malaise, but as the ascendant telos of political science's evolution in America ever since the 1880s. Similarly, where Easton had promoted "systematic theory" in the early 1950s as a decisive break away from prior political science, Martin Landau (1968) argued for leaving behind Easton's "myth of hyperfactualism" to relocate behavioralists' functionalist systems theorizing as only a more explicit and expansive restating of a theoretical orientation that had been common among early APSA presidents. Against the backdrop of such first moves toward plotting continuity between the political science past and behavioral present, Dwight Waldo would, in turn, go on in the mid-1970s to offer a survey of political science "in its origins, its development, and its environing circumstances," which took, both as a "premise … of common sense" and as "a reasonable interpretation of the historical record," that political science is "cumulative" (1975, pp. 2–4).

Emphasizing continuities and cumulation effectively returned disciplinary history as a genre back to moves that had informed its inauguration by Merriam half a century earlier. The result was a departure, not only from the critical history of Crick, but likewise that of Easton, who had also emplotted a wrong turn as pivotal to his narrative of American political science. Looking back on the books of Somit and Tanenhaus (1967) and Waldo (1975) from the standpoint of more recent specialized disciplinary histories we will turn to later, it might be tempting to dismiss them as merely "Whig" histories. Yet, Somit and Tanenhaus (1967) still offer the best one-volume collection of basic institutional facts and trends about the history of APSA and key departments, while Waldo (1975) supplies additional details about the history of subfields, and notably highlights the import of the midcentury hiving off of public administration – until then the largest subfield of American political science – into its own national association and schools.

Disciplinary Histories since the 1980s: Specialization and Globalization

Between the 1950s and 1970s disciplinary history turned from a forward-looking framing of incipient change – whether as novel prescription in Easton (1953) or as rising threat in Crick (1959) – toward a narrative of teleological culmination of the past in the present. Turning to the 1980s, the first major disciplinary histories we find mark a culminating twist on the evolution of the genre since World War II. Accepting the narrative form of an extended unfolding leading up to the present, Ricci (1984) and Seidelman and Harpman (1985) both gave this form a tragic twist. In doing so, both added an account of the Caucus for a New Political Science, which had been founded in 1967 and contested the elections and governance of the APSA up into the late 1970s. The juxtaposition between the caucus's success in achieving organizational reforms of APSA and the failure of progressive political hopes that had initially inspired it provided both books with an ironic close to an overarching tragic narrative of the triumph of professional over practical imperatives in American political science.[7] Both charted century-long histories in which early relevance gave way to professionalizing dynamics whose success appears in both almost as inevitable as it does unappetizing for their authors. Taken alongside the more celebratory works of Somit and Tanenhaus (1967) and Waldo (1975), the despairing narratives of Ricci (1984) and Seidelman and Harpman (1985) suggested that disciplinary history might be getting trapped in a development/progress versus decline dichotomy, which plotted and replotted stock characters and themes under competing narrative forms.

The identification and rejection of such a potential dichotomization during a lively round of historiographical discussion and debate in 1988–91

[7] For a more recent, more detailed, and less despairing account of the motivating goals, internal divides, and impact over time of the caucus, see Barrow (2008).

(Dryzek and Leonard 1988; Farr 1988a; Farr, Gunnell, Seidelman, Dryzek, and Leonard 1990; Gunnell 1991) announced a new agenda in disciplinary histories in American political science. Methodological criticisms of histories from recent decades provided a rallying cry for a younger generation of scholars who assayed and laid claim to disciplinary history as a genre they proposed to refashion, in John Gunnell's words, into "a distinct research specialty" (1991, p. 16). By advocating historiographical norms for disciplinary histories, and writing new histories in light of those norms (for instance, Farr 1988b, 1990; Gunnell 1988, 1992, 1993) these scholars crystallized an agenda for specialized research in disciplinary history that persists to the present. In the first subsection that follows, I revisit the call to write more properly historical disciplinary histories, contextualize it in relation to subfield debates and fragmentation in the American discipline, and explore how fragmentation has also been substantively reflected in the continuing vein of work by political scientists who write histories as nonspecialists, and in the contributions from specialists and nonspecialists alike in the volumes *Discipline and History* (Farr and Seidelman 1993) and *Political Science in History* (Farr, Dryzek, Leonard 1995), and the centennial issue of the *APSR* (Sigelman and Sanders 2006) devoted to disciplinary history. In the concomitant rise of proudly historicist scholarship alongside substantive fragmentation of the foci of disciplinary histories, the history of political science in the late twentieth century paralleled a pairing Charles Camic's chapter in this volume identifies also in the history of sociology.

As notable as the trends outlined previously have been, if we expand our attention beyond America, we can see that arguably the single most significant trend in disciplinary histories of political science in recent decades is the ongoing globalization of the genre. Here a telling parallel is to the transnational turn highlighted by Kevin Passmore in his chapter on history in this volume. In devoting a second later subsection to the globalization of disciplinary histories, I first sketch the rise of disciplinary histories addressing political science outside America and relate these to the creation of national associations and the trajectory of disciplinary projects. Globalization in disciplinary histories has involved, however, not only looking beyond America to other national contexts, but also resituating the history of American political science in transnational and global contexts. In closing this chapter I thus return to the domain I know best – studies of American political science – to chart how the globalizing trend is reshaping disciplinary history as applied to its earliest and most extensively examined case.

Specialization in Disciplinary History and the Fragmentation of American Political Science

The specialized research agenda in American disciplinary history was inaugurated, as I noted, with a fanfare of historiographical conversation in 1988–91. Most contributors to this conversation were located in the political theory subfield, and in the backdrop of their discussion lay the longer-running controversy sparked by Quentin Skinner's (1969) criticisms of much post–World War II scholarship in the history of political thought. The import of this controversy for agendas and identities in the political theory subfield in the 1980s was evident in *Meaning and Context* (Tully 1988), which reprinted Skinner's major critical essays, multiple criticisms of his position, and his rejoinder. Challenging the limited focus of the history of political thought on a canon of figures from Plato to Marx, Skinner had advocated that scholars in this area, to become properly historical, also had to study noncanonical works to reconstruct historically discursive contexts within which to interpret what canonical authors were doing in their classics.

The twin pioneers of disciplinary history as a specialized research agenda – James Farr and John Gunnell – were both actively engaged with Skinner's position. Skinner wrote the lead essay for a volume, *Political Innovation and Conceptual Change* (Ball, Farr, and Hanson 1989), that Farr edited as he was beginning his work in the history of political science, and Farr in turn made historicized conceptual work key to his substantive work in the history of political science (Farr 1988b). Gunnell, by contrast, had directly criticized Skinner (in Gunnell 1982) for jumping from an epistemology based on a contested stance in philosophy of language to methodological preaching for political theorists. For Gunnell, Skinner appeared, in effect, to mimic a mistake of behavioralists whom he (Gunnell 1975) had earlier criticized for leaping from contested stances in philosophy to methodological declarations. Yet, while he rejected the way in which Skinner had *justified* calling for a more historical history of political thought, Gunnell did not reject the call itself (1982, p. 317). Indeed, the admonition to be historical – where being historical is conceived in terms of historically recovering the concepts and conversations of past discursive contexts – was crucial to Gunnell's own developing agenda in disciplinary history.

The trajectory of Gunnell's works from the 1970s on might be seen as using disciplinary history to put the discursive turn on a historical rather than a philosophical basis. In the late 1970s in the *APSR* Gunnell attacked what he labeled "The Myth of the Tradition" (1978) in the political theory subfield. In the 1980s he went on to make the subfield an object of historical research, and thereby expanded his earlier criticism by showing how the subfield's canonical texts and themes, although often treated as a historically given tradition, had been constructed and reinterpreted by academics since the late nineteenth century. Gunnell's findings (1988, 1993) gave fresh heft to concerns regarding the ahistorical character of the subfield, which Skinner had earlier rested on arguments drawn from the philosophy of language. In Gunnell's hands, studying subfield history showed the "History of Western Political Thought" to be less a practice of historical scholarship than a quasi-scholarly refraction of contemporary anxieties. Recovering these subfield twists and turns provides the discursive context in which to locate the call for "histories of political science that are in some significant sense truly historical in attitude" (Gunnell in Farr et al. 1990, p. 592) so prominent in the 1988–91 American metadiscussion about disciplinary histories.

Gunnell's call was applied beyond the political theory subfield when his student Brian Schmidt undertook a history of the international relations (hereafter, IR) subfield. Second only to political theory in the extent to which it shapes intellectual identities among its practitioners via training in a selective theory canon, IR was aptly suited to Schmidt's move. Schmidt pitted specialized disciplinary history in opposition to IR scholars interpreting themselves as extending a lineage of figures stretching onward from ancient Greece. This self-image substituted, Schmidt charged, an "epic rendition of the past" for "attention to the individuals and academic practices that have contributed to the development and current identity of the discipline." He drew a sharp dichotomy between an analytical tradition (a parade of past figures constructed by scholars in the present on the basis of what appear retrospectively and selectively as similar concerns) and a historical tradition (a historical lineage of actual intellectual inheritance and adaptation). It was overlooking this dichotomy that enabled epic narratives common in IR to position present-day scholarship "within a much older ancient lineage without demonstrating the historicity of these claims" (Schmidt 1998, pp. 25–9).

It was, however, not only epic narratives reaching through centuries that the specialist call to be historical could be wielded against. The demand to attend to whether the intellectual links between individuals portrayed or implied by a narrative have a historical grounding can be applied to any narrative structuring device that aggregates individuals, whether that aggregation is conceived as a "tradition," "research program," "network," or something else. This demand's critical edge was also applied to preceding works of disciplinary history. Farr (1988b, p. 1188) criticized Ricci (1984) for giving Karl Popper a prominent role in his tragic narrative of political science without establishing whether major figures of the behavioral era had, as implied, been influenced by Popper's philosophical arguments. Gunnell, in turn, more generally declared about Ricci's book that "the form and content are historical, but the argument is not" (Gunnell in Farr et al. 1990, p. 595).

The call to be historical (commonplace in the historiographical discussion heralding the onset of specialized research in disciplinary history) was a call to attend more closely to who said what to whom, and how he or she actually said it. It was a call, in other words, to attend to the twists and turns of discourse. Specialists are on solid ground when they stress that disciplinary histories should, as histories, be attentive to such twists and turns. But valorizing use of the concept of the historical should be deployed with caution. For example, Schmidt's dichotomous formulation of historical versus analytical traditions appears potentially problematic. Schmidt suggests that a historical tradition is "a pre-constituted and self-constituted pattern of conventional practice through which ideas are conveyed," while an analytical tradition is "a retrospectively created construct determined by present criteria and concerns" (1998, p. 25). The problem here is that no historical recounting of a tradition offers simply a passive picture of a past pattern. Any history unavoidably relies upon choices regarding the selection and synthesis of historical material, and such choices are unavoidably (and, when self-conscious, appropriately), influenced "by present criteria and concerns." Thus it appears that no disciplinary history can avoid being analytical to a certain extent in the sense of being, in some degree, a "retrospectively created construct."

Beyond contextualizing, in light of debates in the political theory subfield, the concern of specialists to offer avowedly more historical histories, we should also appreciate the substantive commonalities in disciplinary histories written by specialists and nonspecialists alike in recent decades. Recent histories continue to refract contemporary identities and concerns of political scientists, just as did histories written in earlier decades. Substantive commonalities in recent American disciplinary histories may, as a result, be discerned in light of the late twentieth century shift in the way that American political scientists understood themselves and their discipline. The intradisciplinary battles that had accompanied the advance of behavioralism in the post–World War II decades ended more in exhausted truces than in victory for any side. Certainly a plethora of quantitative techniques and positivist species of theory had won a major place in the American discipline. But other approaches were far from entirely supplanted, with the methodological balance reached by the 1980s strikingly different in different subfields, and since then, largely stable in each subfield.[8]

Exhaustion with embittering, inconclusive conflict over what political science as a whole should be promoted withdrawal from such conflicts and acceptance of subfield variety. If earlier American political scientists had once infused the discipline writ large with meaning and value – believing there were or should be discipline-integrating intellectual, and perhaps also political, commitments and aims – by the late twentieth century, the locus of scholarly identities had been largely displaced onto subfields, or even more disaggregated sites, such as the ever proliferating organized sections of the APSA. In lamenting this shift as a move to "separate tables," Gabriel Almond (1988) lamented a by-product of the only partial fulfillment of the behavioral revolution he had helped lead in the 1950s and 1960s. Among American political scientists of a more recent vintage, however, the fragmentation that Almond viewed negatively is often simply accepted as a given fact of disciplinary life, or even outright embraced as a healthy symptom of intellectual pluralism and/or specialization. Such pluralism is evident, for example, in the ability of a largely qualitative agenda of historical studies of "American political development" to establish its own distinct niche and identity (Orren and Skowronek 2004) even as the larger subfield of American politics is dominated by ever more technical modes of research.

The reorienting of identities among American political scientists toward a proliferating set of subdisciplinary foci provides an illuminating backdrop in surveying disciplinary histories of recent decades. Given this context it appears unsurprising that the newer specializing agenda in disciplinary history favored a turn away from histories of political science as a whole. Where the older scholar Ricci's (1984) *Tragedy of Political Science* had followed earlier nonspecialist work, such as Somit and Tanenhaus (1967), in taking as its object political science writ large, it was now argued that there was no satisfactory way to encompass the history of the discipline in one manageable narrative (Gunnell 1991, p. 16; Farr and Seidelman 1993, p. 6). This argument resonated well with the ongoing gravitation of American political scientists toward disaggregated scholarly identities and research agendas. When Farr and coeditors (Farr, Dryzek, and Leonard 1995) put together

8 Bennett, Barth, and Rutherford (2003) and Sigelman (2006) document this stabilization as reflected in the methods used in the articles published in major political science journals.

Political Science in History: Research Programs and Political Traditions, the plurals in their subtitle, and their ability to find multiple nonspecialists to author chapters pitched at such disaggregated levels, suggest that the shift in the substantive foci of disciplinary history mapped shifts in the identities and concerns of political scientists.

Replacing the discipline with more disaggregated foci could lead disciplinary histories in many directions. Histories could disaggregate all the way to the individual level (Farr 1990; Farr, Hacker, and Kazee 2006; Gunnell 1992; Fried 2006), or proceed at the midlevel of a cluster of scholars constituting a research program (Ferejohn 1995), or a department if that department held intellectual interest as the breeding ground of a notable research program (Amadae and Bueno de Mesquita 1999) or theory of democracy (Merelman 2003). Alternatively, histories could turn to institutional contexts beyond national associations and departments, as exemplified in a vibrant current of histories delving into foundation archives to study ties between foundation initiatives and the work of political scientists (Parmar 2002; Roelofs 2003; Hauptmann 2006; Hauptmann 2012; Guilhot 2008). Another major vein of studies has charted the history of pivotal concepts, such as "public opinion" (Gunn 1995), "ideology" (Knight 2006), the "state" (Gunnell 1995), "democracy" (Gunnell 2004), "social capital" (Farr 2004), and "political science" itself (Farr 1988). Finally, mapping a late-century trend across the humanities and social sciences, histories have also made gender (Silverberg 1998; Tolleson-Rinehart and Carroll 2006) or race (Walton, Miller, and McCormick 1995; Smith 2004; Fraga et al. 2006; Vitalis 2000, 2008) a core concern.

Amid the broader variety of this disaggregation, perhaps the single most successful move has been to subfield history. The subfields were, as Kaufman-Osborn (2006: p. 68) has observed, "consolidated in the wake of the conflict spawned by the behavioral revolution and express the tacit compromises that attended the collapse of that revolution's disciplinary ambitions." As key structures in the education of students and hiring and promotion of faculty in America subfields have begun to bear much of the identity import displaced from the field as a whole. Disciplinary histories once garnered attention by articulating perspectives on what it means to be a "political scientist," but they often do so better today by articulating perspectives on what it means to be a "political theorist" or a scholar of "international relations." Since Gunnell's *Descent of Political Theory: The Genealogy of an American Vocation* (1993) there has been a continuing subgenre of disciplinary histories of political theory (Castiglone and Hampsher-Monk 2001; Hauptmann 2004, 2005; Kettler 2006; Adcock and Bevir 2007). Yet even more lively is the subgenre of histories of IR that Gunnell's student Schmidt promoted with his book (1998), a review essay (Schmidt 2002), an edited volume (Schmidt and Long 2005), and continuing work (Schmidt 2008). Other scholarship in this vibrant area includes Ashworth (1999, 2006), Bell (2007, 2009), Dunne (1998), Guilhot (2008), Osiander (1998), Sylvest (2004), Schmidt (2011), and Vitalis (2000, 2008).

The Globalization of Political Science and the Globalization of Disciplinary History

The specialization agenda in American disciplinary histories connects, through the figure of Schmidt, to the explosion of histories of IR since the mid-1990s. This explosion is, however, a transatlantic phenomenon only partly fed by, and far from reducible to, American developments. The academics writing IR histories are often not Americans, and the academics and agendas they write histories of are often not American either. The centrality of Europeans as both authors and objects of IR histories calls attention to what is arguably the single most significant recent trend in disciplinary histories: the globalization of the genre. While especially pronounced today, this trend dates back several decades, with the genre's spread following on changes in the institutions and identity of political science outside America during the second half of the twentieth century.

The model of a narrow political science field inaugurated with the founding of the APSA in 1903 remained largely an anomaly in global terms until midcentury. This changed, however, in the aftermath of World War II, when America enjoyed heightened prestige and power due to its newfound military ascendance and its role in creating new international organizations and aiding postwar reconstruction. It was against this backdrop that the newly founded United Nations Educational, Scientific, and Cultural Organization (UNESCO) set out to promote political science internationally in the late 1940s. Its initiative spurred the 1949 creation of the International Political Science Association (IPSA), with national associations in turn founded in France in 1949, Britain in 1950, and West Germany in 1951. Yet, as I observed earlier relative to America, the establishment of a national association was far from tantamount to the creation of a full-fledged discipline. Across European nations during the latter half of the century it again took decades for a disciplinary project, differentiating "political scientists" from members of other academic fields and valorizing professionalized research by political scientists so understood, to advance and gain critical mass (Hayward 1991; Kastendiek 1991; Roux 2004).

As earlier in interwar America, disciplinary history was inaugurated as a genre in Europe during the second generation of national political science associations. With some initial work in the 1970s, such as Kastendiek (1977), the genre took broad flight in the European context during the 1980s. Academics in multiple nations contributed essays on the post-1945 history of political science in their respective countries to the *International Handbook of Political Science* (Andrews 1982). Though the handbook was organized by an American scholar, and for an American press, the next steps in advancing disciplinary histories of political science in non-American countries centered in Europe. In 1985 the Finnish Political Science Association collaborated with IPSA to organize an international conference in Helsinki, The Development and Institutionalization of Political Science, and papers from this conference were subsequently published in the January 1987 *International Political Science Review*, and in *Political Science between Past and Future* (Anckar and Berndtson 1988). During the Helsinki conference, participants also decided to form the International Committee for the Study of the Development of Political Science, under whose auspices another international disciplinary history conference was held in 1987 in Italy. Papers written for this conference made up much of the volume *The Development of Political Science: A Comparative Survey* (Easton, Gunnell, and Graziano 1991). A subsequent round of conferences in Barcelona and Paris in 1990 led, in turn, to the volume *Regime and Discipline: Democracy and the Development of Political Science* (Easton, Gunnell, and Stein 1995), in which the globalization of disciplinary history was notably pushed beyond American and Western European contexts with studies on the history of political science in Eastern Europe, Latin America, and Asia.

By the 1990s disciplinary history had hence become a globalized genre of a globalizing political science discipline. The changes in the genre that we may see as part of its globalization include more, however, than histories being written about political science in countries other than America. They also involve changes in the way histories are told of American political science. What is new here can be suggested by noting that Crick wrote his seminal *American Science of Politics* (1959) as a young British scholar influenced by time spent at Harvard and Berkeley among skeptics of behavioralism. But, by setting up his book in terms of an "American Science," Crick framed political science in a way that tended to cast into shadow the continuing role played in the twentieth century by transatlantic intellectual interaction, such as that from which his own book grew. Over the half-century since Crick wrote, however, the disciplinary project he judged skeptically in midcentury America, and in effect sought to warn fellow

British scholars against, has made huge strides in Britain and elsewhere. The advancing globalization of political science as a discipline has been accompanied within the genre of disciplinary history by expanded attention to transnational influences on political science in America.

In crafting their subfield histories of political theory and IR, Gunnell (1993) and Schmidt (1998) gave major roles to the German *Staatswissenschaften* in the nineteenth century beginning of their narratives, and then in later chapters to émigrés from Nazi Germany who became leading scholars in these subfields in mid-twentieth century America. The first of these moves extended a persistent theme within disciplinary histories of American political science ever since Merriam flagged German influence on early graduate education at Hopkins and Columbia. But in giving a key role also to another intellectual movement westward across the Atlantic during the twentieth century, Gunnell and Schmidt showed that the "American science of politics" did not stop being shaped by transatlantic exchange even during the "American century." Subsequently, Katznelson (2003) and Loewenberg (2006) have extended attention to the mid-twentieth century impact of émigrés beyond the political theory and IR subfields. Much of my own work has sought to push transatlantic histories of American political science in the direction of looking beyond Germany-America exchange – by now well documented for both the nineteenth and twentieth centuries – to Britain-America, and a more limited extent France-America, exchanges (Adcock 2006; Adcock, Bevir, and Stimson 2007; Adcock and Bevir 2010; Adcock 2014). Finally, and especially ripe with potential to reorient disciplinary histories, steps have been taken toward a more fully globalized transnational approach by studies spotlighting how Latin American scholars affected American studies of development and democracy since the 1960s (Packenham 1992; Guilhot 2005).

Looking over the globalizing trend in disciplinary histories from the 1980s to the present, the last decade in particular might ultimately stand out as the period in which this trend pushed beyond its initial comparative, and subsequent transatlantic formulations, to enter its most fully global form.[9] With regard to studies of American political science we have recently seen a string of histories locating developments within the discipline in global contexts of military, political, or economic relations and power. This move was showcased in Oren's (2003) *Our Enemies and US: America's Rivalries and the Making of Political Science*. Oren offered mininarratives of

[9] See Bell (2009) for explicit advocacy of a reorientation of disciplinary histories toward "histories of the global."

political science before and after America's entry into conflict with imperial Germany, Nazi Germany, Fascist Italy, and Soviet Russia, with each narrative charting characterizations of these countries shifting from uncritical or positive to sharply negative. Subsequently, Guilhot's (2005, p. 102) *The Democracy Makers* has exemplified how studies of "the 'fit' between academic social science and the main foreign policy doctrines" of America, as the globe's most powerful nation, can prevent subordinating science to power via attending to "internal scientific struggles … that cannot be entirely reduced to external influence." Other recent studies testifying to growing interest in situating American political science in global contexts include Katznelson (2003), Blyth (2006), Bevir (2007), Vitalis (2008), and Adcock and Vail (2012). Disciplinary histories are thus shifting global contexts to the fore precisely as political scientists have been anxiously pondering America's place in the global order of the twenty-first century. The genre remains, as ever, firmly, and I hope unapologetically, informed by concerns about the present and the place of political science within that present.

References

Adcock, Robert. 2003. "The Emergence of Political Science as a Discipline: History and the Study of Politics in America, 1875–1910," *History of Political Thought* 24.3:459–86.

2006. "The Emigration of the 'Comparative Method': Transatlantic Exchange and the Birth of American Political Science," *European Political Science* 5:124–36.

2007. "Interpreting Behavioralism." In *Modern Political Science: Anglo-American Exchanges since 1870*, ed. Robert Adcock, Mark Bevir, and Shannon Stimson. Princeton, NJ: Princeton University Press.

2014. *Liberalism and the Emergence of American Political Science*. New York: Oxford University Press.

Adcock, Robert and Mark Bevir. 2007. "The Remaking of Political Theory." In *Modern Political Science: Anglo-American Exchanges since 1870*, ed. Robert Adcock, Mark Bevir, and Shannon Stimson. Princeton, NJ: Princeton University Press.

2010. "Political Science." In *The History of Postwar Social Science*, ed. Roger E. Backhouse and Philippe Fontaine. Cambridge: Cambridge University Press, 71–101.

Adcock, Robert, Mark Bevir and Shannon Stimson, eds. 2007. *Modern Political Science: Anglo-American Exchanges since 1870*. Princeton, NJ: Princeton University Press.

Adcock, Robert and Mark Vail. 2012. "Beyond Pluralism? Corporatism, Globalization, and the Dilemmas of Democratic Governance." In *Modern Pluralism: Anglo-American Debates since 1880*, ed. Mark Bevir. Cambridge: Cambridge University Press.

Almond, Gabriel A. et al. 1962. "Political Science as a Discipline," *American Political Science Review* 56.2:417–21.

1988. "Separate Tables: Schools and Sects in Political Science," *PS: Political Science and Politics* 21.4:828–42.

1995. "Political Science: The History of the Discipline." In *A New Handbook of Political Science*, ed. Robert E. Goodin and Hans-Dieter Klingemann. Oxford: Oxford University Press.

Amadae, S. M. 2003. *Rationalizing Capitalist Democracy: The Cold War Origins of Rational Choice Liberalism*. Chicago: University of Chicago Press.

Amadae, S. M. and Bruce Bueno de Mesquita. 1999. "The Rochester School: The Origins of Positive Political Theory," *Annual Review of Political Science* 2:269–95.

Anckar, Dag, and Erkki Berndtson. 1988. *Political Science: Between Past and Future*. Finnish Political Science Association.

Andrews, William G. 1982. *International Handbook of Political Science*. Westport, CT: Greenwood Press.

APSA. 1904. "The Organization of the American Political Science Association," *Proceedings of the American Political Science Association* 1:5–15.

Ashworth, Lucian. 1999. *Creating International Studies: Angell, Mitrany, and the Liberal Tradition*. Aldershot, UK: Ashgate.

2006. "Where Are the Idealists in Interwar International Relations?" *Review of International Studies* 32.2:291–308.

Ball, Terence, James Farr and Russell L. Hanson. 1989. *Political Innovation and Conceptual Change*. Cambridge: Cambridge University Press.

Barrow, Clyde W. 2008. "The Intellectual Origins of New Political Science," *New Political Science* 30.2:215–44.

Bell, Duncan, ed. 2007. *Victorian Visions of Global Order: Empire and International Relations in Nineteenth-Century Political Thought*. Cambridge: Cambridge University Press.

Bell, Duncan. 2009. "Writing the World: Disciplinary History and Beyond," *International Affairs* 85.1:3–22.

Bennett, Andrew, Aharon Barth, and Kenneth R. Rutherford. 2003. "Do We Preach What We Practice? A Survey of Methods in Political Science Journals and Curricula," *PS: Political Science and Politics* 36.3:373–8.

Bevir, Mark. 2007. "Institutionalism and the Third Way." In *Modern Political Science: Anglo-American Exchanges since 1870*, ed. Robert Adcock, Mark Bevir, and Shannon Stimson. Princeton, NJ: Princeton University Press.

Blyth, Mark. 2006. "Great Punctuations: Prediction, Randomness, and the Evolution of Comparative Political Science," *American Political Science Review* 100.4:487–92.

Bryce, James. 1888. *The American Commonwealth*. 3 vols. London: Macmillan.

Collini, Stefan, Donald Winch, and John Burrow. 1983. *That Noble Science of Politics: A Study in Nineteenth Century Intellectual History*. Cambridge: Cambridge University Press.

Crick, Bernard. 1959. *The American Science of Politics: Its Origins and Conditions*. Berkeley: University of California Press.

Dryzek, John and Stephen Leonard. 1988. "History and Discipline in Political Science," *American Political Science Review* 82.4:1245–60.

Dunne, Tim. 1998. *Inventing International Society: A History of the English School*. Basingstoke, UK: Macmillan, 1998.

Easton, Donald. 1953. *The Political System: An Inquiry into the State of Political Science*. New York: Knopf.

Easton, David, John G. Gunnell, and Luigi Graziano, eds. 1991. *The Development of Political Science: A Comparative Survey*. London: Routledge.

Easton, David, John G. Gunnell, and Michael B. Stein, eds. 1995. *Regime and Discipline: Democracy and the Development of Political Science*. Ann Arbor: University of Michigan Press.

Farr, James. 1988a. "The History of Political Science," *American Journal of Political Science* 32.4:1175–95.

1988b. "Political Science and the Enlightenment of Enthusiasm," *American Political Science Review* 82.1:51–69.

1990. "Francis Lieber and the Interpretation of American Political Science," *Journal of Politics* 52.4:1027–49.

1995. "Remembering the Revolution: Behavioralism in Political Science." In *Political Science in History: Research Programs and Political Traditions*, ed. James Farr, John Dryzek, and Stephen Leonard. New York: Cambridge University Press.

2004. "Social Capital: A Conceptual History." *Political Theory* 32.1:6–33.

2007. "The Historical Sciences of Politics." In *Modern Political Science: Anglo-American Exchanges since 1870*, ed. Robert Adcock, Mark Bevir, and Shannon Stimson. Princeton, NJ: Princeton University Press.

Farr, James, John Dryzek, and Stephen Leonard, eds. 1995b. *Political Science in History: Research Programs and Political Traditions*. New York: Cambridge University Press.

Farr, James, John Gunnell, Raymond Seidelman, John Dryzek, and Stephen Leonard. 1990. "Can Political Science History Be Neutral?" *American Political Science Review* 84.2:587–610.

Farr, James, Jacob S. Hacker, and Nicole Kazee. 2006. "The Policy Scientist of Democracy: The Discipline of Harold Lasswell," *American Political Science Review* 100.4:579–88.

Farr, James and Raymond Seidelman. 1993. *Discipline and History: Political Science in the United States*. Ann Arbor: University of Michigan Press.

Ferejohn, John. 1995. "The Development of the Spatial Theory of Elections." In *Political Science in History: Research Programs and Political Traditions*, ed. James Farr, John Dryzek, and Stephen Leonard. New York: Cambridge University Press.

Forman, Paul. 2012. "On the Historical Forms of Knowledge Production and Curation: Modernity Entailed Disciplinarity, Postmodernity Entails Antidisciplinarity," *Osiris* 27:56–97.

Fraga et al. 2006. "*Su Casa* Es *Nuestra Casa*: Latino Politics Research and the Development of American Political Science," *American Political Science Review* 100.4:515–22.

Fried, Amy. 2006. "The Forgotten Lindsay Rogers and the Development of American Political Science," *American Political Science Review* 100.4:555–62.

Gilman, Nils. 2003. *Mandarins of the Future: Modernization Theory in Cold War America*. Baltimore: Johns Hopkins University Press.

Goodnow, Frank J. 1905. "The Work of the American Political Science Association," *Proceedings of the American Political Science Association* 1 (1905):45–6.

Guilhot, Nicolas. 2005. *The Democracy Makers: Human Rights and International Order*. New York: Columbia University Press.

2008. "The Realist Gambit: Postwar American Political Science and the Birth of IR Theory," *International Political Sociology* 2.4:281–304.

Gunn, J. A. W. 1995. "'Public Opinion' in Modern Political Science." In *Political Science in History: Research Programs and Political Traditions*, ed. James Farr, John Dryzek, and Stephen Leonard. New York: Cambridge University Press.

Gunnell, John G. 1975. *Philosophy, Science, and Political Inquiry*. Morristown, NJ: General Learning.

1978. "The Myth of the Tradition," *American Political Science Review* 72.1:122–34.

1982. "Interpretation and the History of Political Theory: Apology and Epistemology," *American Political Science Review* 76.2:317–27.

1988. "American Political Science, Liberalism, and the Invention of Political Theory," *American Political Science Review* 82.1:71–87.

1991. "The Historiography of American Political Science." In *The Development of Political Science: A Comparative Survey*, ed. David Easton, John G. Gunnell, and Luigi Graziano. London: Routledge.

1992. "Continuity and Innovation in the History of Political Science: The Case of Charles Merriam," *Journal of the History of the Behavioral Sciences* 28.2:133–42

1993. *The Descent of Political Theory: The Genealogy of an American Vocation*. Chicago: University of Chicago Press.

1995. "The Declination of the 'State' and the Origins of American Pluralism." In *Political Science in History: Research Programs and Political Traditions*, ed. James Farr, John Dryzek, and Stephen Leonard. New York: Cambridge University Press.

2004. *Imagining the American Polity: Political Science and the Discourse of Democracy*. University Park: Pennsylvania State University Press.

2006. "The Founding of the American Political Science Association: Discipline, Profession, Political Theory, and Politics," *American Political Science Review* 100.4:479–86.

2013. "The Reconstitution of Political Theory: David Easton, Behavioralism, and the Long Road to System," *Journal of the History of the Behavioral Sciences* 49.2:190–210.

Haddow, Anna. 1939. *Political Science in American Colleges and Universities, 1636–1900*. New York: Appleton.

Hauptmann, Emily. 2004. "A Local History of 'The Political,'" *Political Theory* 32.1:34–60.

2005. "Defining 'Theory' in Postwar Political Science." In *The Politics of Method in the Human Sciences: Positivism and its Epistemological Others*, ed. George Steinmetz. Durham, NC: Duke University Press.

2006. "From Opposition to Accommodation: How Rockefeller Foundation Grants Redefined Relations between Political Theory and Social Science in the 1950s," *American Political Science Review* 100.4:643–50.

2012. "The Ford Foundation and the Rise of Behavioralism in Political Science," *Journal of the History of the Behavioral Sciences* 48.2:154–73.

Hayward, Jack. 1991. "Political Science in Britain," *European Journal of Political Research* 20:301–21.

Karl, Barry D. 1974. *Charles E. Merriam and the Study of Politics*. Chicago: University of Chicago Press.

Kastendiek, Hans. 1977. *Die Entwicklung der westdeutschen Politikwissenschaft*. Frankfurt am Main: Campus.

1991. "Political Science in West Germany." In *The Development of Political Science: A Comparative Survey*, ed. David Easton, John G. Gunnell, and Luigi Graziano. London: Routledge.

Katznelson, Ira. 2003. *Desolation and Enlightenment: Political Knowledge after Total War, Totalitarianism, and the Holocaust*. New York: Columbia University Press.

Kaufman-Osborn, Timothy V. 2006. "Dividing the Domain of Political Science: On the Fetishism of Subfields," *Polity* 38.1:41–71.

Kettler, David. 2006. "The Political Theory Question in Political Science, 1956–1967," *American Political Science Review* 100.4:531–8.

Key Jr., V. O. 1958. "The State of the Discipline," *American Political Science Review* 52.4:961–71.

Knight, Kathleen. 2006. "Transformations of the Concept of Ideology in the Twentieth Century," *American Political Science Review* 100.4:619–26.

Landau, Martin. 1968. "The Myth of Hyperfactualism in the Study of American Politics," *Political Science Quarterly* 83.3:378–99.

Loewenberg, Gerhard. 2006. "The Influence of European Émigré Scholars on Comparative Politics, 1925–1965," *American Political Science Review* 100.4:597–604.

Luke, Timothy W. 1999. "The Discipline as Disciplinary Normalization: Networks of Research," *New Political Science* 21.3:345–63.

McCoy, Charles A., and John Playford. 1967. *Apolitical Politics: A Critique of Behavioralism*. New York: Crowell.

Merelman, Richard M. 2003. *Pluralism at Yale: The Culture of Political Science in America*. Madison: University of Wisconsin Press.

Merriam, Charles. 1920. *American Political Ideas, 1865–1917*. New York: Macmillan.

1921. "The Present State of the Study of Politics," *American Political Science Review* 15.2:173–85.

1923. "Recent Advances in Political Methods," *American Political Science Review* 17.2:275–95.

1925. *New Aspects of Politics*. Chicago: University of Chicago Press.

1926. "Progress in Political Research," *American Political Science Review* 20.1:1–13.

Murray, Robert H. 1926. *The History of Political Science: From Plato to the Present*. Cambridge: Heffer and Sons.

Oren, Ido. 2003. *Our Enemies and US: America's Rivalries and the Making of Political Science*. Ithaca, NY: Cornell University Press.

Orren, Karen and Stephen Skowronek. 2004. *The Search for American Political Development*. New York: Cambridge University Press.

Osiander, Andreas. 1998. "Re-Reading Early Twentieth Century IR Theory: Idealism Revisited," *International Studies Quarterly* 42.3:409–32.

Packenham, Robert A. 1992. *The Dependency Movement: Scholarship and Politics in Development Studies*. Cambridge, MA: Harvard University Press.

Parmar, Inderjeet. 2002. "'To Relate Knowledge and Action … ': The Rockefeller Foundation's Impact on Foreign Policy Thinking during America's Rise to Globalism, 1939–1945," *Minerva* 40.3:235–63.

Pollock, Sir Frederick. 1914. *An Introduction to the History of the Science of Politics*, new ed. London: Macmillan.

Ricci, David. 1984. *The Tragedy of Political Science*. New Haven, CT: Yale University Press.

Roelefs, Joan. 2003. *Foundations and Public Policy: The Mask of Pluralism*. Albany, NY: State University of New York Press.

Roux, Christophe. 2004. "Half a Century of French Political Science: Interview with Jean Leca," *European Political Science* 3:25–30.

Schmidt, Brian. 1998. *The Political Discourse of Anarchy: A Disciplinary History of International Relations*. Albany: State University of New York Press.

2002. "On the History and Historiography of International Relations." In *Handbook of International Relations*, ed. Walter Carlsnaes, Thomas Risse, and Beth Simmons. London: Sage.

2008. "Political Science and the American Empire: A Disciplinary History of the "Politics" Section and the Discourse of Imperialism and Colonialism," *International Politics* 45.6:675–87.

Schmidt, Brian, and David Long, eds. 2005. *Imperialism and Internationalism in the Discipline of International Relations*. Albany: State University of New York Press.

Schmidt, Sebastian. 2011. "To Order the Minds of Scholars: The Discourse of the Peace of Westphalia in International Relations Literature." *International Studies Quarterly* 55.3:601–23.

Seidelman, Raymond, and Edward Harpham. 1985. *Disenchanted Realists: Political Science and the American Crisis 1884–1984*. Albany: State University of New York Press.

Sigelman, Lee. 2006. "The Coevolution of the American Political Science and the *American Political Science Review*," *American Political Science Review* 100.4:463–78.

Sigelman, Lee, and M. Elizabeth Sanders, eds. 2006. *Thematic Issue on the Evolution of Political Science, in Recognition of the Centennial of the Review. American Political Science Review* 100.4.

Silverberg, Helene. 1998. "'A Government of Men': Gender, the City, and the New Science of Politics." In *Gender and American Social Science: The Formative Years*, ed. Helene Silverberg. Princeton, NJ: Princeton University Press.

Skinner, Quentin. 1969. "Meaning and Understanding in the History of Ideas," *History and Theory* 8.1:3–53. Reprinted in *Meaning & Context*, ed. James Tully, 29–67.

Smith, Rogers M. 2004. "The Puzzling Place of Race in American Political Science," *Political Science and Politics* 37.1:41–5.

Somit, Albert and Joseph Tanenhaus. 1967. *The Development of American Political Science: From Burgess to Behavioralism*. Boston: Allyn & Bacon.

Storing, Herbert J, ed. 1962. *Essays on the Scientific Study of Politics*. New York: Holt, Rinehart & Winston.

Sylvest, Caspar. 2004. "Interwar Internationalism, the British Labor Party and the Historiography of International Relations," *International Studies Quarterly* 48.2:409–32.

Tocqueville, Alexis de. 2000. *Democracy in America*, trans. Harvey Mansfield and Delba Winthrop. Chicago: University of Chicago Press.

2010. "Speech Given to the Annual Public Meeting of the Academy of Moral and Political Sciences on April 3, 1852." In *Alexis de Tocqueville and the Art of Democratic Statesmanship*, ed. Brian Danoff and L. Joseph Herbert, Jr. Lanham, MD: Lexington Books, Chapter 1.

Tolleson-Rinehart, Sue, and Susan J. Carroll. 2006. "'Far from Ideal': The Gender Politics of Political Science," *American Political Science Review* 100.4:507–14.

Trent, John E., and Michael Stein. 1991. "The Interaction of the State and Political Science in Canada: A Preliminary Mapping." In *The Development of Political Science: A Comparative Survey*, ed. David Easton, John G. Gunnell, and Luigi Graziano. London: Routledge.

Truman, David B. 1965. "Disillusion and Regeneration: The Quest for a Discipline," *American Political Science Review* 59.4:865–73.

Tully, James, ed. 1988. *Meaning and Context: Quentin Skinner and His Critics*. Princeton, NJ: Princeton University Press.

Vitalis, Robert. 2000. "The Graceful and Generous Liberal Gesture: Making Racism Invisible in American International Relations," *Millenium* 29.2:331–56.

2008. "The Noble American Science of Imperial Relations and Its Laws of Race Development," *Comparative Studies in Society and History* 52.4:909–38.

Waldo, Dwight. 1975. "Political Science: Tradition, Discipline, Profession, Science, Enterprise." In *Political Science: Scope and Theory*, ed. Fred I. Greenstein and Nelson W. Polsby. Reading, MA: Addison-Wesley.

Walton Jr., Hanes, Cheryl M. Miller, and Joseph P. McCormick II. 1995. "Race and Political Science: The Dual Traditions of Race Relations and Politics and African-American Politics." In *Political Science in History: Research Programs and Political Traditions*, ed. James Farr, John Dryzek, and Stephen Leonard. New York: Cambridge University Press.

Wilson, Woodrow. 1889. "Bryce's *American Commonwealth*," *Political Science Quarterly* 4.1:153–69.

Index

www.ingramcontent.com/pod-product-compliance
Lightning Source LLC
LaVergne TN
LVHW101500200926
848483LV00001B/182
9781107037724